TOP **10**
BERLIN

CONTENTS

BERLIN

INTRODUCING

Berlin's TV Tower in Mitte

WELCOME TO
BERLIN

Historic, edgy, multicultural: that's Berlin. Here, you can admire world-famous art, explore thought-provoking monuments and party at some of Europe's best clubs – all in one day. Don't want to miss a thing? With Top 10 Berlin, you'll enjoy the very best the city has to offer.

Few cities can rival Berlin's cultural credentials. Boundary-pushing street art and world-renowned clubs speak to the German capital's vibrant modern spirit, while absorbing museums and weighty historic monuments offer insight into its turbulent past. And this city has been indelibly marked by history. Reckoning with the realities of the world wars and the era-defining East–West division is an essential part of any trip to Berlin. Take a deep dive into the history of Germany's Jewish community at the Jüdisches Museum, walk around the glassy

Locals lounging by the Spree

dome of the symbolic Reichstag or revel in the anarchy of the East Side Gallery (a stretch of the Berlin Wall taken over by graffiti artists). To venture even further back in time (2,000 years or so), head to Museumsinsel, where the best of Berlin's mammoth museums await.

The German capital doesn't shy away from its past, nor does it dwell on it. Berliners know how to have fun, and as any bleary-eyed reveller will tell you, this isn't a city of early-birds. Come evening, beer gardens are bustling, while iconic clubs and underground raves keep party-goers dancing until the early hours. Not here for the nightlife? There's still plenty to keep you entertained.

Berlin's food scene is one of its biggest draws, with new Michelin-starred restaurants, legendary fast-food joints and international food markets keeping foodie fans on their toes. And while this city is famed for its hedonism, there's always space to unwind. Vast parks like the Tiergarten offer an oasis amid the buzzy city, while lush green ribbons along the river teem with sunbathers in the summer.

So, where to start? With Top 10 Berlin, of course. This pocket-sized guide gets to the heart of the city with simple lists of 10, expert local knowledge and comprehensive maps, helping you turn an ordinary trip into an extraordinary one.

THE STORY OF
BERLIN

Berlin has gone through a number of significant chapters in its lifetime. It grew from a humble village to a wealthy Prussian town, and survived two world wars and four decades of division. And today? It's one of Europe's most vibrant cities. Here's the story of how it came to be.

The Growth of a City

Berlin's written history began in the early 13th century, when it was a small settlement trading in fish and timber. A little over a century later, in 1411, Friedrich von Hohenzollern became the town's special protector, inaugurating what would become a 500-year reign for the House of Hohenzollern. Despite being hit by the bubonic plague and the Thirty Years' War over the next few centuries, the city grew steadily, and by the time Fredrich Wilhelm became Elector of Brandenburg in 1640, the population had hit an all-time high. After he ratified the Edict of Potsdam, around 15,000 Protestant Huguenots fleeing religious persecution in France were welcomed to Berlin, followed by refugees from Poland, Bohemia and Salzburg.

In 1701, the city became the capital of the new Kingdom of Prussia, one of the independent kingdoms that existed in Germany. The following centuries saw many notable Prussian leaders come to the fore, but Friedrich II (1740–1786), or "Frederick the Great", arguably made the most impact. He was fearlessly dedicated to enhancing Berlin's cultural standing and encouraged merchants to move to the city.

Imperial Capital

As Berlin rapidly industrialized during the 19th century, many of its famous landmarks were built. The driving force behind this explosion of Neo-Classical architecture was Karl Friedrich Schinkel, who built the likes of the Konzerthaus. But it wasn't all grand designs. The 1862 Hobrecht Plan urbanized swathes

An illustration depicting the Thirty Years' War

Friedrich II, King of Prussia from 1740 to 1786

1237
Berlin is founded, and thought to be named after the ruler Albrecht der Bär (Albert the Bear).

of the city to house people from the countryside seeking work in its factories. Modernized sanitation systems, electric street lighting, public transport and telephone lines drastically improved quality of life.

1647
Joining the Stadtschloss with the Tiergarten, Unter den Linden is paved, and swiftly becomes the city's most fashionable boulevard.

At this point, Germany was still made up of kingdoms and principalities. That would all change in 1871, when the prime minister of Prussia, Otto von Bismarck, unified Germany, naming Berlin its capital and Wilhelm I, a member of the House of Hohenzollern, its Kaiser (emperor). The following decades would see Prussia's military and economic influence in Europe grow, until World War I erupted in 1914.

1791
The Brandenburger Tor (Brandenburg Gate), one of Germany's most recognizable landmarks, is completed.

A New Republic

Germany's defeat in the war, the November Revolution and Kaiser Wilhelm II's abdication in 1918 signalled the end of Hohenzollern dominance. It also marked the start of the Weimar Republic, a period of cultural growth and political instability. The arts blossomed against a backdrop of hyperinflation, unemployment and unbridled hedonism. The 1920 Greater Berlin Act also expanded the city's borders and doubled its population to 3.8 million, making it the world's third largest municipality. At this time, the Bauhaus redefined design, writer Christopher Isherwood captured Berlin's pioneering queerness and figures like dancer Anita Berber symbolized its underbelly, a place of cabaret and sexual freedom.

1806
Napoleon's defeat of Prussia places Berlin under French occupation for two years.

1871
The newly appointed chancellor Otto von Bismarck founds the German Empire, naming Berlin as its capital.

1897
Berlin's Scientific-Humanitarian Committee is inaugurated, becoming the world's first gay rights organization.

1939–1945
World War II wreaks destruction on Berlin, culminating in the Battle of Berlin and Hitler's demise.

1948–1949
Allied air forces deliver over two million tonnes (2.3 million tons) of supplies during the Berlin Airlift.

1991
In a narrow vote, Berlin beats Bonn to become the capital of a reunified Germany.

2006
A reconciliatory moment for modern Germany, the country hosts the World Cup final at Berlin's Olympiastadion.

2020
After seven years of reconstruction work, the Berliner Stadtschloss opens its doors to visitors.

World War II

Berlin was still in full swing when the world stock market tanked in 1929, which set in motion the Weimar Republic's collapse and Adolf Hitler's appointment as German chancellor in 1933. Hitler despised Berlin as a place of liberals, communists and loose morals. After he leveraged the Reichstag fire in February 1933 to purge the city of his opponents, Berlin became the nerve centre of the Nazi (National Socialist German Workers') Party when they seized control a month later.

On 9 November 1938, Kristallnacht (Night of Broken Glass), a state-sponsored pogrom designed to violently intimidate Germany's Jewish population, erupted. Thousands were arrested while synagogues, schools and shops were ransacked. Hitler's invasion of Poland in 1939 signalled the start of World War II and three years later in January 1942, the Final Solution indiscriminately condemned millions of Jews to death. By the time two million Soviet Red Army soldiers rolled into Berlin in April 1945, and with Hitler having died by suicide, Berlin was a barely recognizable heap of rubble, its residents destitute and starving.

A Divided City

Germany's defeat by the Allied forces resulted in Berlin being quartered into four sectors administered by Britain, the US, France and the Soviet Union (USSR). This put the city at the

The Reichstag in ruins following the February 1933 fire

Celebrating the fall of the Wall by the Brandenburg Gate

epicentre of the Cold War (1947–1991), an ideological conflict that pitted the US and NATO against the USSR. The birth of two opposing German states in 1949 – the Federal Republic of Germany to the west and the German Democratic Republic (GDR) in the east – divided Germany once more (Britain and France administered their respective sectors until the 1990s). This split was physically cemented when the Berlin Wall went up overnight on 13 August 1961, sealing Berlin off from the West behind the Iron Curtain and cleaving families apart for the next 28 years.

West Berlin became influenced by Western Europe and the US, politically and culturally. Despite a heavy military presence and tales of espionage, artists and intellectuals flooded in, inspired by the anarchic atmosphere. Meanwhile, East Berlin stagnated under the GDR's policies. Food shortages and mass surveillance created dystopian conditions; those who tried to flee over the border were shot at by GDR authorities.

The political changes that swept through the Eastern bloc in 1989 resulted in the fall of the Wall on 9 November, and Germany was officially reunified on 3 October 1990. In many ways, undergoing this hardship allowed Berlin to blossom into the unrestricted place it is today. Progress started slowly in the 1990s; with the former East playing economic catch up with the wealthier West, times were tight. Much of East Berlin was tumbledown and squatting wasn't uncommon, but empty warehouses set the scene for non-stop raves, with techno soundtracking a renewed taste for freedom.

A New Story
People flock to modern Berlin for this unbridled freedom as well as its world-class cultural scene. It's still a safe haven for those in need, too. In response to the 2015 European migrant crisis, then Chancellor Angela Merkel championed the welcoming culture that saw Germany receive over a million refugees. Russia's 2022 invasion of Ukraine forced many Ukranians to the city, too, and Berlin is home to one of Europe's largest Palestinian diaspora communities. While right-wing populism is on the rise, Berliners remain liberal and open-minded; in an uncertain world coloured by conflict and division, this is a place where anyone can live according to their own style.

TOP 10
EXPERIENCES

Planning the perfect trip to Berlin? Whether you're visiting for the first time or making a return trip, there are some things you simply shouldn't miss out on. To make the most of your time – and to enjoy the very best this wonderfully vibrant city has to offer – be sure to add these experiences to your list.

1 Savour some street food
Currywurst, Döner kebab, *Falafel im Brot*: Berlin's street eats are legendary, the sheer variety offering a window into the city's rich cultural make-up. Hit up an *Imbiss* (food kiosk) or time-honoured market to find the comfort food of dreams, and wash your dish down with a frothy beer.

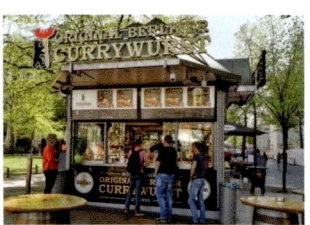

2 Museum-hop around Museumsinsel
With a whole island of museums, Berlin means business when it comes to art and culture. A UNESCO World Heritage-listed complex of five institutions (p34), including the Altes and Neues museums, Museum Island showcases 2,000 years of world history – a day well spent.

3 Look back at World War II
You can't visit Berlin without facing its dark history, and the city doesn't shy away from the impact of World War II. Reflect on the brutal reality of life under the Nazis at the Berlin Holocaust Memorial (p93), and see the city's will to rebuild at the anti-war memorial, Kaiser-Wilhelm-Gedächtnis-Kirche (p40).

4 Climb the Reichstag dome
Berlin overflows with stunning structures, and one of the very best lies atop the parliamentary building (p24). Book in advance to climb the spiral walkway that winds around the Reichstag dome, a glass structure that offers stellar views across the city.

5 Uncover Cold War history

Memories of the Cold War still loom over the capital, having shaped it into the place of solidarity it is today. For an insight into daily life in East Germany, visit the DDR *(p96)* and Stasi museums *(p149)* before stopping by the Berlin Wall Memorial *(p85)*.

6 Seek out street art

Symbolic of Berlin's free-spirited nature, street art is everywhere, and the famous East Side Gallery *(p85)* is just the start. Head to Teufelsberg *(p66)*, a former Cold War spy station that's now a huge canvas, or simply amble around Friedrichshain *(p148)*.

7 Indulge in the city's famed nightlife

Europe's party capital, Berlin is home to some of the world's best techno clubs. Not up for partying at Berghain *(p150)*? Blow off steam another way at a stylish speakeasy, cabaret club or classical music venue.

8 Browse weekend flea markets

Sunday is *Ruhetag* (a day of rest) and the shops are closed, so what to do? Rummage at the flea markets that pop up on squares and along the canal. A favourite is Mauerpark Flohmarkt *(p144)*, which hosts an epic karaoke session.

9 Explore Berlin's parks

Perhaps surprisingly for such an urban city, Berlin's green spaces and access to forests are one of its biggest assets. Cycle through Tempelhofer Feld *(p135)*, an abandoned airport-turned-people's park, or stroll around Tiergarten *(p117)*, a former royal hunting estate.

10 Cruise the Spree

Flowing through the city's heart, the River Spree is a wonderful vantage point to see Berlin in all its glory. Board a boat, order a Berliner Weisse *(p81)* and look out for the likes of the Berliner Dom and the Reichstag. It's the perfect way to bookend your trip.

ITINERARIES

Seeing Brandenburger Tor, enjoying a canal-side stroll, learning about the city's layered history: there's a lot to see and do in Berlin. With places to eat, drink or simply take in the view, these itineraries offer ways to spend 2 days and 4 days in the capital.

2 DAYS

Day 1

Morning
Where better to get acquainted with Berlin than at its most famous square, Alexanderplatz (p108)? Soak up the city skyline from the Fernsehturm observation deck here and look out for Museumsinsel, an island in the Spree where you're heading next. You could spend days exploring the five museums here, but opt for the Neues Museum (p35), where you'll see the stucco-coated limestone bust of Nefertiti. The museum's Allegretto Museum Café is the perfect pitstop for a light lunch.

Afternoon
Admire the Berliner Dom (p58), the city's largest and most striking cathedral, as you leave Museumsinsel and begin to stroll west along shady Unter den Linden (p90). This beautiful boulevard is dotted with colossal examples of Prussian architecture,

> 🚌 **TRANSPORT**
> Since the city is mostly flat, cycling is a great way to get around; bike lanes and rentals are ubiquitous, and you can even take bikes on transport with a bicycle ticket.

Opulent Berliner Dom, located on Museumsinsel

and at its eastern end you'll find the Zeughaus, the oldest and most interesting building here. Admire the sculptures that decorate the exterior then head inside, where the Deutsches Historisches Museum (p27) lies, with over one million objects that explore Germany's past. After you've had your fill of history, continue down Unter den Linden until you reach Brandenburger Tor (p22), a symbolic gate that rulers, statesmen and demonstrators have marched through over the centuries. When the sun starts to set, make for the Reichstag (p24) and climb the dome to admire Berlin bathed in a beautiful glow. It's a quick walk south to your fancy dinner spot, Facil (p121), a two-Michelin-starred restaurant that will set up your evening of classical music at the Berliner Philharmonie (p46) – just make sure to book ahead for both.

Day 2

Morning
The Cold War is a huge chapter in Berlin's story, so dedicate your morning to learning about it. Uncover how the secret police kept a watchful eye on Berliners at the DDR Museum (p96), then jump on a bus to see the remnants of the Wall that once divided the city at the East Side Gallery (p148). Soak up the colourful artwork that has adorned it since 1990, then take a short walk south via the Oberbaumbrücke to Kreuzberg (p132), one of West Berlin's poorest districts during the Cold War and today one of its most vibrant neighbourhoods. Kreuzberg is at the heart of Berlin's Turkish community, the largest in Europe outside of Turkey. It's the perfect spot to sample traditional Turkish cuisine.

Afternoon
Head to the Landwehrkanal (p67) to walk off your lunch, picking up a coffee to go from one of the many cafés lining the canal. It won't be long until you're in Neukölln, a creative district that's also home to one of the few hills in Berlin; climb up and you'll reach Schillerkiez, your access point to the much-loved Tempelhofer Feld (p136). This former airport is your playground for the rest of the day: cycle a loop of the tarmac, join a skating class or chill out in the community garden. Hang around to watch the sunset with a *Späti* beer then wind down for the night at Lavanderia Vecchia (p139), a quirky Italian restaurant set in an old laundry.

> **DRINK**
> Public drinking is legal in Berlin, and buying beers from a *Späti* (convenience store) to drink in a park is a local pastime. You'll find plenty of these surrounding Tempelhofer Feld, and in every district around the city.

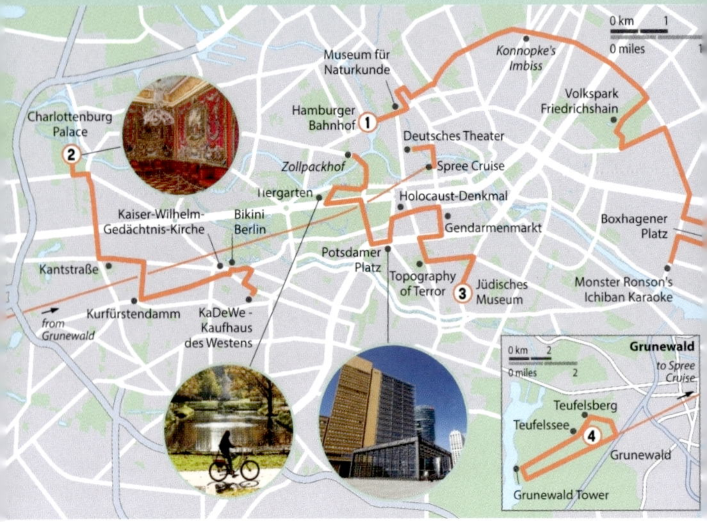

Map labels:
- 0 km   1
- 0 miles   1
- Museum für Naturkunde
- Konnopke's Imbiss
- Volkspark Friedrichshain
- Charlottenburg Palace ②
- Hamburger Bahnhof ①
- Deutsches Theater
- Zollpackhof
- Spree Cruise
- Tiergarten
- Holocaust-Denkmal
- Kaiser-Wilhelm-Gedächtnis-Kirche
- Bikini Berlin
- Gendarmenmarkt
- Boxhagener Platz
- Kantstraße
- Potsdamer Platz
- Topography of Terror ③
- Jüdisches Museum
- Monster Ronson's Ichiban Karaoke
- from Grunewald
- Kurfürstendamm
- KaDeWe - Kaufhaus des Westens
- 0 km   2
- 0 miles   2
- Grunewald
- to Spree Cruise
- Teufelsberg
- Teufelssee
- ④
- Grunewald
- Grunewald Tower

4 DAYS

Day 1

Today begins in Berlin's bustling centre, Mitte, with a visit to the Hamburger Bahnhof (p118). All shows at this railway station-turned-contemporary art gallery are temporary, but they often focus on Expressionism or Pop Art, so it's guaranteed to be a colourful morning. A quick walk away is the Museum für Naturkunde (p102), where you can marvel at the world's largest dinosaur skeleton. When hunger strikes, catch a tram north to Prenzlauer Berg, where the legendary Konnopke's Imbiss (p144) doles out some of the best *Currywurst* in the city. The stand is located right by the tramline, so hop on and head to Friedrichshain, where you can amble through the city's oldest park, Volkspark (p67), where Ludwig

Sculpture on the ornamental Märchenbrunnen fountain

Hoffman's Märchenbrunnen fountain stands, and dip into the shops around Boxhagener Platz (p148). You're well positioned for experiencing Berlin's iconic nightlife (Berghain, p150, is here); whether you succeed in getting into one of Berlin's famed clubs or settle into a slick bar, be sure to end your night belting out some tunes at Monster Ronson's Ichiban Karaoke Bar (p150).

Day 2

It's over to the west of the city this morning, with much to see at Schloss

SHOP
On Sundays in the summer, Mauerpark in Prenzlauer Berg livens up with eclectic flea market stalls, talented buskers and the much-loved Bearpit Karaoke.

Charlottenburg (p42), Berlin's opulent Baroque palace. Once the home of the Hohenzollern dynasty, it features beautiful English-style gardens and two magnificent buildings (each with its own entrance and fee). Spend most of the morning exploring the enchanting grounds and treasures inside, then hop on a short bus ride to Kantstraße (p127) for lunch; this is the city's best street for Asian cuisine, so take your pick from traditional, Chinese or Vietnamese spots. A short walk will take you to the historic boulevard Kurfürstendamm (p38), where the poignant ruins of the Kaiser-Wilhelm-Gedächtnis-Kirche stand. Also here are some of the city's best shops and boutiques; explore Bikini Berlin's (p38) independent stores before heading into KaDeWe (p82), the largest department store in Europe. When all that shopping tires you out, enjoy dinner at KaDeWe's restaurant, the Wintergarten.

Day 3

Spend the morning uncovering the profound impact that World War II had on Berlin, starting with an informative tour at the Jüdisches Museum (p133) to learn about Germany's Jewish population. Next, head to the harrowing Topography of Terror (topographie. de), an exhibition that details Nazi war crimes, before visiting the poignant Holocaust-Denkmal (p93). After a heavy start to the day, get some fresh air on a stroll over to Gendarmenmarkt (p92), choosing from one of the cafés in the pretty square for a leisurely lunch. A quick U-Bahn ride takes you to Potsdamer Platz (p30), Berlin's

modern centre with impressive buildings such as Das Center am Potsdamer Platz. From here continue on to the Großer Tiergarten (p66), Berlin's largest park, to reflect on the day among picturesque meadows and leafy paths. When the sun starts to set, a pint and German-Austrian food call at the riverside Zollpackhof (p121) beer garden.

Day 4

Pack a picnic and jump on the S-Bahn out of the city centre to reach the dense woodlands of Grunewald (p99). Stroll along peaceful paths, climb up the Cold War-era listening station on Teufelsberg (p156) for sweeping views and, if it's a warm day, cool off with a swim in Teufelsee (p67), one of Berlin's many lakes. End up at Grunewaldturm (p156), where you can unwind with a drink at the beer garden beside the tower before catching a bus back into town. See out your trip to Berlin on a cruise along the Spree (p13), looking out over the city's numerous sights, before settling in for a show at the extravagant Deutsches Theater (p72).

Landscaped flowerbeds in the vast Großer Tiergarten

TOP 10 HIGHLIGHTS

The Reichstag Dome

EXPLORE THE
HIGHLIGHTS

There are some sights in Berlin you simply shouldn't miss, and it's these attractions that make the Top 10. Discover what makes each one a must-see on the following pages.

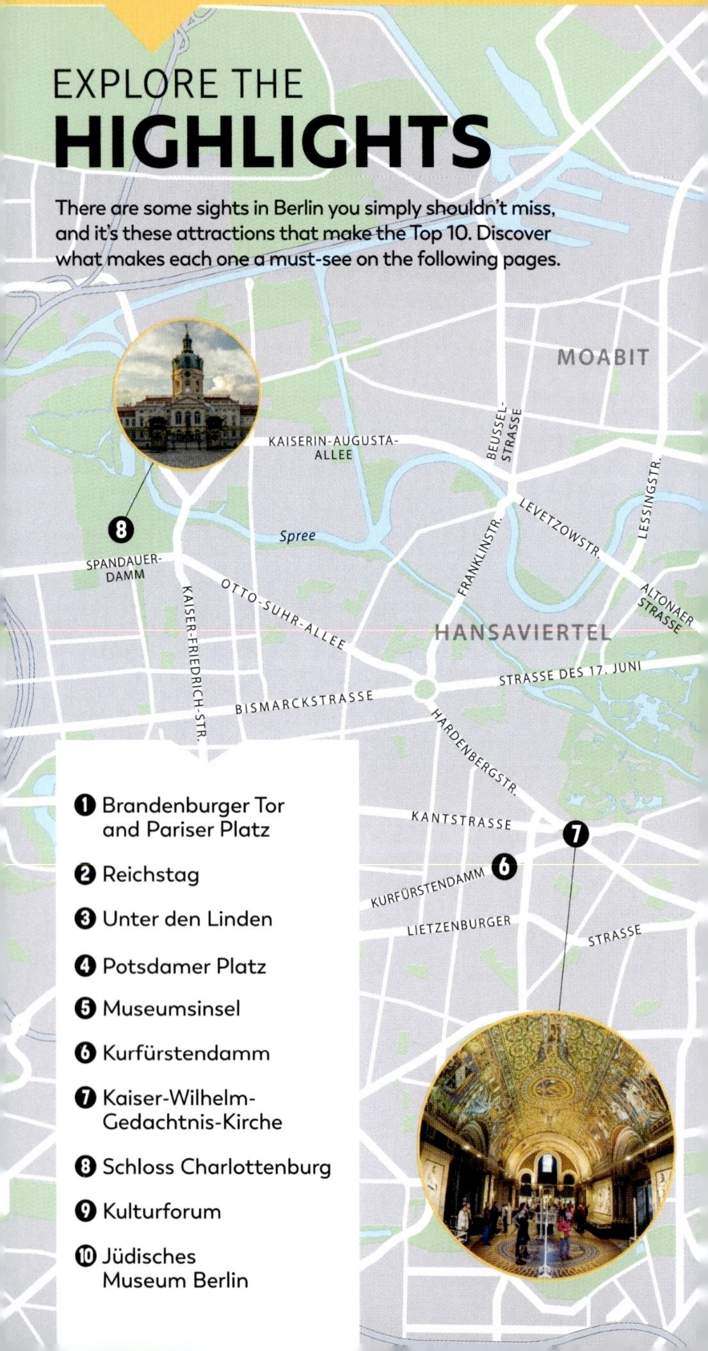

❶ Brandenburger Tor and Pariser Platz

❷ Reichstag

❸ Unter den Linden

❹ Potsdamer Platz

❺ Museumsinsel

❻ Kurfürstendamm

❼ Kaiser-Wilhelm-Gedachtnis-Kirche

❽ Schloss Charlottenburg

❾ Kulturforum

❿ Jüdisches Museum Berlin

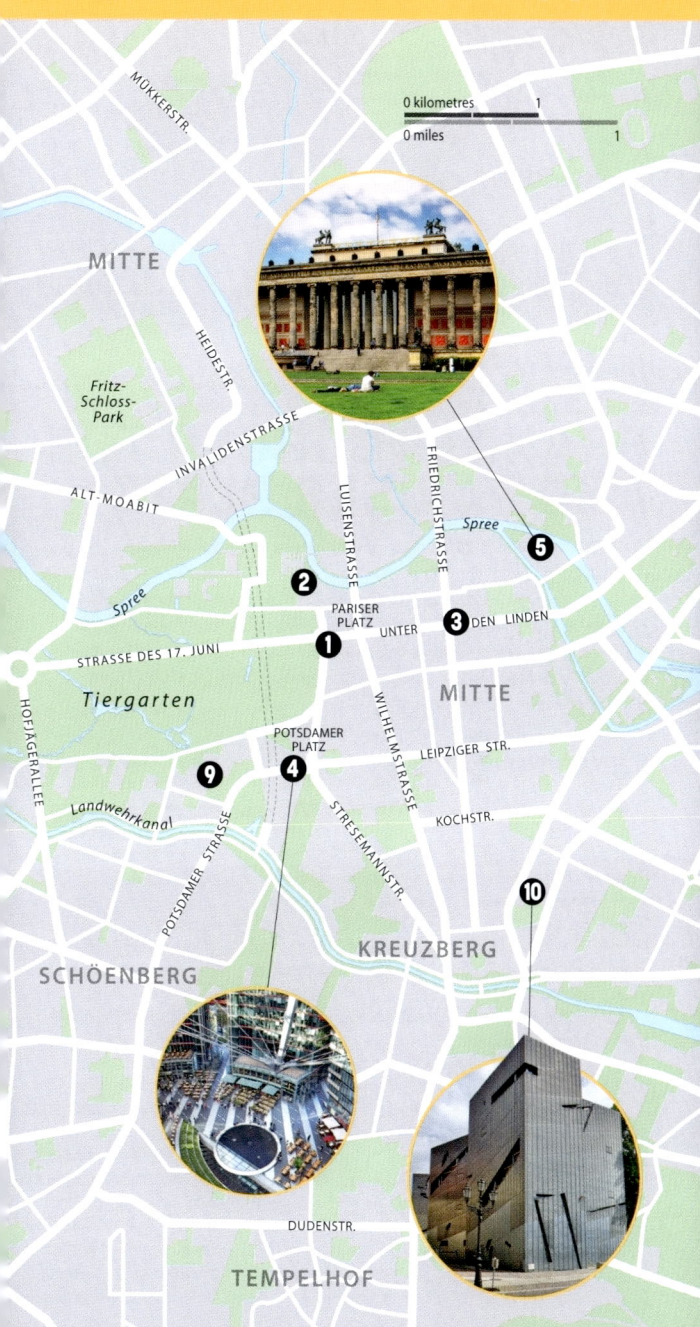

0 kilometres 1
0 miles 1

MITTE

MÜKKERSTR.

Fritz-
Schloss-
Park

HEIDESTR.

INVALIDENSTRASSE

ALT-MOABIT

LUISENSTRASSE

FRIEDRICHSTRASSE

Spree

5

Spree

2

PARISER
PLATZ

3 DEN LINDEN

1 UNTER

STRASSE DES 17. JUNI

Tiergarten

MITTE

HOFJÄGERALLEE

WILHELMSTRASSE

LEIPZIGER STR.

POTSDAMER
PLATZ

4

9

Landwehrkanal

POTSDAMER STRASSE

STRESEMANNSTR.

KOCHSTR.

10

SCHÖENBERG

KREUZBERG

DUDENSTR.

TEMPELHOF

BRANDENBURGER TOR AND PARISER PLATZ

📍 K3 🏠 Pariser Platz ℹ️ Brandenburger Tor southern gatehouse; visitberlin.de

The quintessential icon of Berlin, the Brandenburger Tor stands proudly in the middle of Pariser Platz, asserting itself against the modern embassy buildings that now surround it. Crowned by its triumphant quadriga sculpture, the famous gate has long been a focal point in Berlin's history.

1 Brandenburger Tor

This magnificent Neo-Classical structure was built by Carl Gotthard Langhans in 1789–91 and modelled on the temple porticoes of ancient Athens. A pair of pavilions, once used by guards and customs officers, frames its powerful Doric colonnade.

TOP TIP

Visit in October, when the Festival of Lights transforms the gate into a light sculpture.

2 Quadriga

The 6-m- (20-ft-) high sculpture was mounted in 1793 as a symbol of peace by Johann Gottfried Schadow. The sculpture, which depicts the goddess of victory driving her four-horsed chariot, is the gate's centrepiece.

3 Hotel Adlon Kempinski Berlin

Destroyed in World War II, the city's most elegant hotel is a reconstruction of the original, which hosted celebrities such as Greta Garbo, Thomas Mann and Charlie Chaplin.

4 DZ Bank

🕐 9am–6pm Mon–Fri

The head office of DZ Bank is located in a popular modern building designed by the American architect Frank Owen Gehry. It combines the clean lines of Prussian architecture with some daring elements inside.

5 Akademie der Künste

Built between 2000–2005 and designed by Günter Behnisch and Manfred Sabatke, the Academy of Arts incorporates, behind a vast expanse of windows, the ruins of the old art academy, which was destroyed in World War II.

Brandenburger Tor dominating Pariser Platz

TRANSPORT
The 100, 200 and 300 buses pass several major city sights such as Brandenburger Tor. Buy a day ticket to hop on and off.

6 French Embassy

Architect Christian de Portzamparc completed this building in 2002 on the site of the old embassy, which was ruined in World War II. Its colonnades and windows are a homage to the original.

7 American Embassy

The last gap around Pariser Platz was finally closed in 2008. A dispute had delayed building for years: the US wanted a whole street moved for reasons of security, but had to concede the point in the end.

8 Palais am Pariser Platz

This complex by Bernhard Winking is a modern interpretation of Neo-Classical architecture. Inside there is a café, a restaurant and a souvenir shop around a shaded courtyard.

9 Eugen-Gutmann-Haus

With its clean lines, the Dresdner Bank, built in 1997 by gmp, recalls the style of the New Sobriety movement of the 1920s. In front of it is Pariser Platz's famous original street sign.

10 Haus Liebermann

Completed by Josef Paul Kleihues in 1999, this structure faithfully re-creates the original that stood on the same site. The house is named after the artist Max Liebermann, who lived here. In 1933, watching Nazi SA troops march through the gate, he famously said: "I cannot possibly eat as much, as I would like to puke".

A EYEWITNESS TO HISTORY

The Brandenburg Gate has borne witness to many of Berlin's important events, from various military parades to celebrations marking the birth of the Third Reich and Hitler's ascent to power. It was here, too, that the Russian flag was raised in May 1945, and on 17 June 1953 that 25 workers demonstrating for better conditions were killed.

Clockwise from right **The Pariser Platz street sign; lobby of Hotel Adlon Kempinski Berlin; glass-roofed atrium of the DZ Bank building**

REICHSTAG

◆ K2 ⌂ Platz der Republik 1 ◷ Dome: 8am–midnight daily
(last adm: 9:45pm); Käfer im Reichstag: Hours vary, check
website ⬡ bundestag.de

**No other structure is a more potent symbol of Germany's history
than the Reichstag. Berlin's official parliamentary building has
survived arson, revolution and war, and a tour through its fine
interior is a great way to learn about the country's modern story.**

1 Plenary Chamber
This is the seat of the
Deutscher Bundestag,
the German parliament,
which has convened here
since 20 April 1999.

2 Portico "Dem Deutschen Volke"
The dedication "To the
German People" was
designed in 1916, against
the will of Wilhelm II.

3 The Dome
The Reichstag dome
by Lord Norman Foster
affords breathtaking
views of Berlin. It is
open at the top to
air the building.

4 Restored Façade
Despite extensive reno-
vations, small World War
II bullet holes are still visible in the building's façade.

5 Platz der Republik
Celebrations often take
place on the lawn of this
square in front of the
Reichstag, as in 2006,
the year when Germany
hosted the football
World Cup.

TOP TIP

To visit the dome,
register online two
to three days
in advance.

THE REICHSTAG FIRE

When the Reichstag went up in flames on 27 February 1933, the Dutch Communist Marinus van der Lubbe was arrested for arson. It is, however, believed that the Nazis started the fire themselves as an excuse to get the "Enabling Act" passed.

Tribute at the Weiße Kreuze Memorial

6 Installation "Der Bevölkerung"

Hans Haacke's work of art "To the People" is a counterpoint to the portico inscription opposite and uses the same style of lettering.

7 Weiße Kreuze Memorial

Opposite the southern side of the Reichstag, a memorial recalls the Wall, which stood only a few steps away. The white crosses commemorate the people who died at the Wall while trying to escape to West Berlin.

8 The German Flag

The giant German flag was first raised on the occasion of the official national celebrations of German reunification on 3 October 1990.

9 Memorial by Dieter Appelt

Unveiled in 1992, the memorial in front of the Reichstag commemorates 97 Social Democratic and Communist delegates who were murdered under the Third Reich.

Magnificent glass dome of the Reichstag

10 Käfer im Reichstag

This luxury restaurant (p121) on the Reichstag's roof offers an excellent panorama of the skyline surrounding Alexanderplatz (p108) and beyond.

 EAT
If a meal at the Käfer im Reichstag restaurant exceeds your budget, head to one of the stalls nearby to pick up a classic Berlin *Bratwurst* (sausage).

Käfer im Reichstag atop the historic Reichstag

UNTER DEN LINDEN

📍 K4

Once a royal bridle path linking the king's town residence (the Stadtschloss) and Tiergarten, Unter den Linden became Berlin's trendiest street in the 18th century. Today, it remains one of the city's most important arteries, lined with linden trees and impressive buildings.

Grand Staatsoper Unter den Linden

1 Staatsoper Unter den Linden

📍 K4 🏠 Unter den Linden 7 🌐 staatsoper-berlin.de

The richly ornamented State Opera House is one of Germany's most attractive. Neo-Classical in style, it was built by the Prussian architect Georg Wenzeslaus von Knobelsdorff from 1741–3 as Europe's first free-standing opera house, to plans devised by Frederick the Great (p8) himself.

2 St-Hedwigs-Kathedrale

📍 K4 🏠 Bebelplatz
🕐 11am–6pm Mon–Thu & Sat, 11am–8pm Fri, 1–6pm Sun 🌐 hedwigs-kathedrale.de

Designed by Georg Wenzeslaus von Knobelsdorff in 1740–2 and modelled on Rome's Pantheon, this is the seat of Berlin's Catholic archdiocese. It was commissioned by Frederick the Great to appease Berlin Catholics after the conquest of Silesia.

3 Humboldt-Universität

Berlin's oldest and most highly regarded university was founded in 1810 based on the ideas of Wilhelm von Humboldt. Twenty-nine Nobel Prize winners were educated here, including Albert Einstein.

☕ **DRINK**
Stop for some coffee and pastries at the LePopulaire, located in the Deutsche Bank's Palais-Populaire on Unter den Linden 5.

4 Opernpalais

The building next to the Staatsoper once served as a palace for Friedrich Wilhelm III's daughters. Today it houses a centre for contemporary arts and culture, PalaisPopulaire.

5 Neue Wache

The central German memorial for all victims of war was created in 1816–8 by Karl Friedrich Schinkel. A reproduction of Käthe Kollwitz's moving *Pietà* stands here.

6 Kronprinzen-palais

Created in 1669 as a private residence by Johann Arnold Nering, the building was remodelled in 1732–3 into a Neo-Classical palace by Philip Gerlach. After World War I it became an art museum, before the East German government housed

Stately façade of Humboldt-Universität

Artworks at the German Historical Museum

state visitors there. The German reunification agreement was signed here in August 1990. It now holds cultural events and exhibitions.

7 Statue of Frederick the Great

One of Christian Daniel Rauch's grandest works (*p91*), this equestrian statue shows "Old Fritz"

Statue of Frederick the Great

(13.5 m/44 ft high) in his tricorn and coronation mantle.

8 Deutsches Historisches Museum

🅚 K5 🏠 Zeughaus, Unter den Linden 2 🚫 For renovation until late 2025 🕐 Hours vary, chech website 🌐 dhm.de

Housed in the Zeughaus, the oldest building on Unter den Linden, the country's largest history museum offers an overview of more than 1,000 years of German history.

9 Russische Botschaft

The huge Russian Embassy, built in the Stalinist "wedding-cake style", was the first building to be erected on Unter den Linden after World War II.

GALLERY GUIDE

The ground floor of the Deutsches Historisches Museum houses exhibits from 1918 to the present. The first floor has collections from early civilizations and the Middle Ages to the early 20th century. A pathway links the Zeughaus to the temporary shows in the exhibition hall.

10 Bebelplatz

Originally named Opernplatz, this wide open space was designed by Knobelsdorff as the focal point of his Forum Fridericianum (*p91*). The elegant square was created to introduce some of the lost splendour of ancient Rome to the Prussian capital. In May 1933, it became the scene of the infamous Nazi book burning.

Deutsches Historisches Museum

1. The Dying Warriors
The 22 reliefs by Andreas Schlüter, displayed on the walls of the courtyard rather than in one of the museum's exhibitions, portray the horrors of war in an unusually immediate way.

2. Europe and Asia
This group of 18th-century Meissen porcelain figures reflects the fascinating relationship between the two continents.

3. Steam Engine
A full-sized steam engine from the year 1847 marks the entrance to the exhibition on the Industrial Revolution.

4. Clothes from the Camps
Among the exhibits here that illustrate the years under Nazi rule is the jacket of a concentration camp inmate – a chilling reminder of the Third Reich.

5. Gloria Victis
The moving allegorical figure of *Gloria Victis*, created by the famed French sculptor Marius Jean Antonin Mercié, bears witness to the death of his friend during the conclusive days of the Franco-Prussian War of 1870–71.

Portrait of Martin Luther, painted by Lucas Cranach the Elder in 1529

6. Martin Luther
Luther's portrait, by Lucas Cranach the Elder, is the focal point of exhibition rooms devoted to the Reformation and Martin Luther himself.

7. V2 Rocket
Exhibited in the section on Nazi Germany is a V2 rocket engine, displayed next to an 88-mm (3.5-inches) flak gun. The V2 missile was one of the *Wunderwaffen* ("wonder weapons") used by German troops at the end of World War II.

8. Soldiers Plundering a House
This painting by Flemish-Baroque painter Sebastian Vrancx, dating from around 1600, depicts a scene from the Wars of Religion, which tore the Netherlands apart during the 16th century.

9. Saddle
A valuable saddle, dating from the middle of the 15th century, is decorated with elaborately carved plaques made of ivory.

10. The Berlin Wall
An original section of the Berlin Wall, together with banners of a peaceful pro-unification demonstration in 1989, commemorates the fall of the Wall.

Gloria Victis by Antonin Mercié

ZEUGHAUS UNTER DEN LINDEN

Originally the royal arsenal, the Zeughaus on Unter den Linden was built in 1706 in Baroque style according to plans by the German architect Johann Arnold Nering. It is one of the street's most impressive structures, with the building surrounding a historic central courtyard that is protected by a modern glass cupola roof. Considered especially memorable are Baroque sculptor Andreas Schlüter's figures of 22 dying warriors, which are lined up along the arcades in the courtyard. They portray vividly the horrors of war. Behind the main building stands a cone-shaped glass annexe designed by the Chinese-born architect I M Pei in 2001 for special exhibitions and temporary shows. The permanent exhibition in the main building includes a collection entitled "Images and Testimonials of German History". Highlighting the most significant periods and events in the history of the country, the displays include a surprising variety of exhibits, dating from the days of the early medieval German Empire up to 1994. Featured are the important periods of the Reformation, the Thirty Years' War, the Wars of Liberation and the failed Revolution of 1848, and, of course, the more recent and unforgettable two World Wars.

Entry of Napoleon into Berlin, 27 October 1806 (*1810*) **by Charles Meynier**

POTSDAMER PLATZ

📍 L2

The heart of the metropolis of Berlin beats on Potsdamer Platz. A hub of urban life in the 1920s, the square became a desolate wasteland after World War II, but was revived following the fall of the Wall. Potsdamer Platz has since become a city within the city, packed with an array of entertainment, shopping and dining options that leave visitors spoilt for choice.

1 Das Center am Potsdamer Platz

🏠 Potsdamer Platz
🌐 das-center-am-potsdamer-platz.de

Formerly known as the Sony Center, this complex was designed by Helmut Jahn. It houses a modern workspace and a commercial area offering entertainment venues, a food hall and many hip dining establishments.

2 Weinhaus Huth

The only complete building on Potsdamer Platz to have survived World War II, Weinhaus is now home to a cosy wine bar, Lutter and Wegner.

TOP TIP

The square hosts a Christmas market and a toboggan run.

3 Deutsches Spionage-museum

🏠 Leipziger Platz 9
🕙 10am–8pm daily
🌐 deutsches-spionagemuseum.de

Also known as the "Capital of Spies", this fascinating museum

Weinhaus Huth at Potsdamer Platz

Glassy skyscrapers of Potsdamer Platz

features laser mazes, James Bond-inspired gadgets and thrilling tales of espionage.

4 LEGOLAND® Discovery Centre

🏠 Potsdamer Str. 4 🕐 10am–6pm Mon–Fri, 10am–7pm Sat & Sun 🌐 legolanddiscovery centre.com/berlin 🔗

This LEGO® wonderland features brick models, a miniature Berlin, a train ride to a land of dragons and a DUPLO® Village with bigger blocks for the tots.

5 Theater am Potsdamer Platzr

🌐 tapp.berlin

The theatre at Marlene Dietrich Platz seats 1,800 and hosts theatrical performances, musicals and shows. Every year in February, it transforms into a venue for the Berlinale Film Festival, the "Berlinale Palast".

6 The Playce

Previously known as Potsdamer Platz Arkaden, this shopping mall is now a food and

> 🍽 **EAT**
> The Playce is home to Europe's largest food hub, Manifesto Market, where several restaurants offer everything from Asian to Latin American cuisine.

entertainment venue. Inside, a food market, Manifesto, offers sustainable products and street food.

7 Frederick's

🏠 Bellevuestr. 1 🕐 Hours vary, check website 🌐 frederichs berlin.com

Housed in the former Grand Hotel Esplanade, this 1920s-style spot has a restaurant, two bars, a lounge and deli.

8 Boulevard der Stars

Berlin's walk of fame features stars such as Marlene Dietrich, Werner Herzog, Fritz Lang, Diane Kruger, Hans Zimmer and Romy Schneider.

Marlene Dietrich's star on Boulevard der Stars

Exploring the 25th floor at Kollhoff Tower

9 Kollhoff Tower

🏠 Potsdamer Platz 1 🕐 11am–7pm daily (winter: to 6pm) 🌐 panoramapunkt.de 🔗

Designed by Hans Kollhoff, this building has Europe's fastest lift, which takes visitors to the 25th floor viewing deck in just 20 seconds.

10 Spielbank Berlin

🏠 Marlene-Dietrich-Platz 1 🕐 11am–3am daily 🌐 spielbank-berlin.de 🔗

Roulette and Black Jack can be played, and there are gambling machines too.

Deutsches Spionagemuseum Displays

Outside the entrance to the Deutsches Spionagemuseum

1. Time Tunnel
Covering stories of a wide range of historical figures, from Franciscan monks to conquistadors, this sprawling timeline charts the history of spying as far back as 1500 BCE.

2. Morse Code Station
A hands-on coding station display teaches visitors how to send messages in Morse code on an old World War I module. The encoded messages can even be printed out as souvenirs.

3. Propaganda Grenade
Despite its appearance, this German-designed World War II projectile wasn't built to cause destruction. Instead, it was crammed with anti-Stalinist leaflets that would then rain down behind Soviet lines.

4. Encoding and Decoding Messages
Based on the famous Enigma machine, this interactive display allows visitors to encode top-secret messages.

5. Enigma Machines
The museum's collection of cypher devices includes the iconic Enigma I; of the 40,000 machines used by the Third Reich, this was the most favoured.

6. Bug Finding
In a small room modelled after a historic socialist apartment, visitors can use a bug detector to scan for listening devices and wiretaps.

7. Stasi Trabant
This lime-green replica of the famous East German car shows how the Stasi – the Deutsche Demokratische Republik's secret police force – modified car door panels to include hidden infrared cameras.

8. Lie Detector
Visitors can test their mettle and uncover hidden truths with this easy-to-use digital polygraph.

9. Berlin Spy Map
A huge satellite map of the German capital tells the stories behind numerous locations once linked to Cold War espionage.

10. Laser Maze
This popular laser maze allows visitors to navigate an intricate labyrinth of light while avoiding the beams. There are mazes here designed for both children and adults, each with three difficulty levels.

A coding machine on display

THE NEW CENTRE OF BERLIN

In the 1920s, Potsdamer Platz was Europe's busiest square, featuring the first automatic traffic lights in Berlin. During World War II this social hub was razed to the ground. Ignored for almost 50 years, the empty square shifted back into the centre of Berlin when the Wall came down. During the 1990s, it was Europe's largest building site. New skyscrapers were built, and old structures were restored – some preserved rooms of the ruined historic Grand Hotel Esplanade were even physically moved into the Sony Center. Millions of people came to follow progress from the famous Red Info Box, which was removed in 2001. Altogether, around €17 billion was invested to create the present square.

The Spielbank Berlin casino in Potsdamer Platz

Das Center am Potsdamer Platz dominating Potsdamer Platz

5

MUSEUMSINSEL

📍 J5 🌐 smb.museum 🔗

The UNESCO Word Heritage-listed Museumsinsel is one of Berlin's most unique landmarks: a museum district located on an island formed by the two arms of the Spree River. The world's most diverse museum complex, its five fascinating museums take visitors on a cultural journey through 2,000 years of world history.

1 Altes Museum
⏰ 10am–5pm Wed–Fri, 10am–6pm Sat–Sun
The first building to be completed on Museumsinsel in 1830, the intriguing Altes Museum *(p61)* resembles a Greek temple. Originally meant to hold paintings, it now houses the collection of Classical antiquities.

2 Bode-Museum
⏰ 10am–5pm Wed–Fri, 10am–6pm Sat & Sun
Located at the northern tip of Museumsinsel, the Bode-Museum is a stately structure dominated by a cupola. The building holds the impressive Sculpture Collection, the Museum of Byzantine Art and the Numismatic Collection, made up of an assortment of over 500,000 objects.

3 Ägyptisches Museum
Housed within the Neues Museum, this museum *(p54)* has portraits of Egyptian royals and monumental architecture.

4 James-Simon-Galerie
⏰ 10am–6pm Tue–Sun
Named in honour of James Simon (1851–1932), a patron of the Berlin State Museums, this building was designed by David Chipperfield. The museum was completed and opened in 2019.

> **TOP TIP**
>
> Access all the island's museums by getting a Museumsinsel day pass for €24.

Bust of Nefertiti in the Altes Museum

Alte Nationalgalerie and its grounds

5 Alte Nationalgalerie

⏰ 10am–6pm Tue–Sun

First opened in 1876, the Old National Gallery (*p56*) was restored in the 1990s and now has 19th-century sculptures and paintings, including works by Max Liebermann and Johann Gottfried Schadow.

6 Lustgarten

This "pleasure park", with a fountain in its centre, is located in front of the Altes Museum (*p61*). The lawns are popular with tired visitors.

7 Neues Museum

⏰ 10am–6pm Tue–Sun

Spectacularly revamped by British architect David Chipperfield, the building itself is as fascinating as its exhibits. As well as the Museum of Pre- and Early History, the Ägyptisches Museum is also housed here.

8 Berliner Dom

Easily the island's most commanding structure (*p58*), this Baroque-style cathedral is unusually ornate for a Protestant church. Organ concerts and services can be enjoyed in this exquisitely restored building.

MISSING TREASURES

During World War II, many of the island's exhibits were hidden in bunkers. Some pieces were taken by the Red Army and remain in Moscow. The Neues Museum points out the gaps in the collection.

📷 **VIEW**
Look up at the interior of the Berliner Dom to marvel at Anton von Werner's intricate mosaics, each of which contain over half a million tiles.

9 Colonnade Courtyard

This columned courtyard between the Neues Museum and the Alte Nationalgalerie connects the museums and is an atmospheric venue for open-air concerts.

10 Pergamon-museum

Built in 1909–30, this is one of the world's most important museums (*p54*) of ancient art and architecture, with a vast collection of antiquities.

Striking 6th-century Ishtar Gate, Pergamonmuseum

Collection Highlights

1. Pergamon Altar
The Pergamon Altar from the eponymous Greek city (in modern Turkey) dates from 160 BCE. The altar will remain closed for renovation until 2027.

2. The Mshatta Façade
A gift from Ottoman Sultan Abdul Hamid II to Kaiser Wilhelm II, and now housed in the Pergamonmusem, this stone façade elaborately carved with arabesque and animal forms was the south face of a desert fort built in 744 CE in Mshatta, Jordan.

3. The Berlin Green Head
Little is known about this beautifully crafted ancient Egyptian statue, but experts believe it was crafted around 100–50 BCE. Held in the Neues Museum, it's made from greenshist, a rock with chemicals that give it a green tone.

4. Nefertiti's Bust
The star exhibit in the Neues Museum's Egyptian Museum is a painted limestone bust of Egyptian queen Nefertiti. It was found during excavations in Egypt in 1912, and is believed to date from 1345 BCE.

Admiring the famed bust of Nefertiti in the Neues Museum

5. The Berlin Golden Hat
Part of the Neues Museum's Museum for Prehistory and Early History, this functioning calendar was created between the 9th and 8th century BCE. It's made from a paper-thin single sheet of gold and lavishly decorated with ornaments.

6. The Princesses Group
This iconic example of Neo-Classical sculpture, depicting the Crown Princess Luise of Prussia and her sister Princess Friederike of Mecklenburg-Strelitz, greets visitors at the Alte Nationalgalerie. The life-size marble structure was commissioned in 1797.

7. The Lonely Tree
Of the extensive collection of German Romanticism works held at the Alte Nationalgalerie, this 1822 oil-on-canvas painting by Caspar David Friedrich is a highlight, depicting an ancient oak standing in a romantic landscape.

8. The Praying Boy
Created in 300 BCE, this Greek bronze statue was found on the island of Rhodes in the late 1400s. It's now in the Altes Museum, and depicts a naked male with his arms raised, sculpted in a Hellenistic style.

9. The Pazzi Madonna
This early Renaissance marble relief sculpture is the work of Donatello, and is said to come from the palace of the Pazzi family in Florence. Today it's found in the Bode-Museum's Sculpture Collection.

10. The Portrait Denar of Charlemagne
Held in the Numismatic collection at the Bode-Museum is this rare silver coin, created after 800 CE. One side shows a bust of Holy Roman emperor Charlemagne wearing a laurel wreath; the other shows a church with four columns.

SAVING MUSEUMSINSEL

The island of museums is a treasury of antique architecture, but until recently it had been slowly decaying. Since 1992, however, €1.8 billion has been spent on the renovation and modernization of Museumsinsel. A master plan created by renowned architects that include David Chipperfield and O M Ungers will transform the complex into a unique museum landscape – just as it was first conceived in the 19th century by Friedrich Wilhelm IV, when he established the "free institution for art and the sciences". Once fully completed by 2037, an "architectural promenade" will serve as a conceptual and structural link between various individual museums, except the Alte Nationalgalerie. This promenade will consist of a variety of rooms, courtyards and vaults, as well as exhibition halls. The core of the complex will be the James-Simon-Galerie, a central building opened in 2019. The Pergamonmuseum, which is undergoing extensive restoration, is scheduled to partially reopen in 2027.

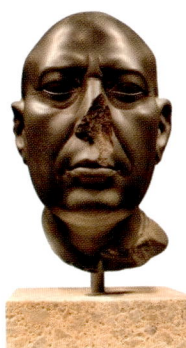

Berlin Green Head, one of the masterpieces in the Neus Museum's Egyptian Museum

Clockwise from left **Visitors at the spectacular Neues Museum; the eye-catching entrance to James-Simon-Galerie**

KURFÜRSTENDAMM

📍 C5

Breathtaking architecture, elegant boutiques and a lively street artist scene around Breitscheidplatz have made this shopping boulevard, known as Ku'damm, one of Berlin's most attractive and well known. At 3.8 km (2.5 miles), it's also the city's longest avenue for strolling, and a perfect way to get a feel for Berlin's vibrant energy.

1 Breitscheidplatz

Here, in the heart of the western city, artists, Berliners and visitors swarm around J Schmettan's globe fountain, known by locals as "Wasserklops" (water meatball).

> 🍴 **EAT**
> Experience bohemian Berlin at Schwarzes Café *(p130)*, a 24-hour café serving up hearty breakfasts and classic cakes, and stronger tipples for the evening crowd.

2 Zoo Palast

w zoopalast. premiumkino.de

This one-of-a-kind cinema was built in 1957 for the Berlinale Film Festival. Today, it is home to seven auditoriums.

3 Traffic Turret

On the corner of Joachimstaler Straße stands an old-fashioned traffic turret or *Verkehrskanzel*, the last one in the city and now a heritage monument. A police officer sat in the raised glass cabin to control traffic lights manually from 1955 until 1962, when the signals went automatic.

4 Kaiser-Wilhelm-Gedächtnis-Kirche

While the church itself was destroyed during World War II, its tower *(p40)* stands in the centre of the square, serving as both a memorial and a stark reminder of the terrors of war.

5 Bikini Berlin

📍 D4 🏠 Budapester Str. 38–50 🕐 10am–8pm Mon–Sat
w bikiniberlin.de

The Bikini-Haus building, built in 1956, was renovated to house the

Clockwise from right
**Neues Kranzler Eck
shopping centre;
the last standing traffic
turret in Berlin at
Kurfürstendamm; the
famous Schaubühne
theatre in Lehniner Platz**

splendid Bikini Berlin, a
hip boutique mall that
also offers great views
of the nearby zoo.

6 Neues Kranzler Eck

This steel-and-glass
building was built in
2000 by architect Helmut
Jahn. The legendary Café
Kranzler was retained
as a bar in front of the
office block. There is
an official Berlin Tourist
Info centre here.

7 Iduna-Haus

The turreted
building at No 59 at the
Leibnitzstraße corner is
one of the few surviving
bourgeois houses from
the late 19th century. The
ornamented Jugendstil
(Art Nouveau) façade has
been lavishly restored.

**Kurfürstendamm, Berlin's
main shopping street**

8 Fasanenstraße

A small street
(p125) off Ku'damm,
Fasanenstraße, with
its galleries, expensive
shops and restaurants, is
one of Charlottenburg's
most elegant areas.

9 Europa-Center

🔲 D4 🏠 Tauent-
zienstr. 9 🕐 10am–8pm
Mon–Sat 🌐 europa-
center-berlin.de

The oldest shopping
centre in West Berlin,
opened in 1962, is
still worth a visit. Here
you will find fashion
boutiques, a comedy
theatre and an official
Berlin Tourist Info centre.

10 Lehniner Platz

The square is home
to the iconic Schaubühne
theatre, built as the
Universum cinema in 1928
by Erich Mendelsohn and
converted in 1978.

**WHEN KU'DAMM
WAS NO MORE
THAN A LOG ROAD**

In 1542, Ku'damm
was just a humble
"Knüppeldamm",
or log road. It served
the Electors as a
bridle path, linking
their town residence
(Stadtschloss) and
their hunting lodge
(Jagdschloss). It was
not until 1871 that
the area around the
boulevard developed
into a fashionable
"new west end".
Chancellor Otto
von Bismarck had
the boulevard
modelled on the
Champs Elysées
in Paris, lined
with houses,
shops, hotels
and restaurants.

KAISER-WILHELM-GEDÄCHTNIS-KIRCHE

📍 D4 🏠 Breitscheidplatz 🕐 Church: 10am–6pm daily; memorial hall: 10am–6pm Mon–Sat, noon–6pm Sun 🔲 gedaechtniskirche-berlin.de 🔳

This ruined Neo-Romanesque church is one of Berlin's most haunting symbols. It was consecrated in 1895 and named Kaiser Wilhelm Memorial Church in honour of Wilhelm I. It stands as both a silent reminder of the destruction of war and a symbol of the city's determination to rebuild.

1 Tower Clock
The tower clock is based on a Classical design, with Roman numerals. At night, it is lit blue by modern light-emitting diodes to match the serene lighting inside.

> **TOP TIP**
> A special music service takes place at 6pm every Saturday.

2 Tower Ruins
Only the church tower survived the Allied bombing raids that razed much of the city to the ground in 1943. Today 71 m (233 ft) high, the tower once rose to 113 m (370 ft). The rough hole in its roof has led to its nickname, "the Hollow Tooth".

3 New Bell Tower
The hexagonal bell tower rises 53 m (174 ft) next to the tower ruins, on the site of the old church's main nave.

4 Russian Orthodox Cross
This gift from the bishops of Volokolomsk and Yuruyev was given in memory of the victims of Nazism.

5 Mosaic of the Hohenzollerns
The vividly coloured mosaic of the Hohenzollerns *(p45)* adorns the vestibule of the church ruins. It depicts Kaiser Wilhelm I together with Queen Luise of Prussia and her entourage.

6 Main Altar
The golden figure of Christ created by Karl Hemmeter is suspended above the main altar in the modern church. In the evening light, the

The only surviving church tower, "the Hollow Tooth"

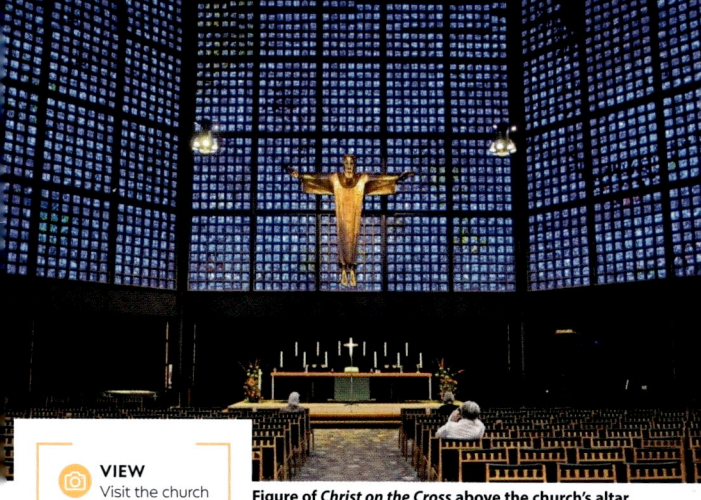

Figure of *Christ on the Cross* above the church's altar

VIEW
Visit the church on a sunny day around lunchtime, when the blue glass window is at its most divine, with light shining through.

windows behind the altar glow an intense dark blue.

7 Kaiser's Mosaic

One of the preserved mosaics shows Heinrich I on his throne, with the imperial orb and sceptre. Originally decorated with scenes from German imperial history, the interior was intended to place the Hohenzollerns within that tradition.

8 Original Mosaics

Glittering mosaics in Jugendstil style showing Prussian dukes and princes are preserved on the walls and ceilings along the stairways.

9 Figure of Christ

Miraculously, the vast, plain sculpture of Christ, which is suspended from the ceiling, survived the bombing of the church.

10 Coventry Crucifix

This small crucifix was forged from old nails that were found in the ruins of Coventry Cathedral in England. It honours the bombing of Coventry by the German Luftwaffe in 1940.

A CHURCH WITH TWO LIVES

The Kaiser-Wilhelm-Gedächtnis-Kirche has the people of Berlin to thank for its preservation: in 1947, the Senate had planned to demolish the tower ruins for safety reasons. In a referendum, however, one in two Berliners voted to preserve it. And so the idea came about to build a new church next to the ruin and to preserve the vestibule of the old church as a striking memorial hall to the horrors of war.

Mosaic showing Kaiser Wilhelm I and the royal family

SCHLOSS CHARLOTTENBURG

📍 B3 🏠 Spandauer Damm 🌐 spsg.de ⤴

One of Berlin's premier royal sights, the former Hohenzollern summer residence offers a glimpse into Prussian history. The palace complex, with its extravagant Baroque buildings, beautifully landscaped gardens, and richly decorated interiors that are unmatched in Berlin, is almost a small village in itself.

1 Schlosskapelle
The splendour of the palace's chapel recalls the once magnificent interior of the complex, before it was destroyed in World War II. Apart from the original altar, the entire chapel is a costly reconstruction.

2 Altes Schloss
🕐 Apr–Oct: 10am–5:30pm Tue–Sun; Nov–Mar: 10am–4:30pm Tue–Sun
The Baroque tower of the oldest part of the palace (c 1695) by Johann Arnold Nering is crowned by Richard Scheibe's golden statue of Fortuna.

3 Neuer Flügel
Built between 1740 and 1747 by Georg W von Knobelsdorff, the New Wing contains Frederick the Great's private quarters, as well as a large collection of 18th-century French paintings.

4 Monument to the Great Elector
The striking equestrian statue of the Great Elector Friedrich Wilhelm is thought to be one of his most dignified portraits. Made by Andreas Schlüter

Friedrich Wilhelm

Stunning Baroque façade of the palace

> ☕ **DRINK**
> With its attractive garden and tree-lined patio, the Orangery Café is the perfect place to relax with a cup of tea or coffee.

TOP TIP

Take a romantic midweek evening stroll to avoid the crowds.

between 1696 and 1703, it originally stood on the Rathausbrücke, near the destroyed Stadtschloss.

5 Käthe-Kollwitz-Museum
⏱ 11am–6pm daily

This museum showcases the works of sculptress and graphic artist Käthe Kollwitz (1867–1945), including 200 drawings and prints, sculptures, a woodcut series about the war and self-portraits spanning 50 years. Kollwitz was the first woman elected to the Prussian Academy of Arts, but was later ostracized by the Nazis.

6 Belvedere
Friedrich Wilhelm II liked to escape to the romantic Belvedere,

a summer residence built in 1788 by Carl Gotthard Langhans, which served as a tea pavilion. Today it houses a collection of precious porcelain objects from Berlin.

7 Schlosspark
⏱ 8am–sunset daily

The palace has a lovely Baroque garden, beyond which lies a vast park, redesigned by Peter Joseph Lenné in 1818–28 in the English style with rivers, artificial lakes and small follies.

8 Porzellankabinett
This small, exquisite mirrored gallery has been faithfully restored to its original glory. Among the exhibits are valuable porcelain items from China and Japan.

9 Neuer Pavillon
This Italianate villa, designed by Karl Friedrich Schinkel for Friedrich Wilhelm III in 1825, was inspired by the Villa Reale del Chiatamone in Naples.

10 Mausoleum
⏱ Apr–Oct: 10am–5pm Tue–Sun; Nov–Mar: 11am–3pm daily

Slightly hidden, this Neo-Classical building by Schinkel is the final resting place of many Hohenzollerns.

BUILDING THE SCHLOSS

The construction of Schloss Charlottenburg began in 1695. The Orangerie was extended and a cupola was added by Johann Friedrich Eosander between 1702 and 1713. Subsequent extensions were undertaken by Frederick the Great, who added the Neuer Flügel in the mid-1700s.

Exquisite ceramics in the Porzellankabinett

Schloss Charlottenburg Rooms

1. Eichengalerie
The wooden panelling of the Oak Gallery is carved with expensively gilded portraits of Hohenzollern ancestors.

2. Gris-de-Lin-Kammer
This small chamber in Friedrich II's second palace apartment is decorated with paintings, including some by his favourite artist, Antoine Watteau. The room was named after its wall coverings in violet-coloured damask.

3. Schlafzimmer der Königin Luise
Queen Luise's bedchamber, designed in 1810 by Karl Friedrich Schinkel, features the clear lines typical of the Neo-Classical style.

4. Winterkammern
Friedrich Wilhelm II's early Neo-Classical rooms contain fine paintings, tapestries and furniture.

5. Grünes Zimmer
The green room in Queen Elisabeth's quarters is an excellent example of royal chambers furnished in 19th-century Biedermeier style.

6. Goldene Galerie
The festival salon in the Neuer Flügel, 42 m (138 ft) long, was designed in

Goldene Galerie, a Rococo garden ballroom from 1746

Rococo style by Frederick the Great's favourite architect, von Knobelsdorff. The richly ornamented room has a cheerful appearance.

7. Bibliothek
Frederick the Great's small but outstanding library has elegant bookcases and a vibrant, light green colour scheme.

8. Konzertkammer
The furniture and gilded panelling in the concert hall have been faithfully recreated as during Frederick the Great's time. Antoine Watteau's *Gersaint's Shop Sign*, considered to be one of his most significant works, hangs here; the king bought the work directly from the artist.

9. Rote Kammer
The elegant chamber, decorated entirely in red and gold, is adorned by portraits of King Friedrich I and Sophie Charlotte.

10. Friedrich I's Audienzkammer
The ceiling paintings and Belgian tapestries depict allegorical figures symbolizing the fine arts and the sciences. There are also magnificent lacquered cabinets, modelled on Asian originals.

Interior of the royal chamber, Gris-De-Lin-Kammer

THE HOHENZOLLERNS AND BERLIN

In 1411, Burggraf Friedrich of the Hohenzollern dynasty of Nuremberg was asked by Sigismund of Luxemburg to support him in a princely feuding before the imperial election for the throne. When Sigismund became king, he gave Friedrich, in 1415, the titles of Margrave and Prince-Elector of Brandenburg as a reward for his services – this is where the histories of the Hohenzollerns and Berlin first became entwined, a relationship that was to last for 500 years. From the start, the family tried to limit the powers of the town and of the Brandenburg nobility. Culture, however, flourished under the new rulers, especially the Great Elector 200 years later, who invited 20,000 Huguenot crafters to Berlin and founded an art gallery and several schools. His grandson Friedrich Wilhelm I, father of Frederick the Great, transformed the city into a military camp, with garrisons and parade grounds, and scoured it for tall men to join his guard unit. In the 19th century, however, relations between Berlin and the Hohenzollerns became decidedly less cordial.

Engraving of the Great Elector welcoming the exiled Huguenots

9

KULTURFORUM

L2 **West of Potsdamer Platz** **smb.museum**

Home to some of the most outstanding European art museums, as well as the famous concert hall of the Berlin Philharmonic Orchestra, Kulturforum attracts millions of visitors interested in culture and music. The complex, based in the former West Berlin, has been growing steadily since 1956 as a counterpoint to Museumsinsel in the former East Berlin.

structure (*p62*) to be built in the Kulturforum in 1960–3. Considered one of the best concert halls in the world, it is the home of the Berlin Philharmonic Orchestra. Kirill Petrenko has been conducting the orchestra since 2019.

1 Musikinstrumen-ten-Museum

Concealed behind the Philharmonie is this fascinating museum (*p55*) of musical instruments. More than 800 exhibits are on show here, including harpsichords and a 1929 Wurlitzer.

2 Neue Nationalgalerie

Designed by German-American architect Ludwig Mies van der Rohe, this spacious gallery (*p62*) occupies two floors and showcases 20th-century art, with a focus on German Expressionism. It also hosts temporary exhibitions regularly.

3 Philharmonie

Herbert-von-Karajan-Str. 1
Hours vary, check website berliner-philharmoniker.de

This tent-like building was the first new

4 Kunstgewerbe-museum

Craft objects from across Europe from the Middle Ages to the present day are on show at this museum (*p54*), including valuable items like the Guelph Treasure, silver from Lüneburg and Renaissance faïence.

5 Kammer-musiksaal

The smaller relative of the larger Philharmonie, this concert hall (*p62*) is one of Germany's most highly regarded chamber music venues.

Vintage harpsichord

TOP TIP

Free lunch concerts are held on summer Wednesdays at the Philharmonie.

Works on display at the Gemäldegalerie

6 Kupferstich-kabinett

🏛 Matthäihirchplatz 8
🕐 10am–5pm Wed–Fri, 11am–6pm Sat & Sun

The Gallery of Prints and Drawings holds more than 550,000 prints and 110,000 drawings from many periods and countries.

7 Gemäldegalerie

🏛 Matthäihirchplatz 4/6
🕐 10am–6pm Tue–Sun

Berlin's largest art museum holds master-pieces of European art by the likes of Bosch, Titian and Rembrandt. They are displayed in the modern Neubau, built in 1998 by Heinz Hilmer and Christoph Sattler.

8 Kunstbibliothek

🏛 Matthäihirch-platz 6
🕐 10am–5pm Wed–Fri, 10am–6pm Sat & Sun

The Art Library has a collection of advertising and art posters and also hosts art and architec-ture exhibitions and design shows.

9 St Matthäus-Kirche

🏛 Matthäihirchplatz 1
🕐 11am–6pm Tue–Sun
🌐 stiftung-stmatthaeus.de 🔗

This church is the only historic building pre-served in the Kulturforum.

Built in 1844–6 by Stüler, it is also a venue for art installations and classical music concerts.

10 Staats-bibliothek

🏛 Potsdamer Str. 33
🕐 8am–10pm Mon–Sat, 10am–6pm Sun
🌐 staatsbibliothek-berlin.de

Built between 1967 and 1978 by Hans Scharoun and Edgar Wisniewski, the National Library is one of the world's largest German-language libraries, with around five million books, manu-scripts and journals.

Glass façade of the Gemäldegalerie

Gemäldegalerie

1. Portrait of Hieronymus Holzschuher
Albrecht Dürer painted this portrait of the mayor of Nuremburg in 1529.

2. Madonna with Child and Singing Angels
A 1477 painting by Sandro Botticelli, this depicts the Madonna and Child, surrounded by angels carrying lilies.

3. The Birth of Christ
Martin Schongauer's altar painting (c 1480) is one of only a few religious paintings by the Alsatian artist that have been preserved.

4. Cupid as Victor
Caravaggio's 1602 painting shows Cupid, the god of love, trampling the symbols of culture, glory, science and power.

5. Portrait of the Merchant Georg Gisze
This 1532 painting by Hans Holbein, showing the Hanseatic League

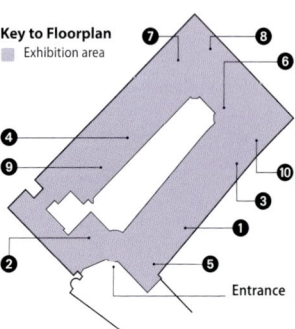

Key to Floorplan
Exhibition area

Gemäldegalerie Floorplan

merchant Georg Gisze counting his money, reflects the rise of the rich citizen during the Renaissance.

6. Portrait of Hendrickje Stoffels
In a 1656–7 portrait of his lover Hendrickje Stoffels, Rembrandt's focus is entirely on the subject.

7. The French Comedy
This painting by Antoine Watteau belonged to the collection of Frederick the Great.

8. The Glass of Wine
A skilfully composed scene, Vermeer's *The Glass of Wine* (1658–61) shows a couple drinking wine.

9. Venus and the Organ Player
Painted by Titian (1550–52), this piece reflects the playful sensuality typical of the Italian Renaissance.

10. Dutch Proverbs
Pieter Brueghel beautifully incorporated and literalized more than 100 proverbs into this 1559 painting.

Hans Holbein's *Portrait of the Merchant Georg Gisze*

ARCHITECTURE IN THE KULTURFORUM

The Kulturforum was planned to fill the area between Potsdamer Straße and Leipziger Platz that had been destroyed during the war. The idea for a townscape of museums and parks is credited to Berlin architect Hans Scharoun, who had designed plans for this between 1946 and 1957. It was also Scharoun who, with the building of the Philharmonie in 1963, set the character of the Kulturforum: the tent-like roofs of the music hall, the Kammermusiksaal and the National Library, designed by him and – after his death – realized by his pupil Edgar Wisniewski, are today among Berlin's top landmarks. All the buildings are characterized by the generously proportioned rooms and, although controversial when they were built, are today considered classics of modern architecture.

**Tent-like roof of the
Berlin Philharmonie**

Philharmonie's auditorium, known for its acoustics

10

JÜDISCHES MUSEUM BERLIN

📍 G5 🏠 Lindenstr. 9–14 🕐 10am–6pm daily (last adm: 5pm) 🌐 jmberlin.de 🔗

The Jewish Museum is one of the most important memorials to the history and culture of Germany's Jewish community. Its displays explore the German-Jewish relationship over the centuries, while the building itself is part of a symbolic design. Together, they create an unforgettable experience. Entry is free for those under 18 years of age.

1 Libeskind Building

Designed by Daniel Libeskind, this building echoes the complex German-Jewish history – its zig-zagging floor plan, concrete "voids", and angled walls and windows sliced into the façade, speak to this complex past.

2 Old Building

This Baroque building, built in 1735 as the Prussian Court of Justice, serves as the entrance to the Libeskind Building. The two buildings are connected via an underground passage. The Old Building houses the ticket counter, visitor information desk, a shop and the Eßkultur café.

3 Permanent Exhibition

The new core exhibition, "Jewish Life in Germany: Past and Present", covers, curates and explicitly presents the culture, traditions, religion and, of course, the history of the Jewish community in Germany, from the Middle Ages to the present day.

4 The Voids

A straight line of five concrete spaces, or the "voids", cut through the entire vertical axis

GALLERY GUIDE

Entrance to the main museum (the Libeskind Building) is via an underground tunnel. The exhibition is divided into 14 sections, taking visitors through German-Jewish history and culture from early history up to the present day.

Libeskind Building housing the museum

of the Libeskind Building. These voids are intended to represent the permanent physical emptiness left behind after the Holocaust.

5 Shalekhet Installation

One of the most poignant exhibits at the museum is the *Shalekhet* (Fallen Leaves) instal-

Artworks showing Jewish life in Germany

lation by Israeli sculptor Menashe Kadishman. It features over 10,000 iron plates, with open-mouthed faces, which visitors must walk over to cross the interesting "Memory Void" on the ground floor of the Libeskind Building.

6 Music Room

This room beautifully celebrates Jewish music and its prominent role in religious and everyday Jewish life. Immerse yourself in mellifluous chantings and soothing compositions.

7 Courtyard

The stunning glass-enclosed courtyard, part of Libeskind's design in the Old Building, and the adjoining garden provide a calm place for reflection.

8 Holocaust Tower

Located along one of the museum's diagonal walkways, the Holocaust Tower lies at the

end of the Axis of the Holocaust. Designed with only one narrow slit for sunlight, it imparts a sense of oppression.

9 The Garden of Exile

Set on a slope, The Garden of Exile represents the disorientation and instability of life in exile. The garden is a perfect square made of 49 concrete columns, with the central column filled with earth from Jerusalem.

10 Objects

A highlight of the museum's permanent exhibition are the objects and personal effects that narrate the history of German Jews. The collection includes art, photographs, applied art and religious artifacts.

Hanukkah candlestick

TOP 10 OF EVERYTHING

The Holocaust Denkmal

MUSEUMS

1 Pergamonmuseum
📍 J5   🏛 Bodestraße 1–3
🌐 smb.museum ✔

This impressive museum on Museumsinsel is a vast treasure trove of antiquities. It is undergoing extensive renovations and will remain closed until a partial reopening in 2027.

2 Ägyptisches Museum
📍 J5   🏛 Museumsinsel, Bodestr. 1   🕐 10am–6pm daily
🌐 smb.museum ✔

The star exhibit displayed at the Egyptian Museum, part of the Neues Museum, is the bust of Nefertiti, wife of Akhenaton. The limestone bust, excavated in 1912, was copied all over ancient Egypt. Another highlight is the Berlin Green Head, a small bust from the 4th century BCE. The museum also holds numerous mummies, sarcophagi, murals and sculptures.

3 Deutsches Historisches Museum
Germany's largest history museum (p27) uses unique exhibits, documents and films

Pei Building home to the Deutsches Historisches Museum

to take the visitor on a journey through German history, from the Middle Ages to the present day.

4 Museum Europäischer Kulturen
This museum (p153) specializes in European folk art, lifestyle, tradition and culture, and, with some 280,000 objects, is one of the largest of its kind in the world. It hosts long-running as well as temporary exhibitions, often in conjunction with museums from other European countries. Among the vast collection of exhibits on display are earthenware items, costumes, handicrafts, jewellery, toys and tools.

5 Kunstgewerbemuseum
📍 L1   🏛 Matthäikirchplatz
🕐 10am–5pm Wed–Fri, 11am–6pm Sat & Sun   🌐 smb.museum ✔

European crafts spanning five centuries are on display at the Museum of Decorative Arts. Its most valuable exhibits are the Guelph Treasure from Braunschweig and the silver treasure of the town council in Lüneburg. The museum also holds Italian tin-glazed earthenware, Renaissance faïence and German Baroque glass and ceramics. Popular displays show Neo-Classical porcelain and furniture, Jugendstil art and Tiffany vases.

6 Haus am Checkpoint Charlie
This museum (p133), set at the former Allied checkpoint, hosts an exhibition documenting events at the Berlin Wall. It screens documentaries relating to the exhibition theme throughout the day. In front of the museum is the famous sign that reads, "You are now leaving the American sector", written in English, Russian, French and German.

Junkers Ju 52 plane at the Deutsches Technikmuseum

7 Deutsches Technikmuseum
The fascinating German Museum of Technology (p133), built on the site of a former railway goods yard, has exciting displays on the history of technology.

8 Jüdisches Museum Berlin
The Jewish Museum (p50), housed in a spectacular building designed by Daniel Libeskind, documents the German-Jewish relationship through the centuries. There are special exhibitions on the influence of Berlin Jews on the city's cultural life, and on the life of the Enlightenment philosopher Moses Mendelssohn. An empty room commemorates the loss of Jewish culture. There is also an excellent programme of special events. The core exhibition opened in 2020.

9 Museum für Naturkunde
With over 30 million intriguing specimens in its grand collection, the Natural History Museum (p102) is one of the largest of its kind in the world. One of the star features is the world's largest dinosaur skeleton, a Giraffatitan found in Tanzania in 1909. There are six more dinosaur skeletons as well as a variety of fossils here. It is also worth making a visit to the glittering exhibition of meteorites and minerals.

10 Musikinstrumenten-Museum
📍L2 🏠Ben-Gurion-Str 1 🕐9am–1pm Tue, 9am–5pm Wed & Fri, 9am–8pm Thu, 10am–5pm Sat & Sun 🌐simph.de ♿

Some 800 musical instruments are on display in this museum, including Frederick the Great's harpsichord. One of the highlights here is the silent film organ, which still works. Saturdays at noon is the best time to visit.

ART GALLERIES

Johannes Vermeer's painting
The Glass of Wine

1 Gemäldegalerie
Berlin's best art museum, the Gemäldegalerie *(p47)* holds European art of the 13th–19th centuries, including Vermeer's *The Glass of Wine* and *The Adoration of the Shepherds* by Hugo van der Goes, and works by Rembrandt, Dürer, Caravaggio and Rubens.

2 Alte Nationalgalerie
The Old National Gallery *(p35)*, built by Friedrich August Stüler in 1866–76, holds a collection of 19th-century, mainly German paintings, including works by Max Liebermann, Wilhelm Leibl, Adolf von Menzel and Arnold Böcklin. It also houses sculptures by Johann Gottfried Schadow and Reinhold Begas, and is one of the many museums set on Museumsinsel *(p34)*, an island in the Spree River.

3 Brücke-Museum
🚇 Bussardsteig 9 🕐 11am–5pm Wed–Mon 🌐 bruecke-museum.de ♿
A must-see collection of German Expressionist works by members of the artists' group Die Brücke (The Bridge), including Kirchner and Pechstein. Many Die Brücke works were labelled "degenerate" by the Nazis and destroyed.

4 Martin-Gropius-Bau
Named after German architect Martin Gropius, this building houses a rotation of popular temporary art exhibitions, on-site studio spaces and a children's play area called BAUBAU.

5 Kunsthaus Dahlem
🚇 N6 🚇 Käuzchensteig 8 🕐 11am–5pm Wed–Mon 🌐 kunsthaus-dahlem.de
This exhibition venue for postwar German Modernism was built from 1939–42 for sculptor Arno Breker. The building was used by US

Artworks displayed at the Alte Nationalgalerie on Museumsinsel

Information Control Division after the war and later became a workspace for artists.

6 C/O Berlin
C4 □ Amerika-Haus, Hardenbergstr 22–24 □ 11am–8pm daily □ co-berlin.org

Located in the former Amerika-Haus, this gallery hosts regularly changing exhibitions, lectures and historical and contemporary photography events.

7 Berlinische Galerie
G5 □ Alte Jakobstr 124–128 □ 10am–6pm Wed–Mon □ berlinischegalerie.de

On display here are collections of German, east European and Russian painters, photographers, graphic designers and architects of the 20th century.

8 Sammlung Scharf-Gerstenberg
B3 □ Schlossstr 70 □ 10am–6pm Wed–Sun □ smb.museum

This gallery has rare works by Surrealists and their forerunners, such as Goya, Klee, Dalí, Max Ernst and Man Ray.

9 Bröhan-Museum
B3 □ Schlossstr 1a □ 10am–6pm Tue–Sun (free 1st Wed of month) □ broehan-museum.de

Set in a late Neo-Classical building, this museum showcases Jugendstil and Art Deco objects from around Europe, and paintings by Berlin artists.

10 Hamburger Bahnhof
The historic Hamburg Station *(p118)* houses modern artworks dating from 1960s up to the present day. The collection includes paintings, installations and multimedia art. Former dispatch warehouses were converted and linked to the old railway building, forming the Rieckhallen, and doubling the exhibition space. Among the many highlights is the Erich Marx Collection, with works by Joseph Beuys. Apart from famous artists like Andy Warhol, Jeff Koons and Robert Rauschenberg, it also showcases works by Anselm Kiefer, Sandro Chiao and others. At night, the museum's façade is lit up by a neon light installation by American artist Dan Flavin.

Neo-Classical façade of the Hamburger Bahnhof

CHURCHES AND SYNAGOGUES

Beautiful main altar and pulpit of the Berliner Dom

1 Berliner Dom
🗺 K5 🏛 Am Lustgarten ⏰ 9am–6pm Mon–Fri, 9am–5pm Sat, noon–5pm Sun (opening hours subject to concert schedule, check website) 🌐 berlinerdom.de ↗

Berlin Cathedral (p35), the largest and most lavish church in the city, was reopened in 1993, after almost 40 years of restoration work. Designed by Julius Raschdorf between 1894 and 1905, the building reflects the empire's aspirations to power. In particular, the black marble imperial stairs are a sign of the proximity of the Hohenzollern residence opposite the cathedral. Members of this powerful ruling dynasty are buried in the crypt. The main nave, topped by an 85-m- (279-ft-) high dome, is remarkable. The church is dominated by a splendid 20th-century Neo-Baroque pulpit and the giant Sauer organ.

2 St-Hedwigs-Kathedrale
Berlin's largest Catholic church (p26) was built by Frederick the Great in 1747–73. Renovation work on the cathedral was completed in 2024.

3 Marienkirche
Work started in 1270 on the Church of St Mary (p110), which nestles at the foot of the Fernsehturm. Gothic and Baroque in style, it has an impressive Neo-Gothic tower, added in 1790 by Carl Gotthard Langhans. The font (1437) and the fresco *Dance of the Dead* (1485) are among the oldest treasures of the church. The richly ornamented Baroque pulpit was made by Andreas Schlüter in 1703.

4 Nikolaikirche
🗺 K6 🏛 Nikolaikirchplatz ⏰ 10am–6pm daily 🌐 stadtmuseum.de/en ↗

Berlin's oldest sacred building, this church was built in 1230 in the Nikolaiviertel quarter. The present structure dates to around 1300. It is particularly famous for the portal on the west wall of the main nave, created by Andreas Schlüter. It is adorned with a gilded relief depicting a goldsmith and his wife. The church was rebuilt in 1987 and completely restored in 2009. It is now a museum exploring the history of the church and the surrounding area. Events and concerts are held here regularly.

5 Synagoge Rykestraße
The largest synagogue (p143) in Berlin, Rykestraße is one of the few Jewish places of worship in Germany to have survived Kristallnacht. It looks the same today as it did 100 years ago.

6 Christi-Auferstehungs-Kathedrale
🗺 B6 🏛 Hohenzollerndamm 166 ⏰ 9:30am–12:30pm daily 🌐 soborberlin.com

Berlin's largest Russian Orthodox church, the Church of Christ's Ascension

Splendid domes of the Neue Synagoge

is known for its green onion domes. Services are held in Russian, following Orthodox rituals.

7 Friedrichswerdersche Kirche

⌂ Werderscher Markt ⌚ 10am–5pm Wed–Fri, 10am–6pm Sat & Sun

This Neo-Gothic church, built between 1824 and 1830 by Karl Friedrich Schinkel, was originally meant to serve the German and French communities of the Friedrichswerder district. Today, the rededicated church holds the splendid sculpture collections of the Alte Nationalgalerie (p35).

8 Kaiser-Wilhelm-Gedächtnis-Kirche

A West Berlin landmark, this iconic Neo-Romanesque church (p40) successfully combines modern architecture with the ruins of the church tower. The church's interior is decorated with mosaics.

9 Neue Synagoge

Once Berlin's largest synagogue, the New Synagogue (p101) was built originally between 1859 and 1866. It was demolished in World War II and partially reconstructed in 1988–95. Its ornate dome is visible from afar.

10 Französischer Dom

⌂ L4 ⌂ Gendarmenmarkt 5 ⌚ Summer: 10am–7pm daily; winter: 10:30am–6pm daily ⓦ franzoesischer-dom.de

Standing at a height of 66 m (216 ft) in the beautiful Gendarmenmarkt, this elegant domed Baroque tower dates back to between 1780 and 1789. It is a magnificent ornamental addition to the Friedrichstadtkirche, which was built to serve Berlin's Huguenot community.

HISTORIC BUILDINGS

1 Reichstag
The seat of the Deutscher Bundestag, the German parliament (*p24*), with its spectacular dome, is a magnet for visitors.

2 Siegessäule
The Victory Column in Tiergarten (*p117*) is topped by a statue of the goddess Victoria. Designed by Heinrich Strack after Prussia's victory in the Danish-Prussian War of 1864, it was refurbished in 2010.

Statue of Victoria on the Siegessäule

3 Rotes Rathaus
Berlin's Town Hall (*p101*), also known as "Red Town Hall" because of the red bricks from Brandenburg province with which it was built, harks back to the proud days when Berlin became the capital of the new Empire. Built in 1861–9 according to designs by Hermann Friedrich Waesemann, the town hall was one of Germany's largest and most magnificent buildings, built to promote the splendour of Berlin. The structure was modelled on Italian Renaissance palaces, and the tower is reminiscent of Laon cathedral in France.

4 Brandenburger Tor
More than a mere monument, the Brandenburg Gate (*p22*) is synonymous with Berlin. It was modelled on the entrance to the Acropolis in Athens, and has stood watch over the city since 1791.

5 Schloss Charlottenburg
Built in 1695, this palace (*p42*) features Baroque and Rococo splendours and a beautiful park, making it one of the most attractive in Germany. It's made up of two magnificent buildings: the Altes Schloss (Old Palace) and Neuer Flügel (New Wing).

The Reichstag, seat of
Germany's parliament

6 Schloss Bellevue
🅿 E3 🏠 Spreeweg 1 🕒 To the public
🌐 bundespraesident.de/EN

Built by Philipp Daniel Boumann in
1785–90, this was the residence of
the Hohenzollerns until 1861. Since
1994 the stately building with its Neo-
Classical façade has been the official
residence of the President of the
Federal Republic. The modern, egg-
shaped Presidential Offices stand
next to the old palace.

7 Konzerthaus
🅿 L4 🏠 Gendarmenmarkt 2
🕒 Apr–Oct: 11am–6pm daily
🌐 en.honzerthaus.de 🌐

The Concert Hall is one of Karl
Friedrich Schinkel's masterpieces.
Built in 1818–21, it was once known
as the *Schauspielhaus* (theatre), and
was used as such until 1945. It was
damaged during World War II, and
then reopened in its new avatar as
the *Konzerthaus* (p92) in 1984. The
building has a portico with Ionic
columns and statues of allegorical
and historical personages.

8 Hackesche Höfe
This complex (p101) of 19th-century
buildings has eight interlinked court-
yards, some of which are decorated in
Jugendstil style, originally by August
Endell. In the early 1990s the complex

was renovated. The first courtyard
is particularly attractive: coloured
glazed tiles with geometric patterns
decorate the house from the foun-
dations up to the guttering. In the
last courtyard, trees are grouped
around an idyllic well. The Hackesche
Höfe is one of Berlin's most popular
spots, especially on weekends, with
restaurants, cafés, a cinema and
the Chamäleon Theatre.

9 Altes Museum and Lustgarten
The façade of the Old Museum (p32),
possibly one of the most attractive Neo-
Classical museum buildings in Europe,
is remarkable for the 18 Ionic columns
supporting a portico. Built in 1830 to
Karl Friedrich Schinkel's design, it was
at the time one of the first buildings
to be created specifically as a museum.
Originally it was to house the royal
collection of paintings; today it is home
to a collection of antiquities. In front of
the museum is a garden (p96) designed
by Peter Joseph Lenné. Conceived as the
king's herb garden, it is now decorated
with a 70-ton granite bowl by Gottlieb
Christian Cantian and a fountain.

10 Zeughaus
Designed by Johann Arnold
Nering as the first Berlin Baroque
building, the former Royal Prussian
Arsenal is now the Deutsches
Historisches Museum (p27), with a
modern addition by I M Pei.

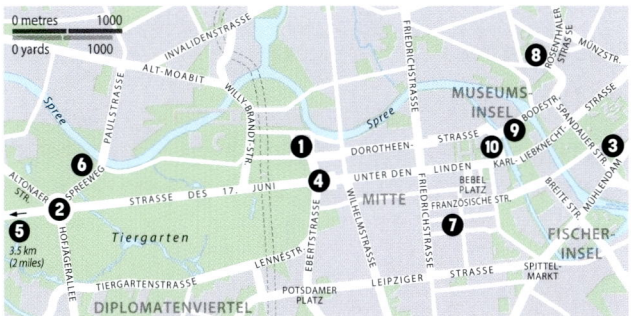

MODERN BUILDINGS

**Shell-shaped roof of the
Haus der Kulturen der Welt**

abandoned after the Cuban Revolution.
The collection here brings together the
best of 20th-century art from Europe
and North America.

3 Das Center am Potsdamer Platz (former Sony Center)
The spectacular building complex (p30),
with its unique roof, is one of Berlin's
largest structures.

4 Hauptbahnhof
📍 J2 🚉 Hauptbahnhof
Europe's largest train station sits on
the site of the historic Lehrter Bahnhof.
This impressive glass-and-steel structure
doubles as a retail and hospitality hub.

5 Philharmonie and Kammermusiksaal
Two modern concert halls (p46) in
the Kulturforum were designed by
Hans Scharoun in 1961 and 1987 respectively – the Kammermusiksaal
(chamber music hall) was completed
after Scharoun's death in 1972 according to his plans by his pupil Edgar
Wisniewski. Both buildings are renowned for their excellent acoustics as well
as for their tent-like roof structures.

1 Haus der Kulturen der Welt
📍 K2 🏛 John-Foster-Dulles-Allee
10 🕐 Noon–7pm Wed–Mon
🌐 hkw.de/en
Designed by American architect
Henry Stubbins in 1957, this building
features a curved roof that resembles
a giant eye gazing over Tiergarten.

2 Neue Nationalgalerie
📍 L1 🕐 10am–6pm Tue–Sat
(to 8pm Thu) 🌐 smb.museum
This impressive structure was constructed
in 1965–8 by Mies van der Rohe. It was
the first building by the pioneering
Bauhaus architect after his emigration
to the US. He made use of his earlier
designs for the Havana head-quarters of
the Bacardi company, which had been

Bundeskanzleramt, home of the offices of the German Chancellor

6 Bundeskanzleramt
K2 Willy-Brandt-Str. 1
To the public

The Chancellor's modern office complex is the only government building to have been designed by a Berlin architect. Axel Schultes developed a vast, elongated office complex, which extends north of the Reichstag, in a bend of the Spree, even stretching across the river. In the centre of the modern building stands a gleaming white cube with round windows, which Berliners quickly nicknamed the "Washing Machine". The interior of the building is decorated with valuable modern paintings. The Chancellor's office on the 7th floor has a view of the Reichstag building.

7 Nordische Botschaften
D4 Rauchstr Gallery: 11am–7pm Mon–Fri, 11am–4pm Sat & Sun
nordicembassies.org

No other embassy building has caused as much of a stir as this one housing five embassies of the Nordic countries: its green shutters open and close depending on the available light. Art exhibitions are held here regularly and there's a canteen and coffee bar.

8 Ludwig-Erhard-Haus
C4 Fasanenstr 85 8am–5pm Mon–Thu, 8am–4pm Fri
ihk.de/berlin/leh

The seat of the Berlin Stock Exchange, Ludwig-Erhard-Haus was designed by British architect Nicholas Grimshaw in 1994–8. Locals refer to it as the "armadillo" because the 15 giant metal arches of the domed building recall the animal's armour.

9 Kant-Dreieck
C4 Kantstr 155

The enormous "shark fin" on top of the KapHag-Group's head-quarters, built by Josef Paul Kleihues in 1992–5, has become a symbol of modern Berlin. The aluminium weather vane is designed to turn in the wind like a sail. Originally, the structure, known as the "Kant Triangle", was to be built one-third higher than it is now, but the plans were vetoed by the Berlin Senate.

10 DZ Bank on Pariser Platz

This elegant building (p23) by Frank Owen Gehry combines Prussian and modern architecture. The giant dome inside is remarkable.

Modern façade of the DZ Bank building

FAMOUS BERLINERS

Acclaimed Berlin-born actress Marlene Dietrich

1 Marlene Dietrich
Born in Schöneberg, Marlene Dietrich (1901–92) launched her career on Berlin's infamous cabaret scene in the 1920s. Her breakthrough role in the film *The Blue Angel* (1931), which was filmed at Babelsberg's legendary UFA Studios *(p162)*, propelled her to international stardom. Dietrich lies buried in the Friedenau cemetery in Steglitz.

2 Albert Einstein
Director of the Kaiser Wilhelm-Institute for Physics, Albert Einstein (1879–1955) was awarded the Nobel Prize for Physics in 1921. He is now better known for his Theory of Relativity, first developed in 1905. Einstein mostly lived and worked in Potsdam, but was connected with Berlin through his lectures and teaching activity. In 1933 Einstein, who was Jewish, emigrated to the US, where he stayed until his death.

3 Bertolt Brecht
Born in Augsburg, Bavaria, Bertolt Brecht (1898–1956) wrote some of his greatest works, such as the *Threepenny Opera*, in a small apartment in Charlottenburg. During the Third Reich, he emigrated to the US, and returned to Germany after the war and founded the Berliner Ensemble in East Berlin in 1949. He lived in Chausseestraße with his wife, Helene Weigel, until his death. His renovated apartment is now a museum.

4 Robert Koch
A pioneer of modern medicine, Robert Koch (1843–1910) was the Director of the Institute for Infectious Diseases. He also taught and researched at the Charité Hospital. In 1905 he received the Nobel Prize for Medicine for his discoveries in the field of tuberculosis research.

5 Käthe Kollwitz
The sculptor and painter Käthe Kollwitz (1867–1945) portrayed the social problems of the poor, and her work provides a powerful, haunting commentary on human suffering. She spent most of her life in a modest abode in the square that is now named after her, in the Prenzlauer Berg district. A monument now celebrates her works and an enlarged reproduction of her *Pietà* now adorns the Neue Wache *(p26)* war memorial.

6 Alexander von Humboldt
Born into an aristocratic Prussian family during the Enlightenment, Humboldt (1769–1859) is widely considered one of the founders of modern geography and ecology. Berlin's oldest university, Humboldt-Universität *(p27)*, is named in his honour.

Alexander von Humboldt

Popular German poet and novelist Theodor Fontane

7 Theodor Fontane
A Huguenot, Fontane (1819–98) was one of the most influential 19th-century novelists and poets in Germany. He also worked as a journalist and critic, penning many of his articles and essays in the Café Josty on Potsdamer Platz. Fontane is particularly well known for his novel *Effi Briest* and five-volume travelogue *Wanderungen durch die Mark Brandenburg (Ramblings through the March of Brandenburg)*.

8 Jacob and Wilhelm Grimm
The brothers Jacob (1785–1863) and Wilhelm (1786–1859) Grimm are known for their classic fairy tales *Little Red Riding Hood*, *Hansel and Gretel* and *Rumpelstiltskin*. Their linguistic output was equally important. Their *German Grammar* and *German Dictionary* are standard reference works even today.

9 Georg Wilhelm Friedrich Hegel
The influential philosopher Hegel (1770–1831) taught at Humboldt University from 1818 until his death. His teachings continue to inspire thinkers today.

10 Nina Hagen
Singer, songwriter and actress Nina Hagen was born in East Berlin in 1955. Known for her eccentric, theatrical style, she was at the forefront of the punk movement in the late 1970s and early 80s. She remains a beloved icon of her time.

TOP 10
INNOVATORS

1. Johann Gottfried Moritz (b 1777) and Wilhelm Wieprecht (b 1802)
Wieprecht and Moritz created the bass tuba and secured a patent for it in 1835.

2. Katharina (Käthe) Paulus (b 1868)
The first professional balloon pilot in Germany, Paulus won a patent for creating the first collapsible parachute in 1921.

3. Otto Lilienthal (b 1848)
A German aviation pioneer, Lilienthal made over 2,000 glider flights and started the first standard production of an aircraft.

4. Ernst Litfaß (b 1816)
Litfaß was a publisher who invented the *litfaßsäule*, a free-standing cylindrical advertising column which still bears his name today.

5. Friedrich von Hefner-Alteneck (b 1845)
While at Siemens, Hefner-Alteneck, an engineer, created a drum armature which played a huge role in the invention of the electric tram.

6. Reinhold Burger (b 1866)
In 1904 Burger patented the Thermos vacuum flask, which was a development of the work of Sir James Dewar *(b 1842)*.

7. Oskar Picht (b 1871)
Director of a school for the visually impaired, Picht developed one of the first Braille typewriters in the world.

8. Maximilian Negwer (b 1872)
A skilled entrepreneur, Negwer invented comfortable ear protection made using wax, Vaseline and cotton wool.

9. Konrad Zuse (b 1910)
German engineer Zuse is known for creating the Z1, the first programmable computer and the first real programming language, Plankalkül.

10. Herta Heuwer (b 1913)
In 1949, Heuwer created the popular German fast food dish *Currywurst* (sausage with curry sauce) at her kiosk.

PARKS AND GARDENS

1 Großer Tiergarten
The Tiergarten (p117) – the green lungs of Berlin – is the most famous park in the city. Set in the centre of town, the park covers more than 200 ha (494 acres). Originally designed in 1833–40 by Peter Joseph Lenné as a hunting estate for the Elector, in the latter half of the 19th century the park became a recreation ground for all Berliners. It attracts cyclists, joggers, sunbathers and families having picnics, especially on weekends.

2 Schlosspark Charlottenburg
📍 B3 🏠 Schloss Charlottenburg, Spandauer Damm 🕐 8am–sunset daily 🌐 spsg.de
The Palace Park is one of the most attractive and charming green spaces in Germany. Immediately behind Schloss Charlottenburg (p42) is a small but magnificent Baroque garden, and beyond this extends a vast park, dating back to the early 19th century. It was landscaped in the English style and features artificial lake and river landscapes, small hidden buildings and idyllic shaded groves on the banks of ponds and streams. The park is ideal for strolling and for sunseekers.

Schlosspark Charlottenburg in front of the palace

3 Grunewald and Teufelsberg
The Grunewald (p152), also known as the "green forest," is the public woods in the southwest of Berlin. It is the least built-up area of woodland in the city. Parts of Grunewald are very quiet, and the woods are home to wild boar. It is also the location of Teufelsberg, a man-made hill topped with a Cold War listening station.

4 Pfaueninsel
Peacock Island (p153), an island in the middle of Großer Wannsee that can be reached only by ferry, is a romantic spot and a leisurely getaway. In the 19th century, the island served as a love nest for King Friedrich Wilhelm II. His charming folly of a palace ruin has been open to the public again since 2025, following extensive renovations. Visitors can enjoy the green spaces, which are home to dozens of peacocks.

5 Viktoriapark
The old municipal park (p134), originally designed in 1888–94 as a recreation area for local workers, is a popular sunset spot. The meadows here which rise to 30 m (98 ft), are great for sunbathing. On top of the hill, a monument recalls the Prussian Wars of Liberation.

6 Botanischer Garten
📍 Königin-Luise-Str. 6–8 🕐 Garden: 9am–sunset daily 🌐 bgbm.org/en ♿
This beautiful Botanical Garden is a paradise of flowers and plants in the southwest of the city. The vast area with 15 greenhouses was built in the late 19th century around gentle hills and picturesque ponds. The Great Palm House by Alfred Koerner has spectacular 26-m- (85-ft-) high giant bamboo from Southeast Asia. The Botanisches Museum, which houses an impressive collection of plant specimens, is closed for renovation until 2026.

Statues at the fountain in Volkspark Friedrichshain

7 Volkspark Friedrichshain

📍 H2 📍 Am Friedrichshain/ Friedenstrasse ⏰ 24 hours daily

Berlin's first public park (1846) is an artificial landscape of lakes, meadows and two wooded mounds, one of which is nicknamed "Mont Klamott", meaning "Mount rubble". There is also a fountain with statues of the most popular fairytale characters.

8 Tierpark Berlin

Founded in 1955, this zoo (p148) is set in the wonderful palace park of Friedrichsfelde. Within its grounds are some 860 animal species.

9 Treptower Park

The 19th-century park and garden (p148) on the banks of the Spree is famous for the Soviet Memorial, which stands next to the graves of 7,000 Red Army soldiers.

10 Schloss Britz and Park

📍 Alt-Britz 73 ⏰ Palace: noon– 6pm Tue–Sun; garden: 9am– sunset daily 🌐 schlossbritz.de

The palace in Britz, dating from 1706 and situated in a lovely park, has been meticulously refurbished with historical furniture from the Gründerzeit period after 1871.

TOP 10
LAKES, RIVERS AND CANALS

1. Spree River
📍 K1–L7
Guided boat tours, romantic evening cruises and relaxing riverside walks are on offer.

2. Teufelssee, Grunewald
This is considered to be one of Berlin's cleanest and most relaxed lakes – nudists and dog lovers enjoy the peaceful banks.

3. Großer Müggelsee
Thousands congregate at Berlin's largest lake (p149) in summer to have a fun time swimming, rowing, sailing or surfing.

4. Schlachtensee
After Wannsee, this small lake is the second most popular. Avoid the crowds by going during the week.

5. Strandbad Wannsee
Europe's largest inland beach (p155) is beautifully white.

6. Lietzensee
📍 A4 📍 Kaiserdamm
Lietzensee is not suitable for swimming, but the surrounding meadows are idyllic.

7. Krumme Lanke, Fischerhüttenweg
Although many consider the lake not clean enough for bathing, it seems cleaner (but colder) than Schlachtensee.

8. Landwehrkanal
📍 C3–G5
Take a boat trip along the canal to see some of Berlin's most attractive bridges, or rent a boat to explore on your own.

9. Tegeler See, Alt-Tegel
The Greenwich Promenade, from Tegeler Hafen (harbour) to Schwarzer Weg, is an attractive walk.

10. Neuer See
📍 M3 📍 Großer Tiergarten
This tranquil lake is hidden in the vast Großer Tiergarten park. On its banks is the Café am Neuen See (p119).

NOTEWORTHY NEIGHBOURHOODS

1 Kreuzberg
Like many of Berlin's neighbourhoods, Kreuzberg *(p132)* has a changing face depending on where you are. To the north lies some of the city's top attractions, such as the Jüdisches Museum *(p50)*, while the east is free-spirited and multicultural, home to an underground nightlife scene and the city's best Turkish food thanks to a huge Turkish community. Then there's the west, a leafier part overlooked by grand 19th-century buildings.

2 Mitte
Meaning "middle", Mitte is Berlin's literal and metaphorical heart. Its importance cannot be overstated: it was here that Berlin was founded, and today it's home to some of its biggest attractions, from Museumsinsel *(p34)* to Potsdamer Platz *(p30)*. Pockets of calm can still be found if you know where to look, like the riverside at Montbijoupark *(p104)* or the street art hub Scheunenviertel.

3 Neukölln
Word about Berlin's coolest borough has long been out, but Neukölln *(p132)* hasn't lost its power to seduce. It's one of the city's fastest-growing districts, home to international expats and young creatives drawn in by the reasonable rents, vintage stores and adult playground Tempelhofer Feld *(p135)*. Though fast-gentrifying, it remains genuinely multicultural, with a strong Middle Eastern community. To explore the heart of the area, stroll down one of the main streets, such as Sonnenalle or Karl-Marx-Straße.

4 Schöneberg
Berlin's LGBTQ+ epicentre since the 1920s, this district *(p132)* has long attracted artists and liberals (David Bowie lived here). It remains a queer stronghold today, home to welcoming bars and rainbow flags flying proudly in restaurants and bookstores. As a leafy residential neighbourhood, it is also wonderful for leisurely strolls and has playgrounds that will keep the kids entertained.

5 Charlottenburg
The city's most well-heeled area *(p122)* holds firmly onto the glitz and glamour of a bygone Berlin, especially along upmarket shopping boulevard Kurfürstendamm *(p38)* and the old-world Schloss Charlottenburg *(p42)*. But it's not all high-end opulence, with cosy cafés and excellent Asian restaurants keeping visitors well-fed.

Catching up over a drink at one of Kreuzberg's street cafés

6 Friedrichshain
Planning to party? Friedrichshain is the thumping centre of Berlin's clubbing scene, where countercultures thrive in dive pubs and iconic clubs like Berghain (p150). It's just as cool in the daytime, with organic food shops, cute cafés and a popular flea market taking over on summer Sundays, all concentrated around Boxhagener Platz (p148).

Boats on the edge of Treptower Park in Treptow

7 Prenzlauer Berg
Before becoming the bougie place it is today, P-Berg (p140) was a bohemian hub in the 1990s. There's still edge to be found amid the leafy parks and genteel boutiques; for one, it's home to some of the city's best beer spots. Things turn up a notch on Sundays when the Mauerpark (p144) flea market hosts an epic open-air karaoke session.

8 Wedding
Not many visitors make it to Wedding, meaning there's all the more reason to visit. Slowly up-and-coming, this multicultural, working-class borough remains largely untouched by gentrification, still offering affordable eating options, eclectic architecture and plenty of green space.

9 Treptow
Often overlooked by visitors heading to the central districts, this green haven in the southeast breathes calm into the hectic city. It feels more like a village than an outer borough, home to a clutch of scenic lakes and lush green spaces, making it the ideal area for a Spree-side walk or picnic.

10 Grunewald
A quick S-Bahn ride to the west lies the sprawling Grunewald (p152), dense woodlands with forest trails and the cooling lake Teufelsee. In true Berlin style, you'll find epic street art even here, with graffiti taking over the former Cold War listening station on Teufelsberg (p156). In short, it makes for a perfect day out from the centre.

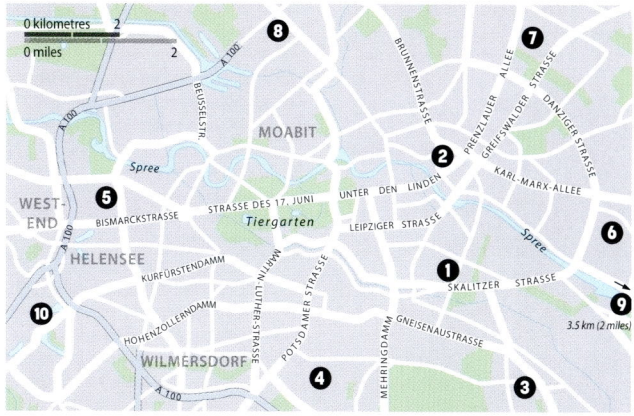

FAMILY ATTRACTIONS

1 Museum für Naturkunde
Berlin's museum of natural history (*p102*) has the biggest dinosaur skeleton on show anywhere in the world. The collections here are well presented.

2 Deutsches Technikmuseum
The technology museum (*p133*) is a giant playground, excellent for learning through play. There are locomotives to clamber over, windmills to play with and the Science Center Spectrum, where older children can conduct their own physics and technology experiments.

3 Filmpark Babelsberg
Exciting shoot-outs, a walk-on film set with a U-boat and a Wild West town are the film park's most popular attractions – and not just with the children. A tour of the former UFA-Film studios (*p162*) takes you behind the scenes: younger visitors can see costumes or admire the Little Sandman (Sandmännchen), a TV figure popular with children in East Germany since 1959. These studios were among the world's most prestigious when they were in operation here in Babelsberg from 1917 to 1945. Everywhere in the park are figures and props from well-known German films. A stunt show features fight scenes, car chases

Dinosaur Hall at the
Museum für Naturkunde

and pyrotechnics like those seen in *Inglourious Basterds*, *Valkyrie* and *Anonymous*, which were all shot here.

4 Labyrinth Kindermuseum
🚇 Osloer Str. 12 🕐 1–6pm Fri (from 11am Sat & Sun) 🌐 labyrinth-hindermuseum.de 🔗
Berlin's lovely Museum for Children is particularly suitable for children at the preschool stage and in the early school years. Three or four themed exhibitions each year deal with subjects in a child-friendly and entertaining way – for example the "Pots and Pans Orchestra". Every exhibition is interactive, allowing kids to experiment. See website for details of special exhibitions and events.

5 Grips-Theater
🗺 D3 🚇 Altonaer Str. 22 🕐 For performance times, check website 🌐 grips-theater.de 🔗
This famous Berlin theatre for children has been showing the hit musical *Linie 1* since 1986. The play, which is best suited to older children and adolescents, uses a U-Bahn line running from Kreuzberg to the Ku'damm as a metaphor for life in the big city. All shows are in German.

Kids playing on a statue at the Filmpark

6 Museum der Illusionen

📍 G3 🏛 Karl-Liebknecht-Str. 9
🕐 10am–8pm daily 🌐 illuseum-
berlin.de 🔗

Specially constructed rooms at this optical illusion museum have visitors believing they are, for example, the size of a giant; each trick is accompanied by scientific explanations.

7 Zeiss-Großplanetarium

Artificial stars, planets and nebulae take you to faraway galaxies under the silvery dome of the planetarium (p144).

8 Puppentheater-Museum

📍 H6 🏛 Karl-Marx-Str. 135
🕐 2–6pm Tue–Sun 🌐 puppentheater-museum.de 🔗

At this excellent Puppet Museum, children are allowed to perform their own puppet shows and have a go at being puppet theatre directors.

9 Futurium

🏛 Alexanderufer 2 🕐 10am–6pm Wed–Mon (to 8pm Thu)
🌐 futurium.de/en

Opened in 2019, Futurium's eye-catching modern building on the Spree has a fantastic educational undertaking that explores the question: "How do we want to live in the future?" The intriguing and interactive exhibition, which is divided into three main sections – nature, man

and technology – is especially worth a visit for those travelling with children. Children of all ages can experiment with 3D printers and laser cutters, or use their creativity to design a city layout and then analyze it for aspects such as mobility, pollution and noise levels.

10 LEGOLAND® Discovery Centre

Apart from the exciting 4D cinema experience and enjoyable rides at the world's first indoor LEGOLAND® (p31) there are also hands-on activities like model-building workshops.

Entrance to LEGOLAND® Discovery Centre

PERFORMING ARTS VENUES

1 Staatsoper Unter den Linden

Both the theatre troupe and the orchestra of the venerable Berlin Opera enjoy top reputations. Founded by Frederick the Great, this opera house (p26) is the place to see the stars of the classical music scene.

2 Philharmonie

Germany's temple of classical music still presents the best performers in the world. Designed by Scharoun, the concert hall (p46) has unique acoustics, much appreciated by artists and audience alike. Concerts by the Berlin Philharmonic Orchestra are very popular and are often sold out for weeks ahead.

3 Deutsche Oper

Berlin's most modern opera house (p128) has an elegant retro design. It was built in 1961 on the site of the former Deutsches Opernhaus, which was destroyed during World War II. The controversial 88 slabs of washed-out concrete, chosen by architect Fritz Bornemann for the main façade, replaced the classic columned portico that once stood here, leading critics to describe the building as lacking artistic formation. Concerts and opera and ballet performances are held here, along with an extensive children's programme.

4 Chamäleon

J5 Rosenthaler 40–1, Hachesche Höfe For performances, check website for details Mon chamaeleon.com/en

Established in 2004, the small, alternative Chamäleon stage is renowned for its innovative and unique programme. Wit and ingenuity are at the forefront of shows here, which tend to be modern circus performances with a mix of music, drama and acrobatics. If you are seated in the front row, you are likely to get pulled onto the stage.

5 Bar jeder Vernunft

C5 Schaperstr. 24 (car park Freie Volksbühne) Box office: noon–6:30pm Mon–Fri; 3–5:30pm Sat, Sun & hols bar-jeder-vernunft.de/en

This venue, whose name means "devoid of all reason", is a popular comedy theatre. The cabaret offers a humorous and, at times, romantic programme of songs, *chansons*, reviews, cabaret, slapstick and comedy, all under an amazing mirror tent dating from the 1920s. Many stars of the international and German cabaret scene can be seen regularly among the performers here, including Tim Fischer, Georgette Dee, the Pfister Sisters and Gayle Tufts, as well as older stars such as Otto Sander.

6 Deutsches Theater

Performances at the German Theatre (p104) – one of the best – include mainly classic plays in the tradition of stage and screen actor

Group of dancers at the Deutsche Oper

and director Max Reinhardt who once worked here. Experimental theatre by young playwrights is performed at the DT Baracke.

7 Theater des Westens
In addition to producing its own shows, such as *La Cage aux Folles*, this theatre *(p128)* also hosts guest productions such as *Blue Man Group* and *Mamma Mia*.

Statue on Theater des Westens' façade

8 Friedrichstadt-Palast
J4 **Friedrichstr. 107** **palast.berlin/en**

Shiny glass tiles and a white, plumed neon sign adorn the eyecatching façade of the Friedrichstadt-Palast, whose long-legged dancers are as popular today as they were in the 1920s. The original venue was damaged during World War II and replaced in the 1980s. Long celebrated as being among the world's best revues, the performances have become even more spirited and entertaining today.

9 Hebbel am Ufer
F5 **Hallesches Ufer 32** **For performances, chech website for details** **hebbel-am-ufer.de/en**

The Hebbel am Ufer has attained cult status in Berlin, thanks to its modern and varied programme of concerts, dance, music and theatre events. The best performers from around the world appear here.

10 Volksbühne
H2 **Rosa-Luxemburg-Platz** **For performances, chech website for details** **volksbuehne-berlin.de**

Opened in 1914 as a "theatre of the people", the iconic, avant-garde Volksbühne offers cosmopolitan theatre, dance and musical performances, and contemporary visual art.

LGBTQ+ BERLIN

Celebrating Christopher Street Day

includes useful information, a round-up of what's on, small ads and interviews from the city's gay scene. It is available for free in LGBTQ+ cafés and shops.

1 Christopher Street Day

Berlin comes alive every summer with Christopher Street Day (p86), Germany's largest Pride festival. The LGBTQ+ community is celebrated with a parade that starts in Mitte (p68) and makes its way to Nollendorfplatz (p135), ending at the Siegessäule (Victory Column). Thousands participate in the festivities, and as day turns to night, the celebration continues in the city's many queer clubs and bars.

2 Siegessäule

W siegessaeule.de
Berlin's oldest and best-selling gay magazine is named after the Victory Column. The monthly magazine

3 Mann-o-Meter

🅓 E5 🅐 Bülowstr. 106
🅞 5–10pm Mon–Fri, 4–8pm Sat & Sun 🅦 mann-o-meter.de
This is Berlin's best-known advice centre for gay and bisexual men that offers all kinds of help. Apart from psychological support relating to AIDS, safe sex and coming out, its counsellors offer help in finding accommodation, give support to those in troubled relationships and provide legal advice. Mann-o-Meter is also a good starting point for gay visitors to Berlin who wish to find out about the LGBTQ+ scene. There's also a café here.

4 SchwuZ

🅐 Rollbergstr. 26 🅞 Hours vary, chech website 🅦 schwuz.de 🅓
Located inside an ex-brewery in Neukölln, this lively queer club has been running since 1977 and is considered to be one of the best venues for parties for the LGBTQ+ community in Berlin. The vibrant parties are often themed, for which details can be found in magazines such as Siegessäule or on the club's social media.

LGBTQ+ history artworks at the Schwules Museum

5 Schwules Museum

📍 E4 🏠 Lützowstr. 73
🕐 2–6pm Mon, Wed–Sun
(to 7pm Sat); 2–8pm Thu
🌐 schwulesmuseum.de 🔗

Situated in Tiergarten, this small Gay Museum documents, through a variety of temporary exhibitions, the high and low points of LGBTQ+ life since the 19th century. The museum was first conceptualized in 1984. Next to the museum is an archive, a small library and a venue for cultural events.

6 Hafen

📍 D5 🏠 Motzstr. 19 🕐 7pm–4am daily 🌐 hafen-berlin.de

This beloved pub located in the heart of Berlin's LGBTQ+ scene on Motzstraße, is a cosy hangout where visitors and regulars can mingle. Although it has a living room vibe, it's also known for its DJ sets.

7 Prinz-Eisenherz-Buchhandlung

📍 D5 🏠 Motzstr. 23 🕐 10am–8pm Mon–Sat 🌐 prinz-eisenherz.buchhatalog.de

Germany's first openly gay bookshop, this place now stocks the entire range of German and international publications relating to the LGBTQ+ community.

Its sales assistants will track down rare or out-of-stock titles at your request. The bookshop also hosts frequent literary readings.

8 SilverFuture

📍 H6 🏠 Weserstr. 206
🕐 5pm–2am daily (to 3am Fri & Sat) 🌐 silverfuture.net

This queer bar welcomes a mixed crowd. It is widely known as a safe, discrimination-free space for all.

9 Stueck

📍 H5 🏠 Schlesische Str. 16, 10997 Berlin–Kreuzberg 🕐 From 6pm Mon–Sat

Stueck is located where the famous queer bar Barbie Deinhoff once stood. The history of the bar survives in Stueck's fresh new interior. The bar continues to be popular for its two-for-one Tuesdays. Thursdays are reserved for women, trans and non-binary guests.

10 SO36

A Kreuzberg classic, this famous – and infamous – dance venue *(p138)* has been very popular for many years and attracts a mixed crowd. The Sunday night club "Café Fatal", when old German chart hits and dance tunes are played, is legendary.

LOUNGES AND CLUBS

1 House of Weekend
🅟 J6 🅐 Alexanderstr. 7 🅞 From 11pm Fri & Sat; closing hours vary, chech website 🆆 weekendclub.berlin

This rooftop spot in an old Soviet block, with great views of the glittering high-rises on Alexanderplatz, is a trendy and surprisingly down-to-earth house, techno and electro pop club, frequented by a young, fashionable crowd.

2 Tresor Club
🅟 L7 🅐 Köpenicher Str. 70 🅞 From 11pm Wed, Fri & Sat; closing hours vary, chech website 🆆 tresor berlin.com

Berlin's first techno club, Tresor opened in 1991 in the vaults of the former Wertheim department store. Today, it is situated in the basement and industrial halls of a giant former power station and continues to deliver the latest in electronic music with a full programme of visiting musicians and DJ sets.

3 Kater Blau
🅟 K7 🅐 Holzmarhstrastr 25 🅞 Hours vary, chech website 🆆 haterblau.de

A techno club with two dance floors, Kater Blau is famous for its dance parties, which start late and continue well into the next day on Fridays and weekends. The outdoor area overlooks the river which features *Agnes*, an anchored ship. Check website for events.

4 SilverWings Club
Housed in the former Tempelhof Airport building *(p136)*, this 1950s US Air Force Officers Club *(p138)* is ideal for dances and events. It hosts legendary theme parties on Saturday nights, which draw a crowd that prefers rock 'n' roll, soul and new wave music.

5 Revier Südost
Housed in a sprawling former brewery, beyond central Berlin, Revier Südost *(p150)* embodies the city's industrial past and its hedonistic party scene, offering a unique space for parties with a distinctly local vibe.

6 Club de Visionäre
🅟 L7 🅐 Am Flutgraben 1 🅞 Hours vary, chech website 🆆 clubdervisionaere.com

This iconic waterside hangout, also known as CDV, is the place to keep the party going late into Sunday night during the summer months. During the week, a mix of locals and visitors come to unwind on the wooden decking beneath a gorgeous weeping willow.

**Fabulous rooftop location
of House of Weekend**

If you're visiting in winter, head to its
sister club, Hoppetosse *(hoppetosse.
berlin)*, housed in an old pleasure boat
moored nearby.

7 Berghain
Set in an East-German-era power
station, Berghain *(p150)* is Berlin's
hottest bastion of electronic music. Its
cavernous main room has a minimal,
industrial design aesthetic. There's also
a smaller Panorama Bar upstairs. Top
DJs perform alongside spectacular light
shows, and the bouncers are notoriously
picky, so be prepared to wait (or not get
in at all). Hardcore partygoers spend
entire weekends here without sleep.
Weekday concerts tend to be ticket-only
and are much easier to get into; check
the website for further details. In the
summer, its garden is open to revellers.

8 Tausend
🚇 E3 🏠 Schiffbauerdamm 11
🌐 tausendberlin.com
A great alternative to techno and
house-dominated clubs, this chic bar
is hidden under the S-Bahn tracks and
has live music. It also plays soul, jazz
and pop music from the 1970s and 80s.
Tausend has an affiliated cantina *(p99)*
and serves excellent mixed cocktails.

**Bartenders whisking cocktails
at the Mein Haus am See**

**9 Mein Haus
am See**
A former bookshop, this retro-chic
club *(p106)* has comfortable seating
and opens daily at 4pm. It attracts
a young, international crowd who
come to relax with coffee and cake
during the day or enjoy cocktails,
DJs and dancing at night, especially
on weekends when it tends to get a
little crowded.

10 Sisyphos
Famous for its weekend-long
parties that start on Friday and
continue until Monday morning,
Sisyphos *(p150)* is housed in a former
factory with a large open-air space.
If you're planning on staying for the
entire duration, you can even buy a
toothbrush here.

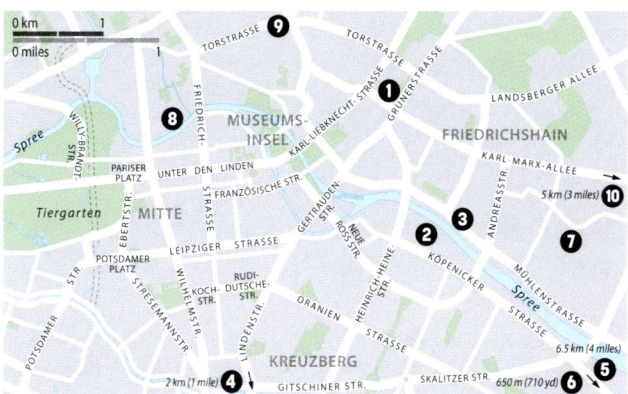

KNEIPEN (PUBS) AND BARS

1 Green Door
This Berlin classic (*p138*) never goes out of style. The interior of this intimate speakeasy bar is well-hidden from the outside. Green Door attracts a young urban crowd that comes here for the cocktails and to mingle at the minimalist retro-style bar as well as along the curved, green walls. There's an outdoor bell, but the door policy is pretty liberal as long as you look sober.

2 E & M Leydicke
This slightly dated bar (*p138*) is still a big hit with tourists as well as groups of students. It regularly hosts concerts and parties featuring swing, blues, jazz and rock 'n' roll bands. Try the sweetish strawberry and raspberry wines.

3 Newton Bar
To see and be seen is the name of the game at this elegant venue (*p98*). The service here is charming, and in summer there's even a fold-down bar on the pavement outside. Heavy leather armchairs make for comfortable sitting, and the walls are adorned with enlarged photographs of nudes by Helmut Newton, after whom the bar is named. Don't miss out on the Caribbean and Latin American cocktails.

4 Beckett's Kopf
⊙ H1 ⌂ Pappelallee 64 ⊙ 7pm–2am Wed–Sun ⊞ becketts-hopf.de
One of Berlin's finest cocktail bars, Beckett's Kopf has a portrait of writer Samuel Beckett in its window. Its dark interior features heavy velvet curtains, as if to keep the secret recipes from prying eyes. The superb concoctions include the "Mother-in-Law", with fruity notes, and the "Prince of Wales", said to be a favourite indulgence of King Edward VII.

5 Weinbar Rutz
Berlin's best (but pricey) wine bar and shop is found downstairs from the award-winning Michelin-star restaurant of the same name (*p107*). It offers over 1,000 wines, but expert staff are on hand to assist you. There's an excellent selection of food, too.

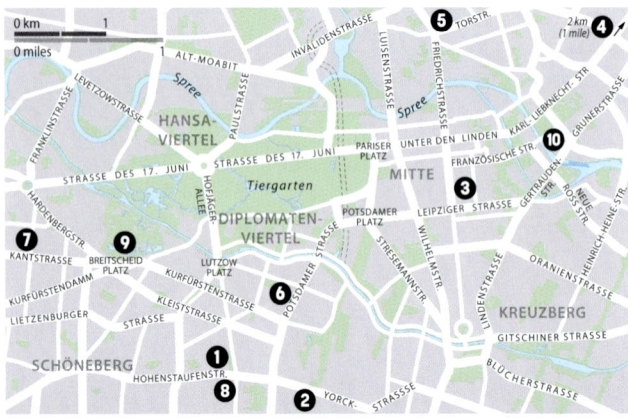

Retro décor of Berlin's Victoria Bar

6 Victoria Bar
🅥 L2 🏠 Potsdamer Str. 102
🕒 6pm–3am Sun–Thu, 6pm–4am
Fri & Sat 🆆 victoriabar.de

This cosy bar, with its understated 1960s ambience, subdued lighting and sophisticated lounge music, is a great place for a relaxing drink and has become a firm favourite among the well-to-do artsy crowd. The cocktails are mixed by the renowned barman Stefan Weber.

7 Zwiebelfisch
🅥 C4 🏠 Savignyplatz 7–8
🕒 Noon–6am daily
🆆 zwiebelfisch-berlin.de

A classic venue reflecting the somewhat ageing Charlottenburg scene, Zwiebelfisch is where the last survivors of the 1968 student revolt generation come to reminisce. Photographs of artists, once patrons of this establishment, are hung on the walls. In summer, there are tables outdoors.

8 Café M
🅥 E5 🏠 Goltzstr. 33 🕒 6pm–
2am Mon–Fri, 1pm–2am Sat, 6pm–
midnight Sun 🆆 cafe-m.de

Noisy yet laid-back, the Café M Kneipe in Schöneberg is a local favourite. Little has changed since it opened more than 40 years ago.

9 Monkey Bar
🅥 D4 🏠 Budapester Str. 40
🕒 1pm–1am Mon–Wed, 1pm–2am
Thu & Fri, noon–2am Sat, noon–
1am Sun 🆆 monkeybarberlin.de

For beer or cocktails try this popular rooftop bar offering spectacular views of the neigh-bouring Berlin Zoo. It also hosts regular DJ and live music events.

10 Zum Nußbaum
One of a few traditional Kneipen in the historic Nikolaiviertel quarter, the old-fashioned Zum Nußbaum (p144) is worth checking out. It serves draught beer and features a selection of flavourful traditional Berlin food.

Patrons enjoying a drink at the Zum Nußbaum

LOCAL DISHES

1 Döner Kebab
While its specific origin story is disputed, many believe that Turkish immigrants introduced Berlin to the Döner kebab in the 1970s, igniting a passion for meat shaved from a rotisserie, paired with salad and sauces in bread. It's a perfect choice for lunch or dinner, but somehow tastes even better as a late-night snack.

2 Eisbein
Not for the faint of heart, this beloved Berlin dish consists of a tender pork knuckle (cured and then gently simmered) served with the skin on a bed of pea purée and sauerkraut. It's fatty and heavy, so a slathering of *Senf* (mustard) can help tackle it, as can a pint of beer from the tap. A classic German restaurant like Zur letzten Instanz *(p114)* serves it up best.

3 Currywurst
Ever since Herta Heuwer started selling it at her *Imbiss* (food stand) in 1949, *Currywurst* has been a city speciality. This fast-food staple consists of grilled, sliced sausage doused in tomato sauce (often ketchup) with a sprinkling of curry powder. Get your fix at any *Imbiss* with a side of *Pommes* (chips), and be sure to ask for your sausage unpeeled, just like the locals.

4 Bratwurst
Not to be confused with *Currywurst*, *Bratwurst* is a grilled sausage served with a white bread roll and *Senf* or ketchup. Cooking methods, varieties and quality of the sausage are numerous, but the long Thüringer Rostbratwurst – a unique sausage from Thuringia – is the most popular. Seek these out at dedicated *Bratwurst* (or *Currywurst*) stands, farmers' markets and traditional German restaurants.

5 Falafel
From baklava to shawarma, Middle Eastern food is hugely popular in Berlin, and a reflection of the city's large Arab communities. For most Berliners, little beats a delicious and affordable falafel snack, whether it's a *Falafel im Brot* (falafel sandwich) or a *Falafel und Hummus Teller* (falafel plate with hummus).

6 Fischbrötchen
A fish sandwich might be more closely associated with the Baltic Coast, but Berlin serves them up just as well. Fishmongers and market stands usually offer a few fish varieties – pickled, grilled or smoked – served with remoulade and onions in a crusty white bun. If you're not squeamish, try one with *Matjes*, a mild pickled herring.

Layered Baumkuchen, which translates to "tree cake"

7 Kaffee und Kuchen

Meeting friends and family for coffee and cake is a long-standing tradition in Germany. While it's mostly a Sunday activity, there's no need to wait to indulge; whether you head to a traditional bakery or hip café, you'll find top brews served with delicious cakes, like *Baumkuchen* spit cake or *Käsekuchen*, a German cheesecake.

8 Königsberger Klopse

Ever-present on East Prussian dinner tables, this traditional German dish shows no signs of falling out of favour, even in modern Berlin. It's the creamy caper sauce poured over the boiled meatballs that has Berliners obsessed, and a traditional inn like Max und Moritz (*p138*) is the place to try it.

9 Seasonal Produce

Eating produce in season borders on an obsession in Berlin, and restaurants follow suit, celebrating whatever is ripe for picking with gusto. Expect menus to change according to the season, where a local dish might centre around *Spargel* (white and green asparagus) in spring and *Pfifferlinge* (chanterelle mushrooms) in autumn.

10 Vegan Food

Berlin has long been celebrated as the vegan capital of Europe, with entire menus dedicated to meat-free fare. Whether grabbing a doughnut or tucking into a Michelin-starred meal, veganism is second nature here.

Currywurst **served with fries and falafel**

TOP 10
BERLIN DRINKS

1. Berliner Weisse mit Schuss
This Berlin specialty consists of a sour wheat beer mixed with raspberry cordial or woodruff syrup, resulting in a bright red or green colour.

2. Club-Mate
Though an acquired taste, this caffeinated herbal tea-flavoured fizzy drink is perfect for a burst of energy.

3. Bier vom Fass
Germany's beers are some of the world's best, and the most highly esteemed is draught beer, enjoyed in a beer garden or *Kneipe* (pub).

4. Radler
Perfect for a summer's day, a Radler is a beer mixed with lemonade; it's often served in a half-litre bottle.

5. Späti-Bier
The lifeblood of Berlin, *Spätis* (convenience stores) offer a generous selection of half-litre bottles of beer for a couple of euros.

6. Berliner Luft
A city classic, this intense peppermint liqueur is enjoyed neat or on ice.

7. German Riesling
Wine isn't produced around Berlin, but varieties from Germany's southern and western regions have made their way here, including popular Riesling.

8. Spezi
A throwback-to-childhood drink, Spezi is a refreshing mix of orange soda and cola concocted in Germany.

9. Glühwein
Mulled wine (hot spiced red or white wine) takes over in the winter, particularly at Christmas markets.

10. Schorle
A mix of fruit juice with sparkling mineral water, Schorle comes in alcoholic and non-alcoholic varieties. *Apfelschorle* is a classic.

A refreshing jug of Schorle

SHOPS AND MARKETS

1 Art and Fashion House Quartier 206
📍 L4 🏠 Friedrichstr 71 🕐 10:30am–7:30pm Mon–Sat

This renowned shopping centre features stunning Art Deco interiors, with mosaic flooring and a marble staircase. Luxury labels such as Moschino, Etro and Bally offer stylish designer clothing and accessories, while the elegant basement and first-floor cafés provide a welcome taste of Berlin coffee culture.

2 Kaufhaus des Westens (KaDeWe)
📍 D5 🏠 Tauentzienstr 21–24 📞 (030) 212 10 🕐 10am–8pm Mon–Sat (to 9pm Fri), 1–8pm Sun

Whatever you are looking for, you will find it here. Over its eight floors, the venerable Kaufhaus des Westens ("department store of the West"), affectionately called KaDeWe, offers more than three million products. On its gourmet floor, West Berlin's former "shop window", you can choose from 1,800 cheeses, 1,400 breads and pastries and 2,000 cold meats. The window displays and inner courtyards are also worth a visit in themselves.

3 Königliche Porzellan-Manufaktur (KPM)
📍 M4 🏠 Wegelystr 1 🕐 10am–6pm Mon–Sat 🌐 kpm-berlin.com

Prussia's glory and splendour to take away – traditional KPM porcelain for your dining table at home. Apart from elegant porcelain dinner services, figures and accessories made in the Berlin factory are also on sale here.

Art Deco interior of Quartier 206, home to luxury boutiques

Antiques and crockery at the des 17. Juni

4 Trödel- und Kunstmarkt Straße des 17. Juni

⚐ K1 **⌖** Str des 17. Juni **⌚** 10am–5pm Sat & Sun

Berlin's largest art and antiques market specializes in antique furnishings and fittings, cutlery and porcelain, books, paintings, clothing and jewellery. The traders are professionals and demand high prices, but in return you are assured of buying something truly special. With its street artists and buskers, the market is an ideal weekend spot for browsing and people-watching.

5 Mauerpark

Visiting the city's largest flea market (p144) is a Sunday pastime, not least because of the bearpit karaoke sessions held in the "bearpit" amphitheatre. Before the singing starts, browse through jewellery, vinyl records and second-hand clothes at the seemingly endless stalls.

6 Modulor

⚐ H5 **⌖** Prinzenstr. 85 **⌚** 10am–6pm Mon–Sat **ⓦ** modulor.de

This two-story emporium offers a wide range of art and design materials for all levels, from hobbyists to professionals. Discover stylish stationery and quality supplies for your next project here.

7 Gipsformerei Staatliche Museen

⚐ A3 **⌖** Sophie-Charlotten-Str 17–18 **⌚** 9am–4pm Tue & Thu **ⓦ** smb.museum

If you fancy a Schinkel statue for your home or a Prussian sculpture from the Charlottenburg Palace gardens, you'll find moulded plaster reproductions here.

8 Antik- und Buchmarkt am Bode-Museum

⚐ J4 **⌖** Am Kupfergraben 1 **⌚** 10am–5pm Sat & Sun

Numerous stalls offering antiques and souvenirs are scattered along the Kupfergraben in front of the Bode-Museum. Occasionally browsers can find a bargain.

9 Türkischer Markt am Maybachufer

Berlin's largest weekday Turkish market (p137) is held on Tuesdays and Fridays along the Landwehrkanal. Pick up a few picnic supplies from the market, and find a shady waterside spot to have lunch while soaking up the sun.

10 Winterfeldtmarkt

The trendiest and also the most attractive weekly food and clothing market (p137) in Berlin has developed into a hotspot with the Schöneberg crowd. On sale are a variety of high-quality goods and produce. This is the place for meeting up on Saturdays.

Potted plants and flowers at the Winterfeldtmarkt

BERLIN FOR FREE

1 Schlosspark Sanssouci
For those who fancy a stroll through a Romantic landscape painting, the Schlosspark Sanssouci *(p160)* is a must-visit. Just a half-hour from Berlin by commuter train, these gardens in Potsdam are strewn with ponds and follies, including an Orangerie, Roman Baths modelled on an Italian villa and a Rococo-style Chinese house.

2 Reichstag
Berlin's biggest freebie happens to be a must-see attraction *(p24)*. There's no topping the fabulous 360-degree view of the city skyline that you get from Lord Norman Foster's beautiful modern dome. Guided tours take in the plenary hall and graffiti left by Russian soldiers in 1945. Register in advance and bring your passport to enter.

3 Tempelhofer Feld
Tempelhof Flughafen was Germany's biggest airport when it was expanded in the 1930s. A powerful symbol of the new Berlin, the grounds of this historic airport were turned into an enormous public green space *(p135)*. You will find urban gardeners, cyclists, in-line skaters, joggers, and people barbequeing, doing Tai Chi, flying kites and playing baseball.

4 Open Monument Day
🕒 Sep 🌐 visitberlin.de
Beautiful private gardens, the interiors of historic monuments, and the hallowed halls of government ministries scattered throughout the city are opened to the public on the second Sunday in September each year. All events are free of charge.

5 Free Concerts
Churches, universities and even renowned classical orchestras give free concerts. Tickets can be booked via email *(ticket@berlinerdom.de)* for concerts at the lavish Berliner Dom *(p58)*. The Berliner Philharmonic's gratis lunchtime concerts *(p46)*, usually with small ensembles, are held every Wednesday at 1pm between September and June.

6 Free Walking Tours
Join a guided walking tour of the city run by Alternative Berlin Tours *(alternativeberlin.com)*, Brewer's Berlin Tours *(brewersberlintours.com)* and New Berlin Tours *(newberlintours.com)*. They're free of charge, although tips are encouraged, and a great way to both explore and learn about the history of the city. The tours are held daily through-out the year. For timings and departure points, please check the individual websites.

7 Museums
Many museums and galleries, including the Alliiertenmuseum *(p154)*, Haus der Wannsee-Konferenz *(p154)* and Knoblauchhaus *(p110)* have no admission charge. Some of Berlin's most prestigious museums, such as

Beautifully landscaped entrance of Schlosspark Sanssouci

the Gemäldegalerie *(p47)*, the Pergamonmuseum *(p35)* and the Alte Nationalgalerie *(p35)* are free for visitors under 18.

8 Holocaust-Denkmal
Designed by New York architect Peter Eisenman, the striking Memorial to the Murdered Jews of Europe *(p93)* consists of 2,711 concrete pillars placed on undulating ground. The underground information centre provides a moving introduction to the horrors that took place during the Holocaust.

9 East Side Gallery
The biggest remaining stretch *(p148)* of the Berlin Wall is now an artistic statement on Germany's division from 1961 to 1989. Famous murals include a Trabant busting through the masonry, *Heads with Big Lips* by Thierry Noir, and Brezhnev and Honecker kissing.

10 Gedenkstätte Berliner Mauer
🅿 G1 🏠 Bernauer Str. 111 🕐 Centre: 10am–6pm Tue–Sun 🌐 stiftung-berliner-mauer.de

The Berlin Wall Memorial is well worth a visit for its recreated "death strip", excellent documentary centre and dramatic stories of how East Germans escaped over (or under) the deadly barrier. Listening stations and displays are spread along the former border.

Browsing exhibits at the Gedenkstätte Berliner Mauer

TOP 10
MONEY-SAVING TIPS

1. The city's public museums, including the comprehensive complex on the Museumsinsel, are covered by the popular Berlin Museum Pass (€32). This pass offers free entry to all participating institutions for three consecutive days.

2. Many of Berlin's neighbourhoods are perfect for a peaceful, leisurely walk, and you will be surprised by how quick and convenient it is to travel between the city's main sights on foot.

3. Theatres and opera houses sell discounted tickets at the door on the day of the performance.

4. Go gallery-hopping in the arty Mitte district. Here, Auguststrasse and Linienstrasse teem with alluring collections open to the public.

5. Buy a refreshing drink from a *Späti* (late-night convenience store) and do as the locals do: sit and unwind in one of the city's scenic parks or by the canal for a break any time the sun shines.

6. Buy discounted public transport tickets (such as a four-pack or a day pass) or hire a bicycle to get around the city and see the lovely sites, just like a local.

7. Bus lines 100 and 200 take in Berlin's best sights for the price of a single fare.

8. Take advantage of the affordable yet delicious set menus in Berlin's cafés and restaurants, particularly at lunchtime.

9. Comb through the expansive Mauerpark flea market *(p144)*, where you can find unique vintage and retro treasures. The market runs all day on Sundays.

10. If you are a visitor from outside the EU and are leaving the EU with purchased goods, remember to get a refund on Germany's 19 per cent sales tax. Simply enquire with sales staff at stores for an *Ausfuhrbescheinigung* (export papers).

FESTIVALS AND EVENTS

1 Fashion Week
Jan & Jul ⓦ fashionweek.berlin
Top designers and local talent present their new collections at various venues throughout the city.

2 Grüne Woche
2nd half of Jan ⓦ gruene woche.de/en ⚡
The largest gourmet feast in the world, Green Week is an agricultural and gastronomical fair for everyone. Embark on a culinary journey at the Messe Berlin exhibition grounds.

3 Internationale Tourismus Börse (ITB)
Mar ⓦ itb.com/en ⚡
Messe Berlin hosts the world's largest tourism fair, which offers up-to-date travel information to the general public, often at elaborately designed stalls. The nighttime shows put on by many of the exhibiting countries are especially popular.

4 Berlinale
2nd & 3rd week in Feb
ⓦ berlinale.de ⚡
The Berlinale is the top German film festival, and is attended by Hollywood and German stars alike. Until 1999, the film festival took place around the Zoo-Palast cinema; today the area around Potsdamer Platz takes centre stage for the festivities.

5 Karneval der Kulturen
Whitsun (varying date in May or early Jun)
For three full days, the streets of Kreuzberg come alive with song and dance displays and street carnival parades – all celebrating Berlin's multicultural heritage.

6 Christopher Street Day
ⓦ csd-berlin.de/en
A colourful Pride parade jubilantly meanders through west Berlin on Christopher Street Day, in what is one of Europe's most widely attended celebrations of LGBTQ+ identity. Smaller festivities take place in other venues too, as some 500,000 people from all around the world boisterously drink and dance in the streets of Central Berlin.

7 Lange Nacht der Museen
Last weekend in Aug ⓦ lange-nachtdermuseen.berlin ⚡
For one night, one ticket gives access to all the city's museums until well after midnight, offering visitors an

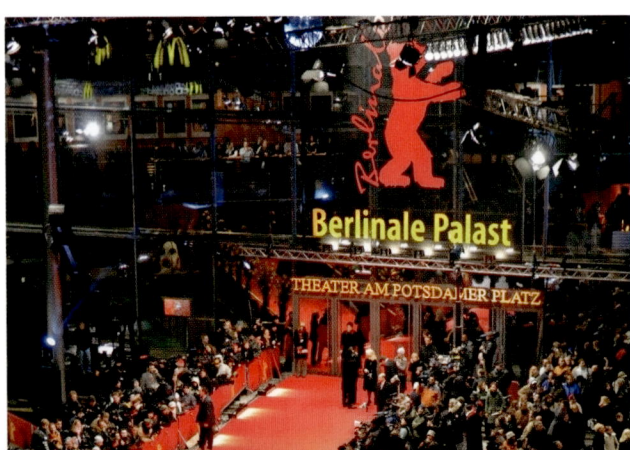

Exploring the pavilions in the Internationale Funkausstellung

unusual experience. Many institutions also put on special events, and street artists and sellers entertain the patiently queueing public.

8 Internationale Funkausstellung (IFA)

Early Sep 🛱 ifa-berlin.com 🔗

The latest in high-tech toys and entertainment technology are show-cased from over 1,800 global exhibitors at the IFA (International Broadcasting Exhibition). It is held annually in the Messe Berlin exhibition grounds.

9 Pop-Kultur

End Aug/early Sep
🛱 pop-kultur.berlin

As a successor of the Berlin Music Week, this entertaining festival for bands, musicians, artists, producers, labels and audiences is held at various venues in Kulturbrauerei in the Prenzlauer Berg district. This is a great platform to discover local musicians.

10 Festival of Lights

Oct 🛱 festival-of-lights.de

For 10 days, dozens of Berlin's modern and historical buildings are illuminated with magnificent light displays created by a number of renowned artists from across the globe.

Exciting red carpet event at the Berlinale

TOP 10 SPORTS HIGHLIGHTS

1. Tempelhofer Feld
Berlin's expansive recreational spot (p136) is a must-visit.

2. Berliner Neujahrslauf
1st Jan
A New Year's day run in the cold takes place at Brandenburger Tor.

3. Sechstagerennen
2nd half of Jan 🛱 sixdayweekend.com/en
This six-day race is one of Berlin's most popular cycling events.

4. VeloCity Cycling Races
End of Jun/early Jul
🛱 velocity.berlin
Don't miss this adrenaline-fuelled cycling race that passes through seven Berlin districts.

5. DFB-Pokalfinale
May
The huge Olympiastadion hosts Germany's knockout football cup final.

6. Berlin Half Marathon
Early Apr 🛱 generali-berliner-halbmarathon.de
This is Berlin's largest and most high-profile half marathon.

7. Berlin Triathlon
Early Jun 🛱 berlin-triathlon.de
Register online for this triathlon, held every year at Treptower Park.

8. Internationales Stadionfest (ISTAF) and ISTAF Indoor
Feb and early Sep 🛱 istaf.de
Germany's biggest athletics festivals draw a large crowd. Events are held across the Uber Platz and the Olympiastadion.

9. Berlin Marathon
3rd/4th Sun in Sep
🛱 bmw-berlin-marathon.com/en
The Berlin Marathon, held at Straße des 17. Juni, attracts thousands of international runners.

10. Deutsches Traberderby
1st week in Aug
The derby for professional trotter racing takes place at Trabrennbahn Mariendorf, which houses an Art Nouveau grandstand.

AREA BY AREA

Berliner Dom and the Spree River

CENTRAL BERLIN: UNTER DEN LINDEN

The boulevard of Unter den Linden at the heart of historic Mitte. Many of Berlin's sights are set along this significant avenue and around Bebelplatz, creating a picture of Prussian and German history from the early 18th century onwards. To the south of this avenue is the Neo-Classical Gendarmenmarkt, which is considered one of Europe's most attractive squares; the area around it is filled with elegant restaurants and cafés. Nearby is Friedrichstraße, which is lined with luxury stores, modern offices and apartments.

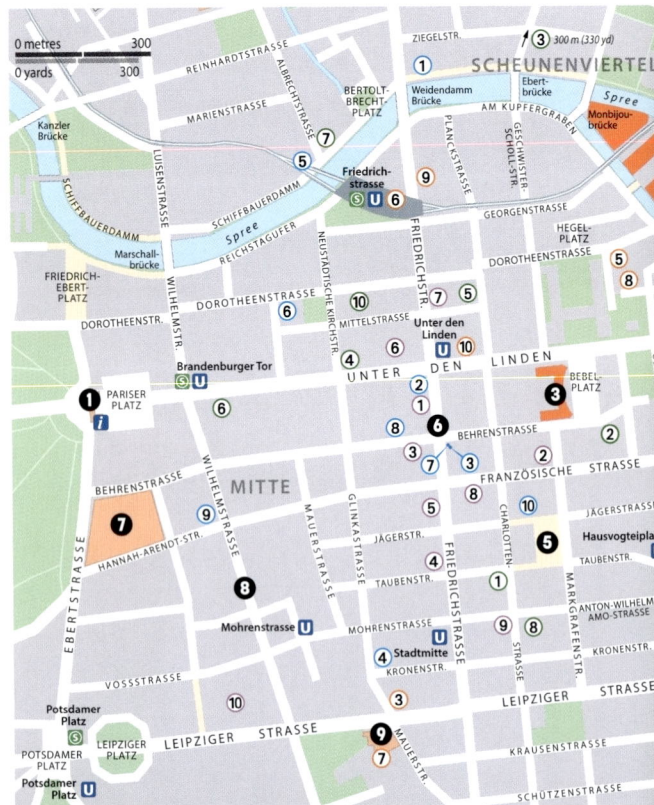

For places to stay in this area, see p174

1 Brandenburger Tor

Berlin's best-known landmark (*p22*) is located on Pariser Platz and leads through to the fashionable Unter den Linden.

2 Humboldt Forum

🔲 K5 🏛 Schloßplatz ⏰ 10:30am–6:30pm Mon, Wed–Sun 🌐 humboldt-tforum.com

Designed by Franco Stella and opened in 2021, this museum and cultural complex features a rooftop terrace offering spectacular views. The exhibits on show here include artifacts from sub-Saharan Africa, Asia, Oceania and the Americas.

Magnificent Brandenburger Tor on Pariser Platz

3 Forum Fridericianum

🔲 K4 🏛 Unter den Linden and Bebelplatz

The historic structures of this complex are among the city's finest. In 1740, Frederick the Great commissioned architect von Knobelsdorff to design and construct the prestigious Neo-Classical buildings for the area around today's Bebelplatz. Frederick personally influenced their designs of Deutsche Staatsoper, Prinz-Heinrich-Palais, Alte Bibliothek and the Catholic St-Hedwigs- Kathedrale, and later the Humboldt University. The opera house was the first to be built. A memorial at Bebelplatz recalls its dark past – in 1933, it was the site of the Nazi book burning. Frederick's successors commissioned the Altes Palais and a statue of "Old Fritz", surrounded by his buildings. Christian Daniel Rauch created the bronze figure in 1840, portraying Frederick wearing his tricorn hat and coronation mantle.

HISTORIC UNTER DEN LINDEN

A symbol of Neo-Classical glory and Prussian power, Unter den Linden also plays a significant role in more recent history. On the night of November 9, 1989, East and West Berliners celebrated the fall of the Berlin Wall by dancing on its remains, with the Brandenburger Tor's Doric columns serving as a backdrop.

4 Museumsinsel

Museum Island (p34), a UNESCO World Heritage Site, is one of the most significant complexes of museums in the world, holding major arts collections and imposing, full-scale ancient structures across five key museums. Based here are the Pergamonmuseum (closed for renovation until 2027), the Bode-Museum, the Alte National-galerie and the Altes and Neues Museums, including the famous Ägyptisches Museum. The iconic Berliner Dom, the original Berlin Cathedral, is also located in this area.

5 Gendarmenmarkt

This square, whose strict layout is reminiscent of an Italian Renaissance piazza, is probably the most beautiful in Berlin. Named after a regiment of *gens d'armes* stationed nearby, Gendarmenmarkt was built at the end of the 17th century as a market square. The Schauspielhaus (theatre) on the west side of the square was reopened as the Konzerthaus (concert hall) in 1984 (p61). A statue of the playwright Friedrich Schiller stands in front of the building. To the left and right of the Konzerthaus stand the twin towers of the Deutscher and Französischer Doms (German and French cathedrals), dating back to the late 18th century. Französischer Dom, to its north, is a prestigious late Baroque building (p59); concealed behind it is the Französische Friedrichstadtkirche, a church serving Berlin's French community. The Deutscher Dom opposite, built in 1708 on the south side of the square for the Reformed Protestant Church, did not receive its first tower until 1785. An exhibition on democracy in Germany is on display here.

THE HUGUENOTS IN BERLIN

In 1685, the Great Elector issued the famous Edict of Potsdam, granting asylum in Berlin to around 20,000 Huguenots, who were persecuted in their native France because of their Protestant faith. Skilled academics and crafters, they moulded Berlin's social and cultural life and enriched it with the French art of living. Today, the city's French community still worships at the Friedrichstadtkirche, part of the Französischer Dom complex.

6 Friedrichstraße

🗺 J4–L4 🚇 Mitte

Friedrichstraße has regained some of the glamour and vibrancy it possessed before World War II. Today, Berlin's Fifth Avenue is once again home to elegant shops and upmarket restaurants and cafés. Especially worth visiting are the three Quartiers 205, 206 and 207 (the latter designed by

Museumsinsel's Bode-Museum overlooking the River Spree

architect Jean Nouvel) within the building of Friedrichstadtpassagen and Art and Fashion House Quartier 206 *(p82)*. At the northern end of the street is the famous Dussmann store (books, music, events), the S-Bahn station Friedrichstraße and the former entertainment district, which includes the striking Friedrichstadt-Palast *(p73)* and the impressive Admiralspalast *(p96)*.

7 Holocaust-Denkmal

🚇 L3 🚏 Ebertstr 🅾 Information Centre: 10am–6pm Tue–Sun
🌐 stiftung-denkmal.de

The Memorial to the Murdered Jews of Europe serves as Germany's national Holocaust memorial *(p85)*. After years of debate, US star architect Peter Eisenman completed the monument in 2005. It consists of a large field with dark grey steles of varying heights up to 2 m (6 ft), which symbolize the six million Jews and others murdered by the Nazis in concentration camps between 1933 and 1945. Below the memorial, an information centre explains the causes and history of the genocide.

Sprawl of steles at the Holocaust-Denkmal

🕐

HISTORIC MITTE WALK

Morning

Turn back the clock on **Wilhelmstraße** *(p94)*, Berlin's political nerve centre until 1945. Starting at **Hotel Adlon Kempinski**, head south past the modern British Embassy. Turn right at Behrensstraße to visit the **Holocaust-Denkmal**, then carry on along Wilhelmstraße, where signs point out the old ministries. The Prussian State Council was in the Neo-Classical building at No 54; its last president was Konrad Adenauer, who became West Germany's first chancellor. At the corner of **Vossstraße** were Hitler's main offices in the Neue Reichskanzlei. Continue down to No 97, the giant structure of the former Ministry of Aviation. Today the **Federal Ministry of Finance** is based here. Retrace your steps north, turn right into **Leipziger Straße** then left into **Friedrichstraße**.

Afternoon

After lunch, pop into the concept store **The Square** *(p97)* just down the street. Then head to the **Gendarmenmarkt** square nearby. Admire its Konzerthaus and the imposing Deutscher and Französischer domes. The latter holds regular classical music concerts – check their website for the schedule. Round off your day with a hearty meal at the historic **Borchardt** *(p99)* on Französische Straße.

8 Wilhelmstraße

🔲 L3 🔲 Between Unter den Linden and Leipziger Str.

In imperial Berlin, the centre of the German Empire's governmental power was based in Wilhelmstraße. Around 100 years later, nothing remains of the prestigious historic buildings which represented the equivalent of No 10 Downing Street in London or Quai d'Orsay in Paris. All political decisions were made at Wilhelmstraße: both Chancellor (at No 77) and President (No 73) of the German Reich lived here in old townhouses. Their gardens became known as "ministerial gardens". Adolf Hitler had the street systematically developed into the nerve centre of Nazi power. The Neue Reichskanzlei (the Chancellor's office) was built in 1937–9 to plans by Albert Speer, at the corner of Voßstraße and Wilhelmstraße. It was blown up in 1945. Behind the Reichskanzlei was the so-called "Führerbunker" where Adolf Hitler committed suicide on 30 April 1945. It is now a car park. Of the historic buildings, only the former Reichsluftfahrtministerium (Ministry of Aviation) remains. Today, Wilhelmstraße is lined by modern residential and office buildings; the British Embassy, built in 2000 by Michael Wilford, creates a link with the international importance of this street.

9 Museum für Kommunikation

🔲 L4 🔲 Leipziger Str. 16 🔲 9am–5pm Tue–Fri (to 8pm every 3rd Wed in month), 10am–6pm Sat & Sun 🔲 mfk-berlin.de 🔲

The world's largest Post Office Museum opened in 1872. Its excellent displays document the history of communication from the first postage stamps of the Middle

Postmodern façade of the British Embassy on Wilhelmstraße

Vintage European letterbox at the Museum für Kommunikation

Ages to today's satellite technology. Particularly worth seeing are a blue and a red stamp from Mauritius, one of the first telephone installations (dating back to 1863) and three talking robots who interact with the visitors. Younger visitors always enjoy the digital exhibits, where they can learn and gain new insights while playing.

10 Schlossplatz
K5 **Mitte**

The Stadtschloss (town residence) of the Hohenzollerns once stood here. It was blown up by the East German government in 1950–51, and today just a few historic fragments of the original can be seen. Remains include the façade of the doorway where Karl Liebknecht is said to have proclaimed the Socialist Republic in 1918. The portal has been incorporated into the former Staatsratsgebäude (State Council Building) on the south side of the square. On its eastern side, the square used to be bordered by the Palast der Republik (Palace of the Republic), the former seat of the East German parliament demolished in 2008. The Humboldt Forum cultural centre (p91) was opened in 2021 and is set in the reconstructed Berlin Palace. It features a façade reminiscent of the old Hohenzollern Palace (p162) and a library. The non-European collections of the former Dahlem Museums (of Asian Art and of Ethnology) are housed in the building.

A DAY OF CULTURE

Morning

Start your stroll on Unter den Linden, which begins in front of the **Brandenburger Tor** on Pariser Platz (p22). Once Berlin's prestigious royal avenue, it remains a popular promenade for both locals and visitors. Head east and pass by the **Russian Embassy**, built in 1952. Stop for breakfast at **Einstein Unter den Linden** (p98), then continue along the boulevard to the 13.5-m-(44-ft-) high equestrian statue of Frederick the Great at **Forum Fridericianum** (p91). This area and Bebelplatz are right in the centre of old Berlin, with the Staatsoper, Altes Palais, St-Hedwigs-Kathedrale and Humboldt-Universität around them. Stop for an early lunch at **PalaisPopulaire** (Unter den Linden 5) or **Café Felix at Staatsbibliothek** (Unter den Linden 8).

Afternoon

In the early afternoon continue east along Unter den Linden. At the end of the street lies the **Museumsinsel** (p34). Cross the Schloßbrücke to explore the wealth of treasures in the island's museums. If you have time, visit the **Berliner Dom** (p58). Opposite the impressive cathedral you will see **Schlossplatz**, with the **Humboldt Forum** (p91). Return to the intersection at Freidrichstraße, and head to either **Bocca di Bacco** (p99) or **Grill Royal** (p99) to end your day with a delicious meal.

The Best of the Rest

1. DDR Museum
📍 K5 🏛 Karl-Liebknecht-Str. 🕐 9am–9pm daily 🌐 ddr-museum.de/en
This museum of everyday life in East Germany recreates socialist-era interiors and displays examples of East German design, including a Trabant car that visitors can sit in.

2. Lustgarten
📍 K5 🏛 Unter den Linden 1
Used as a parade ground for the German Democratic Republic, Lustgarten (Pleasure Garden) is now a popular park to take a break and relax after visiting the Museumsinsel. It is also a pleasant place for sunbathing.

3. WMF-Haus
📍 L4 🏛 Leipziger Str., corner Mauerstr.
The former headquarters of the porcelain and cutlery manufacturer WMF has remarkable façades deco-rated with beautiful mosaics.

4. Alte Kommandantur
📍 K5 🏛 Unter den Linden 1
Rebuilt with the original Classicist façade, this impressive building houses the Berlin offices of the media giant Bertelsmann.

5. Maxim-Gorki-Theater
📍 K4 🏛 Am Festungsgraben 2 🌐 gorhi.de
This renowned theatre was once Berlin's Singakademie, or singing school. Paganini and Liszt, among other great performers, are showcased here.

6. S-Bahnhof Friedrichstraße
📍 K4 🏛 Friedrichstr.
Remodelled several times, this has always been one of Berlin's most famous stations. Between 1961 and 1989, it was the principal crossing point between East and West.

Display of transport at the DDR Museum

7. Kinemathek
🏛 Mauerstr. 7 🕐 Hours vary, check website 🌐 deutsche-kinemathek.de
Housed temporarily in a former electrical substation, this institution celebrates the rich history of German cinema.

8. Palais am Festungsgraben
📍 K4 🏛 Am Festungsgraben 1 📞 (030) 20 45 34 50
The 1753 Baroque palace has retained its original elegant interior and magnificent ceiling frescoes.

9. Admiralspalast
📍 J4 🏛 Friedrichstr. 101 🕐 Hours vary, check website 🌐 admiralspalast.theater
Berlin's most legendary venue stages musicals and comedy shows.

10. Memorial to the Persecuted Homosexuals Under Nazism
📍 F4 🏛 Ebertstraße 🕐 10am–8pm Mon–Sun 🌐 stiftung-denkmal.de
Across Ebertstrasse from the Holocaust-Denkmal (p93), this solemn memorial in Tiergarten serves as a poignant reminder of the LGBTQ+ people persecuted by the Nazis.

Shops

1. KPM Store
🅥 K4 Friedrichstr. 158 🕒10am–7pm Mon–Sat 🅦 hpm-berlin.com

The finest porcelain of the famous Royal Porcelain Manufacture (KPM) is on offer at this elegant store. Shop for vases, candle holders, cups and plates here.

2. The Square
🅥 K4 Französiche Str. 🕒10:30am–7pm Mon–Sat 🅦 thesquareberlin.de

This trendy concept store offers newcomer fashion and luxury labels such as Christian Louboutin and Stella McCartney.

3. Jack Wolfskin
🅥 K4 Behrenstr. 23 🕒10am–6pm Mon–Sat 🅦 jack-wolfshin.com

Make sure you stock up on clothing, equipment and footwear before setting out on any outdoor activities at this branch of Germany's famous outfitter.

4. Bucherer
🅥 K4 Friedrichstr. 171 🕒10am–7pm Mon–Fri, 10am–6pm Sat 🅦 bucherer.com

A luxury outlet selling excellent quality watches and jewellery.

5. Karl Lagerfeld
🅥 K4 Friedrichstr. 172 🕒10am–7pm Mon–Sat 🅦 karl.com

Find refined, elegant accessories, shoes, bags and sunglasses at this luxury fashion label's store.

6. Nivea Haus
🅥 K4 Unter den Linden 28 🕒10am–7pm Mon–Sat 🅦 nivea.de

The Berlin flagship store of the German skin care brand Nivea offers a range of day spa services alongside selling Nivea products. Book facial treatments, massages and manicures, or simply buy some products to take home with you.

7. Kulturkaufhaus Dussmann
🅥 K4 Friedrichstr. 90 🕒10am–midnight Mon–Fri, 9am–11:30pm Sat 🅦 hulturhaufhaus.de

Kulturkaufhaus Dussmann has a large section on classical music. The English-language section here is also excellent.

8. Ritter Sport Bunte Schokowelt
🅥 K4 Französiche Str. 24 🕒10am–6:30pm Mon–Sat 🅦 ritter-sport.com/de/berlin

The chocolate maker's flagship store has fun merchandise, a chocolate-themed exhibition and workshops.

9. Rausch Schokoladenhaus
🅥 L4 Charlottenstr. 60 🕒10am–8pm Mon–Sat 🅦 rausch.de/en/chocolate-house

Giant chocolate sculptures of the Reichstag and Brandenburger Tor adorn this chocolatier's windows. The café on the upper floor offers a selection of the store's delicious creations.

10. Mall of Berlin
🅥 L3 Leipziger Platz 12 🕒10am–8pm Mon–Sat 🅦 mallofberlin.de

With 270 shops and restaurants, the Mall of Berlin occupies an entire block and connects Leipziger Straße and Wilhelmstraße through a passage.

Mall of Berlin home to many shops and restaurants

Pubs and Bars

1. Newton Bar
🅿 L4 🏠 Charlottenstr. 57 🕐 11am–2am daily (to 3am Thu–Sat) 🌐 newton-bar.de
One of the trendiest bars in town. Sink into the deep leather armchairs and sip your cocktails, surrounded by enlarged photographs of nudes by Helmut Newton.

2. Rooftop Hotel de Rome
🅿 K4 🏠 Behrenstr. 37 🕐 Noon–11pm daily 🌐 roccofortehotels.com/hotels-and-resorts/hotel-de-rome
The stylish bar on the roof of Hotel de Rome offers spectacular views of Bebelplatz and excellent Italian fare.

3. Zosch
🅿 J4 🏠 Tucholshystr. 30 🕐 4pm–2am Sun 🌐 zosch-berlin.de
An old-fashioned pub in Mitte, Zosch has an unpolished charm. Concerts hosted in the brick vaulted cellar range from folk to jazz music.

4. Einstein Unter den Linden
🅿 K4 🏠 Unter den Linden 42 🕐 8am–10pm Mon–Fri, 10am–10pm Sat, 10am–6pm Sun 🌐 einstein-udl.com
This Viennese coffeehouse-inspired bistro is popular with politicians, artists and journalists. Excellent wines and beer brands are on offer.

5. Freundschaft
🅿 K4 🏠 Mittelstraße 1 🕐 6pm–1am Mon–Fri 🌐 istdeinbesterfreund.com
Enjoy a range of drinks at this cosy wine bar. This place specializes in mostly natural wines, mainly from Austria and France. Take a seat at the oval bar counter and order a glass, along with small dishes.

6. Café LebensArt
🅿 K4 🏠 Unter den Linden 69A 🕐 9am–7pm daily 🌐 cafe-lebensart.de
More like a café than a bar, LebensArt offers tasty breakfast and after-noon cakes.

7. Ständige Vertretung
🅿 K3 🏠 Schiffbauerdamm 8 🕐 11am–1am daily 🌐 staev.de
The name harks back to the permanent West German repre-sentation in East Berlin. Ständige Vertretung is famous for its Rhineland specialities, such as Kölsch beer.

8. Bellboy Bar
🅿 L4 🏠 Mohrenstr. 30 🕐 6pm–2am Sun–Thu, 6pm–3am Fri & Sat 🌐 bellboybar.com
Located on the ground floor of the Hilton Berlin, this plush bar has a wide range of food and drink.

9. Das Lemke
🅿 K7 🏠 Dirchsenstr. S-Bahn arch No 143 🕐 Noon–11:30pm Mon–Sat, 1–10:30pm Sun 🌐 hm.lemke.berlin
Berlin's first craft brewery, this pub has a relaxed ambience and a variety of beers.

10. Windhorst
🅿 K3 🏠 Dorotheenstr. 65 🕐 6pm–1am Mon–Fri, 8pm–1am Sat 🌐 windhorst-bar.de
Sophisticated jazz bar with bartenders whipping up your cocktail of choice.

Einstein Unter den Linden, a Viennese-style bistro

Restaurants

Enjoying the view from the waterfront at the Grill Royal

PRICE CATEGORIES

For a three-course meal for one with half a bottle of wine (or equivalent meal), taxes and charges included.

€ under €30 €€ €30–60 €€€ over €60

1. Grill Royal
 K4 Friedrichstr. 105b 5pm–midnight daily grillroyal.com · €€
Steak-lovers can choose from a range of cuts from around the world.

2. Crackers
 K4 Friedrichstr. 158 6pm–midnight Mon–Thu, 6pm–1am Fri–Sat, 6–11pm Sun crackersberlin.com · €€€

The brainchild of Heinz Gindullis, Crackers is known for its exceptional dishes and extravagant drinks menu, making it the perfect spot for a late-night cocktail.

3. Bocca di Bacco
 K4 Friedrichstr. 167–8 Noon–midnight Mon–Sat boccadibacco.de · €€€
A sophisticated Italian diner, Bocca di Bacco offers a wide range of fresh fish and meat dishes. This is also an excellent enoteca with a good wine list.

4. Liu Nudelhaus
 L4 Kronenstr. 72 11:30am–3pm Mon–Fri & 5–7:30pm Wed–Fri chengduweidao.de · €€
The Sichuan noodles here are widely regarded as some of the city's best. Expect to wait a while for a table.

5. Tausend Cantina
 K3 Schiffbauerdamm 11 9pm–late Thu–Sat tausendberlin.com · €€€
Top-notch Asian and Ibero-American cuisine by celebrated chef Duc Ngo.

6. Restaurant & Café 1687
 K4 Mittelstr. 30 8am–6pm Mon–Fri 1687.berlin · €€€
Enjoy modern European cuisine with Franco-Mediterranean influences. There's an extensive wine list on offer.

7. Borchardt
 K4 Französische Str. 47 11:30am–midnight daily borchardt-restaurant.de · €€€
A beautiful dining room makes for a stunning setting for the modern French dishes and schnitzel served here. Reservations are a must.

8. Cookies Cream
 K4 Behrenstr. 55 6:30–11pm Tue–Thu, 5–11pm Fri & Sat cookiescream.com · €€€
This is one of the first vegetarian restaurants in Germany to get a Michelin star.

9. Rotes Kamel
 L3 Hannah-Arendt-Str. 4 3–11pm Sun–Thu, 3pm–midnight Fri–Sat roteskamel.com · €€
Fresh, satisfying meals with flavours from the Middle East, are on offer here.

10. Hugo & Notte
 L4 Gendarmenmarkt 5 Noon–10pm Tue–Sun hugo-und-notte.de · €€€
Enjoy French cuisine at this restaurant on the premises of the French cathedral.

CENTRAL BERLIN: SCHEUNENVIERTEL

From the mid-19th-century onwards, the Scheunenviertel ("barn quarter") became a refuge for thousands of Jewish migrants fleeing Russia and Eastern Europe. After World War II the area was entirely neglected and that caused it to inevitably fall into decay. It has been rejuvenated in recent decades and many historic merchants' yards and narrow side streets have been restored, reviving the quarter's unique and lively character. With its many restaurants, galleries and shops, the district has become a beautiful and pleasant place to live and visit. The tragic history of its former inhabitants, however, remains unforgotten.

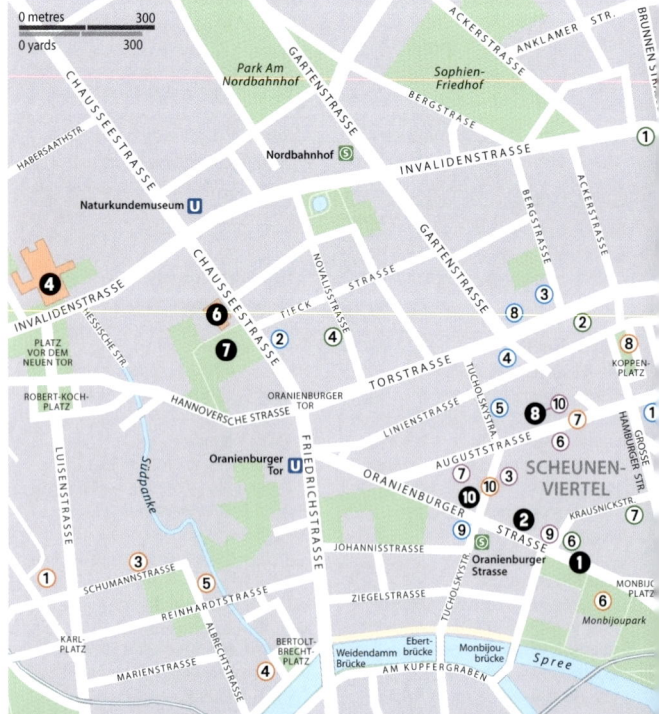

For places to stay in this area, see p174

1 Oranienburger Straße

🗺 J4 🚇 Mitte, between Friedrichstr. & Rosenthaler Str.

Located in the centre of old Scheunenviertel, Oranienburger Straße symbolizes the rise and fall of Jewish culture in Berlin like no other street. Traces of its Jewish past are visible at the Neue Synagoge *(p101)* and several Jewish cafés and restaurants. Some 18th- and 19th-century buildings attest to the street's former splendour – the Postfuhramt *(p103)* with its ornate façade, for example, or the house at Nos 71–72, built in 1789 by Christian Friedrich Becherer for the Grand Lodge of the German Freemasons. The area is also great for a night out – visit one of the many bars and restaurants *(p106)* lining the street.

Glittering carved dome of the Neue Synagoge

2 Neue Synagoge

🗺 J4 🚇 Oranienburger Str. 28–30 🕐 Summer: 10am–6pm Mon–Fri, 10am–7pm Sun; winter: 10am–6pm Sun–Thu, 10am–3pm Fri 🌐 centrumjudaicum.de ⧉

Once the largest in Europe, the New Synagogue was opened in 1866. In 1938, it survived Kristallnacht, when Jewish homes were vandalized across Germany, thanks to a brave police officer Wilhelm Krützfeld, but it was damaged by bombs during World War II. Behind the splendid Moorish façades are a prayer room and the Centrum Judaicum.

3 Hackesche Höfe

🗺 J5 🚇 Rosenthaler Str. 40–41

Berlin's largest and most attractive group of restored commercial buildings, Hackesche Höfe extends from Oranienburger Straße to Rosenthaler Straße. The complex, comprising eight interconnecting courtyards, was designed around the turn of the 20th century by August Endell and Kurt Berndt, two leading exponents of the Jugendstil. The first courtyard especially has elements typical of the style: geometric motifs on vibrant glazed tiles cover the building. The complex is a popular centre of nightlife.

Various species displayed at the Museum für Naturkunde

4 Museum für Naturkunde
F2 Invalidenstr. 43
9:30am–6pm Tue–Fri (from 10am Sat & Sun) museumfuer-naturkunde.berlin

The Museum of Natural History (p55) is one of the biggest of its kind and features the largest dinosaur skeleton to have ever been discovered: a Giraffatitan found in Tanzania and housed in the museum's glass-roofed courtyard. Other smaller reconstructed dinosaur skeletons are also on display, as are taxidermist Alfred Keller's insect models, various types of fossils, meteorites and minerals.

5 Sophienstraße
J5 Große Hamburger Str. 29

Narrow Sophienstraße has been beautifully restored and looks just as it did in the late 18th century. The buildings and courtyards now have shops and arts and crafts workshops. Nearby, the Baroque Sophienkirche (p104), the first Protestant parish church, was founded by Queen Sophie Luise in 1712. Next to it is a cemetery with some tombs dating back to the 18th century.

6 Brecht-Weigel-Museum
F2 Chausseestr. 125 Hours vary, chech website adh.de/en/archiv/museen/brecht-weigel-museum

Bertolt Brecht, one of the greatest playwrights of the 20th century, lived here with his wife, Helene Weigel, between 1953 and 1956. On display are original furnishings, documents and photographs.

7 Dorotheenstädtischer Friedhof
F2 Chausseestr. 126 Summer: 8am–8pm daily (winter: to sunset)

This is a striking cemetery dating back to 1762. To the left of the entrance are the graves of Heinrich Mann (1871–1950) and Bertolt Brecht (1898–1956); further along are the pillar-like tombstones of Johann Gottlieb Fichte (1762–1814) and Georg Wilhelm Friedrich Hegel (1770–1831).

8 KW Institute for Contemporary Art
G2 Augustr. 69 11am–7pm Wed–Mon (to 9pm Thu) hw-berlin.de

Housed in a former margarine factory, this gallery displays works by established as well as up-and-coming artists.

JEWISH BERLIN

In the 19th century, Berlin had a population of 200,000 Jews, the largest such community in Germany. Apart from the wealthier Jews who lived in the west of the city, it included many Jewish migrants from Eastern Europe. They settled in Spandauer Vorstadt, primarily in Scheunenviertel, an impoverished part of the district. Later, Nazi propaganda used that name to denote the whole area to tarnish all Jews by association.

9 Gedenkstätte Große Hamburger Straße

J5 · Große Hamburger Str.
· jg-berlin.org

Before 1939, this was a thoroughly Jewish street, with Jewish schools, the oldest Jewish cemetery in Berlin and an old people's home. The latter achieved tragic fame during the Nazi period – it was used as a detention centre for Berlin's Jews before transporting them to concentration camps. A monument commemorates the thousands who were sent to their death from here. To the left of the home is a Jewish school, on the site of an earlier school founded in 1778 by the Enlightenment philosopher Moses Mendelssohn (1729–86). To the right is the Alter Jüdischer Friedhof (old Jewish cemetery), where some 12,000 of Berlin's Jewish people were buried between 1672 and 1827. It was destroyed by the Nazis in 1943, and in 1945 it was converted into a park. Only a few Baroque tombstones or *masebas* survived. The spot thought to be Mendelssohn's tomb is marked by a *maseba*.

10 Postfuhramt

J4 · Oranienburger Str. 35

The richly ornamented Postfuhramt (post office transport department) dates from the 19th century. The building houses the head office of a medical technology firm.

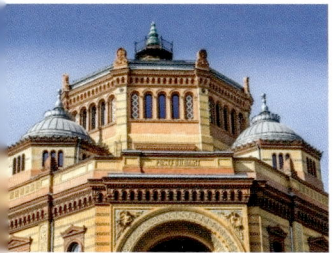
Intricately designed façade of Postfuhramt

A DAY IN SCHEUNENVIERTEL

Morning

Take the S-Bahn to Berlin's former entertainment district at Friedrichstraße. Then walk north up to Reinhardtstraße, opposite the Friedrichstadt-Palast, and turn left here towards Bertolt-Brecht-Platz. Continue south to Albrechtstraße to the **Berliner Ensemble** (p104). Admire the theatre where Bertolt Brecht used to work, then make a detour to visit his home, the **Brecht-Weigel-Museum**, by returning to Friedrichstraße and walking north to Chausseestraße. Then retrace your steps and turn left into **Oranienburger Straße** (p101) to fashionable Scheunenviertel. About a seven-minute walk down the street will bring the dome of the **Neue Synagoge** (p101) into view.

Afternoon

Walk down Tucholskystraße and turn right into Auguststraße for some refreshments at Strandbad Mitte (*Kleine Hamburger Straße 16*). After lunch return to Auguststraße. Picturesque courtyards are found here, such as the old-world **Schulhof** (p105) at No 21. Just across the street is the **KW Institute for Contemporary Art**. Continue along Auguststraße then turn right for the **Gedenkstätte Große Hamburger Straße** and the **Hackesche Höfe** (p101). Round off your tour by enjoying a spot of shopping in Scheunenviertel.

The Best of the Rest

1. Charité
🔟 J3 🅰 Schumannstr. 20–21
🆆 charite.de

Many renowned physicians, such as Rudolf Virchow and Robert Koch, worked and taught at this world-famous hospital, founded in 1710. The Museum of Medical History (closed Mondays) has some 750 remarkable exhibits on display.

2. Alte and Neue Schönhauser Straße
🔟 J5 🅰 Weinmeisterstraße

Alte Schönhauser Straße is one of the oldest streets in Mitte. It is characterized by a colourful jumble of traditional and modern fashion shops.

3. Deutsches Theater
🔟 J3 🅰 Schumannstr. 13A
🆆 deutschestheater.de

Once the place of work of Max Reinhardt, this theatre – considered one of the best German-language theatre – shows mainly German classics, often in new interpretations.

4. Berliner Ensemble
🔟 J3 🅰 Bertolt-Brecht-Platz 1
🆆 berliner-ensemble.de

This theatre, established in 1891–2 by Heinrich Seeling, was the main venue for Bertolt Brecht's plays, including *The Threepenny Opera*.

5. Reichsbahnbunker
🔟 J3 🅰 Reinhardtstr 20
🆆 sammlung-boros.de

One of the few surviving World War II bunkers in Berlin, it is now home to the Boros Collection contemporary art gallery.

6. Monbijoupark
🔟 J5 🅰 Oranienburger Str./Spree

This lovely park was once the grounds of the little Monbijou Palace.

7. Auguststraße
🔟 G2 🅰 Between Oranienburger Str. & Rosenthaler Str.

The area around this road harks back to old Scheunenviertel, with courtyards and art galleries.

8. Koppenplatz
🔟 G2 🅰 Near Auguststr.

In this small square, a monument of a table and an upturned chair recall the forced expulsion of Jewish people.

9. Sophienkirche
🔟 G3 🅰 Große Hamburger Str. 29

This 18th-century parish church preserves its old Berlin charm.

10. Tucholskystraße
🔟 J4

This street is typical of the transformation of Scheunenviertel, with trendy shops next to renovated façades.

Strolling through the pleasant Monbijoupark

Old Courtyards

Ivy-covered exterior of the Sophie-Gips-Höfe

1. Sophie-Gips-Höfe
🅿 G3 🚇 Sophienstr. 21–22
Famous for the Hoffman art collection, which is based here, this former sewing machine factory is a popular meeting place.

2. Sophienhöfe
🅿 G3 🚇 Sophienstr. 17–18
The 19th-century red-brick artisans' workshops have been beautifully transformed into artists' studios and a theatre.

3. Heckmann-Höfe
🅿 G3 🚇 Between Oranienburger Str. 32 & Auguststraße 9
These lavishly restored yards in a candy factory attract a lot of visitors. There's also a restaurant and trendy shops on the premises.

4. Sophienstr. 22 and 22A
🅿 G3
Two small inner courtyards, partially planted, are surrounded by yellow and red-brick walls.

Haus Schwarzenberg, a hot spot for Berlin street art

5. Rosenthaler Straße 37
🅿 J5
This green-tiled courtyard is unique. Once part of the Wertheim department store, it now houses a boutique and tapas bar. The 1775 townhouse through which it is accessed has a beautiful wooden staircase.

6. Schulhof
🅿 G2 🚇 Auguststr. 21
Time seems to have stood still around 1900 in this courtyard, which houses an elementary school.

7. Hof Auguststraße 5A
🅿 G3
The extensive courtyard of the former Postfuhramt permits a glimpse of the original façade of the building.

8. Haus Schwarzenberg
🅿 J5 🚇 Rosenthaler Str. 39
Berlin's post-Wall subculture of edgy art collectives is still alive and well in this unrenovated courtyard.

9. Kunsthof
🅿 J4 🚇 Oranienburger Str. 27
A courtyard full of nooks and crannies, which is today occupied by a number of workshops, offices and cafés.

10. KW Courtyard
🅿 G2 🚇 Auguststr. 69
Large-scale installations by the resident artists are regularly on display in the leafy courtyard of the KW Institute for Contemporary Art *(p102)*.

Pubs, Bars and Nightclubs

1. Buck and Breck
🗺 G2 🏠 Brunnenstr. 177 🕐 7pm–2am Sun–Fri 🌐 buckandbreck.com

A bar with an intimate setting, this place specializes in fine cocktails.

2. Pawn Dot Com Bar
🗺 G2 🏠 Torstr. 164 🕐 6pm–2am daily (to 3am Fri & Sat) 🌐 pawndotcombar.berlin

Whimsical cocktail bar in the yard of a former royal pawnshop.

3. B-flat
🗺 G3 🏠 Dirchsenstr. 40 🕐 From 8pm daily, chech website for events 🌐 b-flat-berlin.de

Live jazz, and occasionally dancing, are on offer at this small venue.

4. Reingold
🗺 F2 🏠 Novalistr. 11 📞 (030) 54 90 66 080 🕐 From 8pm Tue–Sat

A relaxed bar with a 1920s ambience, Reingold is perfect for a nightcap.

5. Hackbarth's
🗺 G2 🏠 Auguststr. 49A 📞 (030) 282 77 04 🕐 10am–4am daily

This breakfast café transforms into a bar by sundown, serving beer on tap.

6. Mr. Susan
🗺 J5 🏠 Krausnichstr. 1 🕐 6pm–1am Tue–Sat 🌐 mrsusan.com

A cocktail bar serving creative drinks. It hosts occasional pop-up events as well.

Entrance to the Mein Haus am See, a chic retro bar/club

7. Anna Koschke
🗺 J5 🏠 Krausnichstr. 11 🕐 5pm–1am Tue–Thu, 5pm–3am Fri & Sat 🌐 anna-hoschke.de

This neighbourhood pub is popular with locals and students. The *bouletten* (meatballs) here are legendary.

8. Yosoy
🗺 J5 🏠 Rosenthaler Str. 37 🕐 From 11am daily 🌐 yosoy.de

Tasty tapas, wines and exciting cocktails are served at this attractively furnished Spanish restaurant – which is why it is usually crowded late into the night.

9. Mein Haus am See
🗺 G2 🏠 Brunnenstr. 197-198 🕐 From 4pm daily 🌐 mein-haus-am-see.club

With its flexible opening times, this café and bar is popular with locals, especially on weekends. Arrive early to get a table.

10. Oxymoron
🗺 J5 🏠 Rosenthaler Str. 40–41 🕐 9:30am–11pm Mon–Sat 🌐 oxymoron-berlin.de

This lounge bar and restaurant in popular and lively Hackesche Höfe (p101) features chintz decoration and serves light French and Italian meals.

Enjoying a meal in the courtyard of the Oxymoron

Restaurants

1. Shiso Burger
G2 · Auguststr. 29C · Noon–11pm daily · shisoburger.com · €

Succulent Asian-style burgers and crispy sweet potato fries are served at this trendy spot.

2. Rutz
F2 · Chausseestr. 8 · From 6pm Mon–Fri · rutz-restaurant.de · €€€

Enjoy exceptional dishes created using local ingredients at this high-end restaurant.

3. Bandol sur Mer
G2 · Torstr. 167 · From 6:30pm Mon–Fri · bandolsurmer.de · €€€

A prestigious Michelin-starred restaurant, Bandol sur Mer is casual with a bistro-style open kitchen. It offers flavourful French dishes that are beautifully plated.

4. Frea
G2 · Torstr. 180, corner of Kleine Hamburger Str. · 5:30pm–midnight daily · frea.de · €€

This sustainable restaurant serves organic, plant-based food made using zero-waste practices.

5. Beth-Café
G2 · Tucholskystr. 40 · 11am–8pm Sun–Fri (to 5pm Fri) · adassjisroel.de/heute/beth-cafe · €

This small Jewish café, part of the Adass-Jisroel community, serves Jewish snacks alongside kosher wines and beers.

6. Hackescher Hof
J5 · Rosenthaler Str. 40–41 · 9am–11pm daily · hackescherhof.de · €€€

One of the neighbourhood's most popular restaurants, Hackescher Hof serves tasty local food.

PRICE CATEGORIES

For a three-course meal for one with half a bottle of wine (or equivalent meal), taxes and charges included.

....

€ under €30 €€ €30–60 €€€ over €60

---

7. Monsieur Vuong
G2 · Alte Schönhauser Str. 46 · Noon–midnight daily · monsieurvuong.de · €€

This Vietnamese restaurant is known for its traditional dishes.

8. Gärtnerei
G2 · Torstr. 179 · 6–11:30pm daily · gaertnerei-berlin.com · €€€

A chic Michelin-starred restaurant, Gärtnerei serves German dishes, accompanied by Austrian wines. The menu also offers plenty of vegetarian options.

9. Kamala
J4 · Oranienburger Str. 69 · (030) 283 27 97 · Noon–11:30pm daily · €€

This hidden gem offers traditional Thai cuisine alongside an impressive wine list.

10. Coccodrillo
G2 · Veteranenstr. 9 · Noon–3pm & 5:30pm–11pm Mon–Thu, noon–11pm Fri & Sat, noon–10pm Sun · bigsquadra.com/en · €€

The all-Italian staff here serves traditional Italian food in a gleaming 1950s-style setting.

Tender pork knuckle presented elegantly at Rutz

CENTRAL BERLIN: AROUND ALEXANDERPLATZ

The area around Alexanderplatz – "Alex" to locals – is one of the city's oldest parts. It was here that the twin towns of Cölln and Berlin merged in the 13th century. The square defined the heartbeat of the city before World War II; after the ravages of war, it seemed vast and a little forlorn, but its vibrancy, described by Alfred Döblin in his novel *Berlin Alexanderplatz*, has slowly returned. A short walk away is the city's oldest coherent quarter – the historical Nikolaiviertel – with its medieval Nikolaikirche.

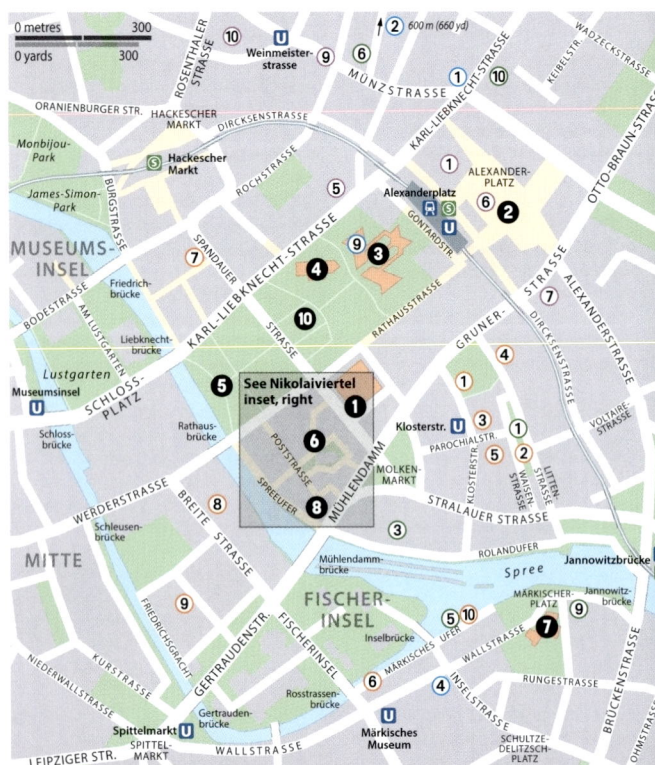

1 Rotes Rathaus

📍 K6 🏛 Rathausstr. 15
📞 (030) 90 26 20 32
🕐 9am–6pm Mon–Fri

Berlin's proud town hall (p61), the office of the Governing Mayor, is the political centre of power in Greater Berlin. It was built in 1861–9 to a design by Hermann Friedrich Waesemann on the site of an older town hall. The Rathaus was intended to demonstrate the power and the glory of Berlin, and the architect took his inspiration for the new building from Italian Renaissance *palazzi*. The building is known as the "Rotes Rathaus" (Red Town Hall) – not a reference to its Socialist past, but to the red bricks from Brandenburg province with which it was built.

Berlin's Alexanderplatz beside the Berliner Fernsehturm

2 Alexanderplatz

📍 J6 🏛 Mitte

This huge, commercial square in the centre of East Berlin, called "Alex" by Berliners, was one of the most vibrant places in Berlin before World War II. Alfred Döblin beautifully captured the rhythm of the city in his famous novel *Berlin Alexanderplatz* (1929). While the square remains a hub of activity, especially around the Galeria department store (p113), its vibe today is noticeably different from its pre-war heyday. Alexanderplatz was originally a cattle and wool market. Not many of the prewar buildings have survived – only Berolinahaus and Alexanderhaus remain, next to Alexanderplatz, the historic S-Bahn station, both dating back to 1929. The square was almost completely laid to waste in World War II, and most of the surrounding concrete tower blocks were built in the 1960s.

3 Berliner Fernsehturm

📍 J6 🏛 Panoramastr. 1a
🕐 Mar–Oct: 9am–11pm; Nov–Feb: 10am–11pm 🌐 tv-turm.de/en ♿

This 368-m- (1,207-ft-) high TV tower is the tallest building in Berlin, affording views of up to 40 km (25 miles). There is a viewing platform at 203 m (666 ft). The Sphere restaurant above rotates around its own axis once every 30 minutes. The tower, visible from afar, was erected in 1965–9 by the East German government to signify the triumph of their capital East Berlin.

Colourful buildings lining a street in Nikolaiviertel

4 Marienkirche

📍 J6 🏠 Karl-Liebknecht-Str. 8 ⏰ 10am–6pm Mon–Sat, noon–6pm Sun 🌐 marienkirche-berlin.de

Originally built in 1270, Marienkirche was extensively remodelled in the 15th century. Thanks to its Baroque church tower, it is one of Berlin's loveliest churches. Inside, the alabaster pulpit by Andreas Schlüter (1703) and the main altar (1762) are highlights. The 15th-century Gothic font and a 22-m-(72-ft-) long fresco from 1485, *Der Totentanz* (The Dance of Death), are its two oldest treasures.

5 Marx-Engels-Forum

📍 K5

This public park was founded by the East German authorities shortly after German reunification in 1989. The words "Next time it will all be different" were scrawled onto the bronze monument to Friedrich Engels and Karl Marx, the fathers of Socialism, erected in 1986.

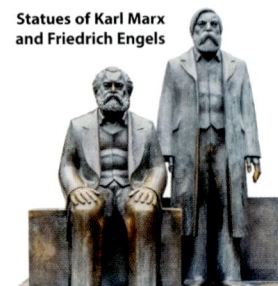
Statues of Karl Marx and Friedrich Engels

6 Nikolaiviertel

📍 K6 🏠 Mitte Knoblauchhaus: Poststr. 23 ⏰ 10am–6pm Tue–Sun 🌐 stadtmuseum.de/museum/museum-hnoblauchhaus 🔗

Centred around the medieval Nikolaikirche *(p161)*, the small and quaint Nikolaiviertel quarter with its nooks and crannies, souvenir shops and old Berlin restaurants is one of the most charming parts of the city. The area extending between the banks of the Spree River and Mühlendamm was razed to the ground in World War II. East Germany restored it after the war, but unfortunately not always successfully: some houses were covered in prefabricated façades. Knoblauchhaus was one of few to escape wartime destruction. Dating from 1759, it was the former home of the Knoblauch family (Neue Synagoge was designed by architect Eduard Knoblauch). Today it houses a museum depicting everyday life in Berlin, and includes a fully furnished apartment in the Biedermeier style.

7 Märkisches Museum

📍 L6 🏠 Am Köllnischen Park 5 🔧 For renovation until 2028 🌐 stadtmuseum.de/en/museum/maerkisches-museum

Berlin's municipal museum holds several artifacts relating to the city's culture and history, including architectural treasures such as door-ways and the head of one of the horses from the top of the Brandenburg Gate. There is also a Gothic Chapel room with a collection of medieval sculptures.

8 Ephraim-Palais
🔲 K6 🏠 Poststr. 16 🕐 10am–6pm Tue–Sun 🌐 stadtmuseum.de/en/ museum/museum-ephraim-palais 🔗

This Rococo palace, built in 1766 for the merchant, court jeweller and mint master Nathan Veitel Heinrich Ephraim, was once regarded as the city's most beautiful spot. Rebuilt using original elements after the old palace was demolished, it houses a museum on local history and Berlin art history.

9 Karl-Marx-Allee and Frankfurter Allee
🔲 H3 🏠 Mitte/Friedrichshain

This avenue was built as a showpiece for Socialism in 1949–55. Known then as "Stalinallee", it provided ultra-modern apartments that are again in high demand today.

10 Neptunbrunnen
🔲 K6 🏠 Am Rathaus

The green Neo-Baroque fountain, dating from 1895, depicts the sea god Neptune. He is surrounded by four female figures, symbolizing Prussia's main rivers at the time: the Rhine, Weichsel, Oder and Elbe.

Magnificent Neo-Baroque Neptunbrunnen

A DAY AROUND ALEXANDERPLATZ

Morning

Start your day at Strausberger Platz, where you can admire the Socialist architecture lining Frankfurter Allee and **Karl-Marx-Allee**. Then take the U-Bahn (or continue on foot) to **Alexanderplatz** *(p109)*, where you can indulge in a bit of shopping before heading to the beautiful **Marienkirche**. Step back outside to admire the lovely **Neptunbrunnen** fountain, then walk to the **Berliner Fernsehturm** and – if the weather is nice – take the lift. Afterwards, stroll past **Rotes Rathaus** *(p101)* towards **Marx-Engels-Forum**, and head to **Zille-Stube** *(p115)* for lunch; the outdoor seating here is a particular draw.

Afternoon

After lunch, pop by the Schlüterhof, then cross **Schloßplatz** to walk along Friedrichsgracht and have a look at the old Jungfernbrücke. Then turn left into Sperlingsgasse to find **Brüderstraße** *(p112)*, which features two historic townhouses. Continue towards Scharrenstraße and Breite Straße and cross the Spree at Mühlendammbrücke. To the left is the old **Nikolaiviertel** quarter. The Nikolaikirche museum is especially worth a visit. End your day with a meal at **Zur Gerichtslaube** *(p115)*.

The Best of the Rest

1. Franziskaner-Klosterkirche
K6 **Klosterstr. 74** **Apr–Sep: 10am–6pm daily** **hlosterruine.berlin**
This picturesque spot, ideal for a break, features the remnants of a 13th-century Franciscan abbey surrounded by lawns.

2. Historische Berliner Stadtmauer
K6 **Waisenstr.**
A fragment of the 13th–14th-century town wall that once surrounded the twin towns of Berlin and Cölln.

3. Palais Podewil
K6 **Klosterstr. 68** **hultur-projehte.berlin/en/podewil**
The light yellow Baroque palace, built in 1701–4, has been transformed into Podewil, a cultural centre and a subsidiary of the Grips-Theater (p70).

4. Stadtgericht Mitte
K6 **Littenstr. 13–15** **9am–1pm Mon–Fri**
The imposing municipal courts building features extravagant stairs in the lobby area, with curved balustrades and elegant columns.

5. Parochialkirche
K6 **Klosterstr. 67** **9am–3:30pm Mon–Fri**
Parochialkirche, by Johann Arnold Nering and Martin Grünberg, was one of Berlin's most charming Baroque churches, but the interior and bell tower were destroyed in World War II. In 2016, a replica of the tower was mounted, bearing a new carillon with 52 bells.

6. Märkisches Ufer
L6
This picturesque riverside promenade gives a good impression of the city in the late 18th century. Look out for No 12, a typical Berlin Baroque house that was initially built on Fischerinsel in 1740 and transplanted here in 1969.

7. Heilig-Geist-Kapelle
J5 **Spandauer Str. 1**
A beautiful example of Gothic brick architecture, this hospital church was built around 1300.

8. Ribbeckhaus
K5 **Breite Str. 36**
The only Renaissance house in central Berlin, with a remarkable, lavishly ornamented façade.

9. Brüderstraße
L5
This little street behind Petriplatz has a rich, historic past. Galgenhaus at Brüderstraße 10 now houses the art gallery Kewenig.

10. Historischer Hafen
L6 **Märkisches Ufer** **historischer-hafen-berlin.de**
Moored at this port are several examples of the barges and tug-boats that once operated on the Spree. The *Renate-Angelika* hosts a historical display on inland shipping.

Grand atrium and staircase of Stadtgericht Mitte

Shops and Markets

Sleek Alexa shopping centre, home to top brands

1. Galeria
Ⓟ J6 **Ⓜ** Alexanderplatz 9 **Ⓞ** 9:30am–8pm Mon–Sat **Ⓦ** galeria.de

The largest department store in eastern Berlin stocks everything your heart could desire. Its food department entices with a range of international gourmet foods.

2. Die Puppenstube
Ⓟ K6 **Ⓜ** Propststr. 4 **Ⓞ** 9am–6:30pm Mon–Sat, 11am–6pm Sun **Ⓦ** puppen-eins.de

Adorable dolls made from porcelain and other materials await, as do mountains of cute fluffy teddy bears.

3. Teddy's
Ⓟ K6 **Ⓜ** Propststr. 4 **Ⓞ** 10am–6pm Mon–Sat **Ⓦ** teddy-laden.de

An old-fashioned toy store with probably the city's best selection of teddy bears, including brands like Steiff. It also has bear clothing and accessories.

4. Schmuck und Kunsthandwerk Berlin
Ⓟ K6 **Ⓜ** Am Nußbaum 8 **Ⓞ** 11am–7pm Mon–Sat **Ⓦ** berlin-kunsthandwerh.de

A beautiful jewellery shop selling pretty rings, necklaces, bracelets and earrings, handcrafted using crystals from Swarovski and Polaris.

5. Manga-Mafia Store
Ⓟ J6 **Ⓜ** Karl-Liebknecht-Str. 13 **Ⓒ** (030) 61 65 34 57 **Ⓞ** 10:30am–7pm Mon–Fri, 10am–7:30pm Sat

A haven for manga and anime fans, this store offers a vast array of Japanese comics, art books as well as merchandise.

6. U- and S-Bahnhof Alexanderplatz
Ⓟ J6 **Ⓜ** Alexanderplatz

This bustling area has a selection of shops for daily needs, plus late-opening fast food outlets and German *Imbisse* (food stands).

7. Alexa
Ⓟ K6 **Ⓜ** Am Alexanderplatz, Grunerstr. 20 **Ⓞ** 10am–8pm Mon–Sat **Ⓦ** alexacentre.com

One of the largest shopping malls in Berlin, this centre features a wide range of brands, dining options, and entertainment venues, including a bowling alley.

8. Erzgebirgischer Weihnachtsmarkt
Ⓟ K6 **Ⓜ** Propststr. 8 **Ⓞ** 11am–7pm Mon–Sat, 1–6pm Sun & public hols **Ⓦ** das-sachsenhaus.de

A vast array of shelves laden with German handicrafts, including traditional wooden nutcrackers and Plauen lace.

9. Münzstraße
Ⓟ J6

This tiny street is full of original fashion boutiques and designer stores. A real hotspot for fashion aficionados.

10. Birkenstock
Ⓟ J6 **Ⓜ** Neue Schönhauser Str.6–7 **Ⓞ** 11am–7pm Mon–Sat **Ⓦ** birkenstoch.com

A German institution, this is where Berliners go to stock up on summertime footwear.

Wooden nutcracker

Pubs, Cafés and Beer Gardens

1. Zur letzten Instanz
📍K6 🏠Waisenstr. 14–16 🕐Noon–3pm & 5:30–11pm Mon–Sat 🌐zurletzteninstanz.com/en/start-en

Berlin's oldest pub dates back to 1621, and former guests include Napoleon, Beethoven and Angela Merkel.

2. Zum Nußbaum
📍K6 🏠Am Nußbaum 3 📞(030) 242 30 95 🕐Noon–10pm

This charming historic pub in Nikolaiviertel serves draught beers and *Berliner Weiße* in summer.

3. The Greens
📍H3 🏠Am Krögel 2 🕐10am–6pm Mon–Fri, noon–6pm Sat & Sun 🌐the-greens-berlin.de

A hidden café offering coffee, tea and snacks amid potted plants.

4. Brauhaus Georgbräu
📍K6 🏠Spreeufer 4 🕐10am–midnight daily (winter: from noon daily) 🌐georgbraeu.de

This beer garden offers rustic fare and beer from both Berlin and Munich.

5. Hafenbar-Fischerinsel
📍H4 🏠Märkisches Ufer 28 🕐May–Oct: noon–11pm Wed–Sun 🌐hafenbar.business.site

This restaurant is on the deck of an old tugboat, the *Renate-Angelika*. Enjoy a beer here with potato salad.

6. Café Oliv
📍J6 🏠Münzstr. 8 🕐9am–5pm Mon–Fri, 9:30am–5pm Sat, 9:30am–3pm Sun 🌐oliv-cafe.de

Trendy Berliners get their organic sandwiches, flat whites and home-baked cakes from this sleek venue.

7. Café Ephraim's
📍K6 🏠Spreeufer 1 🕐Noon–11pm daily 🌐ephraims.de/en

Hearty German food, excellent coffee, and cakes, served on a riverside terrace next to the Spree, attract both locals and tourists.

8. tigertörtchen
📍K6 🏠Spandauer Str. 25 🕐8am–6pm Thu–Tue 🌐tigertoertchen.de

Come here for inventive cupcake creations such as date and walnut or crab and dill.

9. Marinehaus
📍L6 🏠Märkisches Ufer 48–50 🕐Noon–late daily 🌐marinehaus.de

This traditional pub with maritime decor serves German food.

10. Hofbräu Wirtshaus
📍H3 🏠Karl-Liebknecht-Str. 30 🕐Noon–11pm Mon–Fri, 10pm–midnight Sat & Sun 🌐hofbraeu-wirtshaus.de/berlin

Enjoy southern German dishes at this Bavarian beer garden.

Relaxing on a bench outside the Zur letzten Instanz

Restaurants

Colourful exterior of Mutter Hoppe, lit up at night

1. Beast

☑ J6 ☐ Karl-Liebhnecht-Str. 29 ☐ 5pm–1am Sun–Thu, 5pm–2am Fri–Sat ☑ beast-berlin.com · €€€

This stylish restaurant serves juicy steaks and delicious cocktails.

2. Alois Moser – Alpenküche

☑ J5 ☐ Anna-Luise-Karsch-Str. 2 ☐ 10am–10pm Mon–Sun ☑ alois-moser.de · €

A cosy restaurant with an Austrian menu, Alois Moser has views of the Museum Island and the Berliner Dom.

3. Zur Gerichtslaube

☑ K6 ☐ Poststr. 28 ☐ 11:30am–1am daily ☑ gerichtslaube.de · €€

The former court building is a stylish setting for traditional Berlin specialities such as Prussian sausages.

4. MAMMAM Street Food Mitte

☑ L6 ☐ Inselstr. 8 ☐ 11am–9pm daily ☑ mammam-berlin.de · €€

Sample street-food-inspired dishes from Vietnam and Thailand at this cosy spot.

5. Zum Paddenwirt

☑ K6 ☐ Niholaihirchplatz 6 ☐ From noon daily ☑ paddenwirt.de · €€

A must visit for fans of traditional Berlin food. The menu includes fried herrings and brawn, and a strong beer.

6. Zillestube

☑ K6 ☐ Spreeufer 3 ☐ From 11am daily ☑ zillestube-nikolaiviertel.de/en · €

Named after the 19th-century Berlin illustrator and photographer Heinrich Zille, this rustic pub serves hearty Berlin food and beers.

7. Fischer & Lustig

☑ K6 ☐ Poststr. 26 ☐ 11:30am–midnight Mon–Sat, 11:30am–11pm Sun ☑ fischerundlustig.de · €€

With a large menu of fish dishes, Fischer & Lustig serves regional cuisine made with locally sourced ingredients. The courtyard tables are especially popular during summer.

8. Balthasar Spreeufer 2

☑ K6 ☐ Spreeufer 2 ☐ Noon–10pm daily ☑ balthazar-restaurant.de · €€

Enjoy German and international cuisine with fusion dishes such as tagliatelle with a ginger and tomato sauce, and many more meat- and fish-based mains.

9. Fernsehturm Sphere

☑ J6 ☐ Panoramastr. 1a ☐ 10am–midnight daily ☑ tv-turm.de/restaurant-sphere · €€

This revolving restaurant in the TV Tower offers superb views and Berlin-Brandenburg specialities, including cod with beetroot and potato purée.

10. Mutter Hoppe

☑ K6 ☐ Rathausstr. 21 ☐ From 11:30am daily ☑ mutterhoppe.de · €€

Gigantic portions of delicious German food make up for the brisk service.

THE TIERGARTEN AND FEDERAL DISTRICT

In 1999, Berlin's green centre became the government district. Around the Tiergarten, Berlin's largest park, stand the Reichstag, the Bundeskanzleramt and Schloss Bellevue, the official residence of the President of the Federal Republic of Germany. The sprawling Tiergarten itself is a great place for strolling and cycling, and it also offers access to the Landwehrkanal, the Neuer See, the Spree River and Berlin's zoo. In summer, its lawns are used for picnics, sunbathing and casual sports.

1 Top 10 Sights
p117

1 Restaurants
p121

1 Hidden Treasures
p120

For places to stay in this area, see p175

Reichstag, topped with its modern glass dome

1 Reichstag
More so than any of the other landmarks in Berlin, the Reichstag (p24), the seat of the German parliament, has come to symbolize German history.

2 Kulturforum
This unique complex (p46) of modern buildings features the best museums and concert halls in western Berlin.

3 Großer Tiergarten
🚇 L1 🚇 Tiergarten
The Großer Tiergarten is Berlin's largest park, straddling an area of more than 200 ha (494 acres) between the eastern and western parts of the city. Formerly the Elector's hunting grounds, it was redesigned in the 1830s as a park by Peter Joseph Lenné. At the end of the 19th century, the Siegesallee was established in the east of the park, more than 500 m (1,640 ft) in length, lined by statues of monarchs and politicians. After World War II, the starving and freezing population cut nearly all the trees for firewood and dug up the lawns to grow food. Thanks to reforestation since the 1950s, the Tiergarten, today, is one of Berlin's favourite green spaces.

4 Siegessäule
🚇 D4 🚇 Großer Stern 🚇
In the middle of the Tiergarten stands the 67-m- (220-ft-) high Victory Column (p61), erected to commemorate Prussia's victory against Denmark in the war of 1864. After victory over Austria in 1866 and France in 1871, the structure was crowned by a 35-ton gilded statue of the goddess Victoria. There are great views from the viewing platform, 285 steps up.

5 Diplomatenviertel
📍 E4 🅐 Between Stauffenbergstr. and Lichtensteinallee as well as along Tiergartenstr.

In the late 19th century, an embassy district sprang up. Most structures were destroyed during World War II, and the buildings were left to decay until German reunification. After the government moved back to Berlin from Bonn in 1999, new life was breathed into the diplomats' quarter. Especially worth seeing are the Austrian and Indian embassies on Tiergartenstraße, the Nordic embassies on Rauchstraße and the Mexican embassy on Klingelhöferstraße.

6 Hamburger Bahnhof
📍 F2 🅐 Invalidenstr. 50–51 🕙 10am–6pm Tue–Fri (to 8pm Thu), 11am–6pm Sat & Sun 🌐 smb.museum ♿

This former railway station is now the Museum für Gegenwart (Museum of the Present Day) and holds contemporary works of art. One of the highlights is the private collection of Erich Marx, with works by Beuys and others.

7 Sowjetisches Ehrenmal
📍 K2 🅐 Str. des 17. Juni

This somber site, the first of Berlin's three Soviet Memorials, was opened on 11 November, 1945. It is flanked by two tanks, supposedly the first to reach Berlin. The memorial commemorates the 80,000 Red Army soldiers who died during World War II in the fight to liberate Berlin. A legend persists that the large column was made from the marble blocks of Hitler's Reich Chancellery. Designed by Nicolai Sergijevski, the column is crowned by a bronze statue created by Lev Kerbel. Behind the memorial, 2,000 Russian soldiers are buried.

8 Potsdamer Platz
Ravaged by World War II, Potsdamer Platz (p30) remained a wasteland for the next 40 years. In the 1990s, redevelopment began making it one of Europe's largest construction sites, taking five years to build. Today, it is one of Berlin's busiest squares. Adjoining it is Leipziger Platz, which is home to the Mall of Berlin. To the southwest is the Kulturforum, where you can find the Philharmonie (p46) and the Gemäldegalerie (p47).

PETER JOSEPH LENNÉ
Lenné (1789–1866), one of Germany's most influential landscape architects, was born into a family of gardeners in Bonn. He studied in Paris and joined the Royal Gardens in Potsdam as an apprentice in 1816. There he met Schinkel and together they set out to design the parks of Berlin and Potsdam in the harmonious style of the time.

Exhibition on Nazi Germany
at Bendlerblock

9 Gedenkstätte Deutscher Widerstand

📍 E4 🏠 Stauffenbergstr. 13–14
🕐 9am–6pm Mon–Fri, 10am–6pm
Sat & Sun 🌐 gdw-berlin.de/en

Today known as Bendlerblock, this
1930s complex lies behind the former
Prussian Ministry of War. During World
War II it served as the army head-
quarters. It was here that a group of
officers planned the assassination of
Adolf Hitler. The attempt failed on 20
July 1944 and Claus Schenk Graf von
Stauffenberg and others were arrested.
Many of them were shot in the courtyard during the night. A memorial,
created by Richard Scheibe in 1953,
commemorates these events. On the
upper floor is a small exhibition documenting the German resistance against
the Nazi regime. The Bendlerblock
has been incorporated into the Berlin
branch of the Federal Ministry of Defence.

10 Villa von der Heydt

📍 E4 🏠 Von-der-Heydt-Str.
16–18 🌐 preussischer-kulturbesitz.
de/en

This late Neo-Classical villa, built
in 1860–62 by architects Hermann
Ende and G A Linke for one of the
city's most elegant residential areas
at the time, is one of the few extant
examples of the architectural villa
style typical of the Tiergarten. The
Prussian Heritage Foundation now
has its headquarters here.

Sowjetisches Ehrenmal memorial
to the Soviet Armed Forces

A DAY OUT AROUND TIERGARTEN

Morning

Start your tour of Tiergarten near
the **Reichstag** (p24). Explore the
government district with the
Bundeskanzleramt (Federal
Chancellor's Office). Stop at **Käfer
im Reichstag** (p121) for breakfast.
You will pass the **Carillon** (p122)
and the Haus der Kulturen der
Welt (p62) on the way to **Großer
Tiergarten** (p66). Continue along
one of the paths into the park,
until you reach Straße des 17. Juni.
Turn right to go towards
Siegessäule (p117). From there
continue along Fasanerieallee
until you reach **Café am Neuen
See** (p67) for lunch.

Afternoon

After lunch, take a stroll through
the Diplomatenviertel. From
Neuer See, it is only a few steps
east along Lichtensteinallee and
Thomas-Dehler-Straße until
you get to Rauchstraße with
its Scandinavian embassies. On
Tiergartenstraße you will pass
the embassies of Japan, Italy,
India and Austria. Head towards
the **Kulturforum** (p46), then walk
along Reichpietschufer until you
reach **Neue Nationalgalerie**
(p46) to view works by artists
such as Edvard Munch, Gerhard
Richter and Andy Warhol.
Stop for a meal at the
Michelin-starred **Vox** (p121)
at the Grand Hyatt.

Hidden Treasures

1. Neuer See
🅿 D4 🚇 S-Bahn station Tiergarten
The largest lake in the Tiergarten is perfect for rowing. Afterwards you can unwind in the Café am Neuen See.

2. Löwenbrücke
🅿 D4 🚇 Großer Weg
The Lion Bridge, which leads across a small stream near Neuer See, was built in 1838 and is "suspended" from the sculptures of four lions. This idyllic spot is a favourite meeting point in Berlin.

3. Lortzingdenkmal
🅿 L1 🚇 Östlicher Großer Weg
There are 70 statues of philosophers, poets and statesmen in Tiergarten. The statue of the composer Lortzing, at one end of Neuer See, is one of the most beautiful.

4. Houseboats
🅿 K1 🚇 Str. des 17. Juni, Tiergartenufer
Docked on the banks of the Spree River are some of the few remaining houseboats in Berlin – an idyllic haven in the middle of the city's bustle.

5. Open-Air Gas Lantern Museum
🅿 L1 🚇 At S-Bahn station Tiergarten
With over 90 beautiful lamps from different cities illuminating the paths, an evening stroll in the Tiergarten can be a romantic affair.

Relaxing on the bank of the Landwehrkanal

6. Landwehrkanal
🅿 C3–G5 🚇 Tiergartenufer.
Relax on the grassy banks of the 11-km (7-mile) long Landwehrkanal.

7. Englischer Garten
🅿 D3 🚇 An der Klopstockstr.
The lovely English-style landscaped garden near Schloss Bellevue is ideal for strolling or relaxing at the Teehaus.

8. Locks
🅿 L1 🚇 At the Zoo, S-Bahn station Tiergarten
The two Landwehrkanal locks and the quirky Schleusenkrug beer garden are very popular with locals and visitors.

9. Swiss Embassy
🅿 F3 🚇 Otto-von-Bismarch-Allee 4a
This chocolate box building, a mix of Neo-Classical and modern architecture, symbolizes the turbulent past of the area.

10. Carillon
🅿 K1 🚇 John-Foster-Dulles-Allee (Haus der Kulturen der Welt)
The *Carillon*, officially dedicated in 1987, is one of the largest of its kind in Europe. The 68 bells are rung everyday at noon and 6pm in the 42-m- (138-ft-) high black tower. Open-air concerts are held on Sundays from May to September.

Carillon bell tower, looming over the Tiergarten

Restaurants

1. Café am Neuen See
📍 D4 🏠 Tiergarten, Neuer See, Lichtensteinallee 2 🕐 Beer garden: Mar–Oct: 9am–11pm daily; restaurant: 9am–midnight daily 🌐 cafeamneuensee.de · €

On the shore of the lake, this is a restaurant, café and beer garden.

2. Schleusenkrug
📍 D4 🏠 Tiergarten-Schleuse 🕐 Noon–midnight Mon–Sat (from 11am Sun, winter: to 6pm) 🌐 schleusenkrug.de · €

This café, next to a lock, has a beer garden and is popular with students.

3. Zollpackhof
📍 J1 🏠 Elisabeth-Abegg-Str.1 🕐 Noon–11pm daily 🌐 zollpackhof.de · €€

Huge beer garden with views of the Spree River, serving German-Austrian food and Bavarian beer.

4. Käfer im Reichstag
📍 K2 🏠 Platz der Republik 🕐 Hours vary, check website 🌐 feinhost-haefer.de/berlin · €€

An ambitious restaurant, known for its views.

5. Joseph-Roth-Diele
📍 E5 🏠 Potsdamer Str. 75 🕐 10am–10pm Tue–Fri 🌐 joseph-roth-diele.de · €

This popular restaurant and bar features a traditional German menu and live piano music. Cash only.

6. Konditorei G Buchwald
📍 D3 🏠 Bartningallee 29 🕐 11am–6pm daily 🌐 onditorei-buchwald.de · €

Berlin's oldest pastry shop is well-known for its decadent Baumkuchen.

7. Vox
📍 F4 🏠 Marlene-Dietrich-Platz 2 🕐 6:30–11pm daily 🌐 vox-restaurant.de · €€€

An elegant restaurant in the Grand Hyatt Hotel, Vox serves a modern

PRICE CATEGORIES

For a three-course meal for one with half a bottle of wine (or equivalent meal), taxes and charges included.

€ under €30 €€ €30–60 €€€ over €60

fusion of Asian and international dishes. Do not miss the sushi.

8. Hugos
📍 D4 🏠 Budapester Str. 2 🕐 6:30–midnight Tue–Sat 🌐 berlin.intercontinental.com · €€€

Excellent gourmet food, stellar views and superb service combine to make this Michelin-starred spot one of the best. There's also a wine bar and private dining rooms available.

9. Paris-Moskau
📍 J1 🏠 Alt-Moabit 141 🕐 Noon–3pm & 6pm–midnight Mon–Fri 🌐 paris-moskau.de · €€

A classic restaurant with a focus on seasonal dishes featuring game and seafood, complemented by an excellent selection of special wines.

10. Facil
📍 L2 🏠 Potsdamer Str. 3 🕐 Noon–3pm & 7–11pm Mon–Fri 🌐 facil.de · €€€

This two-Michelin-starred gourmet restaurant focuses on Mediterranean cuisine. The rooftop dining area is surrounded by bamboo gardens.

Patrons enjoying traditional food in the Zollpackhof

CHARLOTTENBURG AND SPANDAU

The sophisticated haute bourgeoisie enclave of Charlottenburg was the only Berlin district that did not touch the Wall. The historical streets off Ku'damm feature a range of stunning galleries, independent boutiques and tempting cafés and restaurants, many set within stout early 20th-century residential houses. The central section of this area and the proud town hall remind visitors that this was once Prussia's richest town, and was only incorporated into the city of Berlin in 1920. Spandau, on the other side of the Spree and Havel, is almost regional in comparison. Its late medieval core and hulking citadel make it seem like a small, independent town, far from the buzz of central Berlin.

1 Käthe-Kollwitz-Museum

This amazing museum (p43) provides a unique opportunity for visitors to become acquainted with the phenomenal works of the famous German graphic artist and sculptor Käthe Kollwitz (p64). Her drawings and sculptures portrayed the social problems of the poor, as well as human tragedy and suffering. The museum perfectly exhibits her work, including posters, sculptures and drawings, as well as letters and photographs.

2 Zitadelle Spandau

🏛 Am Juliusturm 🕐 10am–5pm Fri–Wed, 1–8pm Thu 🌐 zitadelle-berlin.de 🔗

This citadel, built between 1560-94 by Francesco Chiaramella de Gandino and Rochus zu Lynar, is sited at the strategic confluence of the Havel and Spree. The Juliusturm, a remnant of a fortress that stood here as early as the 12th century, was used as a prison in the 19th century. Later, the reparations paid by France after its defeat in the Franco-Prussian War of 1870–71 were kept here. The City History Museum of Spandau is located in the former arsenal of the citadel.

Admiring the Schloss Charlottenburg in the palace's gardens

3 Kurfürstendamm
This famous Berlin boulevard (p38) was known to be frequented by writers, directors and painters in the interwar years. Today it is a lively avenue lined with designer stores and elegant cafés.

4 Schloss Charlottenburg
The beautiful Baroque and English-style gardens of this lovely Hohenzollern summer residence (p42) are perfect for a stroll. After the damage caused by World War II, the palace's stunning interiors were restored.

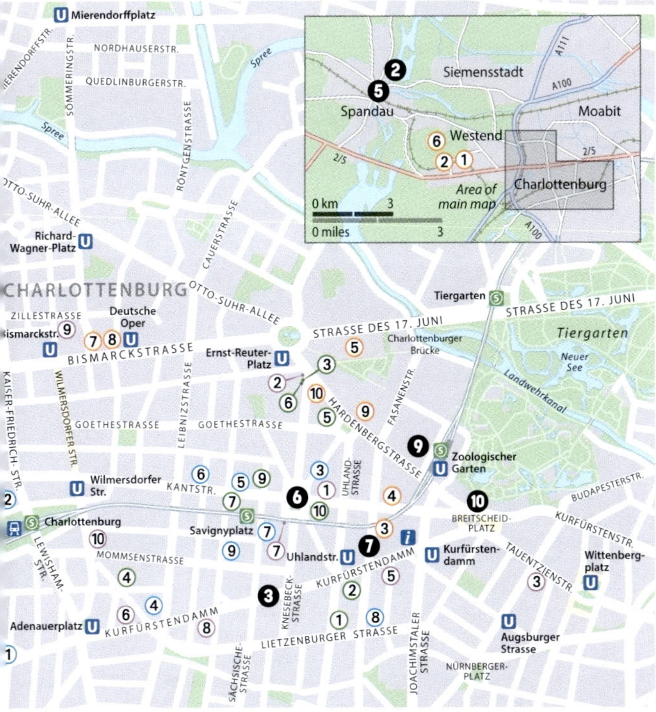

For places to stay in this area, see p176

Red-brick Gotisches Haus in Spandau Old Town

5 Spandau Old Town
📍 Breite Str., Spandau

When walking around Spandau's pedestrianized Old Town (Altstadt), it is easy to forget that you are still in Berlin. The old town preserves its historical charm while offering modern amenities and a vibrant atmosphere. The narrow alleyways and nooks and crannies around the 13th-century Nikolaikirche are lined by late medieval houses, a reminder that Spandau was founded in 1197. The Gotisches Haus – the oldest house in Berlin, dating back to the late 15th century – stands at Breite Straße 32. It was built of stone at a time when most houses were made of wood. It is now the Visitor Information Centre, and some of its rooms are used to showcase finds from the house and other artifacts of the period.

6 Savignyplatz
📍 C4 📍 An der Kantstr.

One of Berlin's most well-known squares is right in the heart of Charlottenburg. Savignyplatz, named after a 19th-century German legal scholar, is known as a district for artists and intellectuals and for its vibrant nightlife. It has also long been associated with Berlin's cultural life. The square has two green spaces, either side of Kantstraße, which was built in the 1920s as part of an effort to create parks in the centre of town. Small paths, benches and pergolas make it a pleasant place for a rest. Dotted all around Savignyplatz are street cafés, restaurants and shops, especially in Grolman-, Knesebeck- and Carmerstraße. Many have lost their way here after a night out, which is why the area is jokingly known as the "Savignydreieck" (the Savigny Triangle). This is still a thriving Charlottenburg community; the shops, bookshops, and cafés are always busy, especially on Saturdays.

SPANDAU AND BERLIN

One of the oldest towns within the area of greater Berlin, Spandau is 60 years older than the German capital, and Spandauers proudly point to their independent history. For a long time, a mutual mistrust existed between Berliners and Spandauers, but this was not just a result of Spandau's geographical location, isolated from the remainder of the city by the Havel and Spree rivers. It was also due to the fact that Spandau was only incorporated into Berlin in 1920. Spandauers today still say they are going "to Berlin", even though the city centre is only a few U-bahn stops away.

7 Fasanenstraße

C5 Charlottenburg

Elegant Fasanenstrasse is the trendiest of the streets off Kurfürstendamm. Designer shops, galleries and restaurants are tucked away here, along with a retail strip catering to the masses. The junction of Fasanenstraße and Ku'damm is one of the liveliest spots in Berlin. One of the best-known places here is the Hotel Bristol Berlin, formerly known as the Kempinski, at the northern end of Fasanenstraße. Nearby is the Jüdisches Gemeindehaus (p128), the Jewish community house, and a little further along, at the junction with Kantstraße, is the Kant-Dreieck (p63). The Berliner Börse (stock exchange), based in the ultramodern Ludwig-Erhard-Haus (p63), is just above, at the corner of Hardenbergstraße. The southern end of the street features the Literaturhaus and Villa Grisebach, one of Berlin's oldest art auction houses. In addition to a few cosy restaurants worth visiting, you'll also find some very expensive fashion stores. The street leads to picturesque Fasanenplatz, where many artists lived before 1933.

Beautiful garden café in the Literaturhaus on Fasanenstraße

A DAY IN CHARLOTTENBURG

Morning

Begin your tour of Charlottenburg at Breitscheidplatz and head west along **Kurfürstendamm** (p38). At **Fasanenstraße** turn left to visit the Literaturhaus. You could stop for a mid-morning breakfast at **Café Wintergarten** (p130) in the Literaturhaus, before going back up Fasanenstraße in a northerly direction. You will pass the **Hotel Bristol Berlin** (p176) on the left, and on the right is the Jüdisches Gemeindehaus and the Ludwig-Erhard-Haus. Diagonally opposite across Kantstraße stands the **Theater des Westens** (p128). Turn left and head west along Kantstraße until you reach Savignyplatz. Explore the streets around the square, such as Knesebeck-, Bleibtreu- and Mommsenstraße. Kanststraße is the centre of Berlin's Asian culinary scene. Try **Lon Men** (p131) for Taiwanese classics or **Good Friends** (Kanststraße 30) for stellar Cantonese.

Afternoon

A short bus ride west along Kantstraße gets you to **Lietzensee** (p67), a picturesque lake surrounded by lush lawns. On your way back, visit **Der Kuchenladen** (Kantstraße 138) for cake and coffee. Head up Kantstraße and Jebensstraße to end your tour at the **Museum für Fotografie** (p126) and marvel at Helmut Newton's iconic Big Nudes.

Funkturm, with the ICC building in the foreground

8 Funkturm and Messegelände

A4/5 ▣ Messedamm 22 ◷ Tower: 11am–10pm Tue–Sun ⊕ messe-berlin. de ⬀

The 150-m- (480-ft-) high Funkturm (radio tower), reminiscent of the Eiffel Tower in Paris, is one of the landmarks of Berlin that can be seen from afar. Built between 1924–26 to plans by Heinrich Straumer, it served both as an aerial and as an air-traffic control tower. The viewing platform at 125 m (410 ft) provides magnificent views, while the restaurant, situated at 55 m (180 ft), overlooks the oldest part of the complex, the exhibition centre and the surrounding pavillions. In the east is the Hall of Honour, designed by Richard Ermisch in 1936 in the colossal Fascist architectural style. On the opposite side rises the silver ICC, the International Congress Centrum, built in 1975–9 by Ralf Schüler and Ursulina Schüler-Witte. Once considered one of the world's most advanced conference centres, the building is due to be renovated into a cultural hub. Nearby is the two-tier CityCube, Berlin's new trade fair and conference facility. The sprawling ExpoCenter grounds around it host International Grüne Woche (Green Week, an agricultural fair), Internationale Tourismus Börse (ITB, a tourism fair) and Internationale Funkausstellung (IFA, the consumer electronics fair).

THE HISTORY OF CHARLOTTENBURG

The magnificent Charlottenburger Rathaus (town hall) on Otto-Suhr-Allee is a reminder of the time when this district of 200,000 people was an independent town. The town, named after the eponymous palace, arose in 1705 from the medieval settlement of Lietzow. Towards the end of the 19th century, Charlottenburg – then the wealthiest town in Prussia – enjoyed a meteoric rise following the construction of the Westend colony of villas and of Kurfürstendamm. Thanks to its numerous theatres, the opera and the Technical University, the district developed into Berlin's west end during the 1920s.

9 Museum für Fotografie

C4 ▣ Jebensstr. 2 ◷ 11am–7pm Tue–Sun (to 8pm Thu) ⊕ smb. museum ⬀

Helmut Newton (1931–2004), the world-famous photographer, has

posthumously returned to his home city. This museum presents changing exhibitions of his early fashion and nude photography, as well as his photos of the famous, rich and beautiful, artfully captured from 1947 onwards.

10 Kaiser-Wilhelm-Gedächtnis-Kirche

☑ D4

This Neo-Romanesque church is locally known as the Hollow Tooth, due to its wrecked condition caused by bombings during the war. A popular landmark church (p40) in west Berlin, it is also an anti-war memorial. The original western tower was the only building left standing on Breitscheidplatz after the 1943 air raids. Several efforts have been made over the years to preserve this grand ruin.

Mosaic at the Kaiser-Wilhelm-Gedächtnis-Kirche

A SPANDAU AND WESTEND WALK

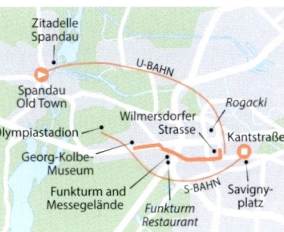

Morning

Start with a journey on the U-Bahn. From the centre of town, take a U2 train in the direction of Ruhleben, and at Bismarckstraße station change to the U7 in the direction of Rathaus Spandau. Ten minutes later you will have reached the centre of **Spandau Old Town** (p124), where you can visit Breite Straße and Nikolaikirche. Before returning to Charlottenburg, visit the **Zitadelle Spandau** (p122). Return by U-Bahn, getting off at the Wilmersdorfer Straße station, which is great for high-street shopping. Stop for a fish lunch and a glass of Riesling at **Rogacki** (p129).

Afternoon

From Wilmersdorfer Straße a 30-minute walk west along Neue Kantstraße will take you to the **Funkturm and Messegelände** with the "Ehrenhalle". Take a coffee break above the city's rooftops at the **Funkturm-Restaurant** and enjoy the views from the observation deck. The Haus des Rundfunks (broadcasting house) nearby and the **Georg-Kolbe-Museum** (p128), a 25-minute walk away, are worth visiting. Then, take the S-Bahn to the **Olympiastadion** (p128). In the evening, return to Savignyplatz by S75 from S-Olympiastadion. End your day at **Dicke Wirtin** (p131) with some classic Berlin dishes and beer.

The Best of the Rest

1. Georg-Kolbe-Museum
⌂ Sensburger Allee 25 ⏲ 10am–6pm Wed–Mon ⊠ georg-kolbe-museum.de
Sculptures by Kolbe (1877–1947) are exhibited in his home and workshop.

2. Corbusierhaus
⌂ Flatowallee 16
This innovative block was built for the 1957 Interbau trade fair. French architect Le Corbusier lived here.

3. Jüdisches Gemeindehaus
📍 C4 ⌂ Fasanenstr. 79–80 ⊠ jg-berlin.org
The Jewish community house stands on the site of the Charlottenburg synagogue. It was damaged during Kristallnacht on 9 November 1938 and mostly destroyed during World War II. Only the portal remains.

4. Theater des Westens
📍 C4 ⌂ Kantstr. 12 ⊠ stage-entertainment.de
Located in a building from 1895–6, this theatre is regarded as one of Germany's best musical theatres.

5. Technische Universität
📍 C4 ⌂ Str. des 17. Juni ⊠ tu.berlin/en
Berlin's Technical University was founded in 1879. It became a major intellectual centre and home to some of the greatest minds of the world.

6. Olympiastadion
⌂ Olympischer Platz ⏲ Hours vary, chech website ⊠ olympiastadion.berlin/de/start
Built for the 1936 Olympic Games, the stadium is an example of the Fascist architecture favoured by the Nazis.

7. Deutsche Oper
📍 B4 ⌂ Bismarchstr. 34–37 ⊠ deutscheoperberlin.de
One of the most significant national cultural venues, this opera house specializes in Italian and German classics.

8. Denkmal Benno Ohnesorg
📍 B4 ⌂ Bismarchstr.
Alfred Hrdlicka's 1971 sculpture honours student Benno Ohnesorg, who was shot dead here during a protest in April 1967.

9. Universität der Künste
📍 C4 ⌂ Hardenbergstr. 32–33 ⊠ udh.de
The School of Art is one of the best German universities for courses on fine arts, architecture and design.

10. Renaissance Theater
📍 C4 ⌂ Knesebechstr. 100 ⊠ renaissance-theater.de
A gem of Art Deco architecture, this little venue has been run as an actors' theatre since the 1920s. A range of international and contemporary dramas are performed here.

Dancers' fountain inside Georg-Kolbe-Museum

Antique shops lining Suarezstraße

Shops and Markets

1. LIVING BERLIN
C4 Kantstr. 17 10am–7pm Mon–Sat living-berlin.com
This interior design emporium has been serving Berlin's style-conscious for 25 years.

2. Manufactum Store
C4 Hardenbergstr. 4–5 10am–8pm Mon–Fri, 10am–6pm Sat manufactum.com
A unique store with a selection of classic textiles, furniture, garden tools, lamps and office supplies.

3. Peek & Cloppenburg
D5 Tauentzienstr. 19 10am–8pm Mon–Sat peek-cloppenburg.de
Offering five floors of men's, women's and children's clothing, this is one of Berlin's most popular department stores.

4. TITUS Berlin Zoopreme
C5 Meinekestr. 2 10am–8pm Mon–Sat titus.de
The latest must-have labels are stocked at this streetwear store along with sports accessories and shoes.

5. Veronica Pohle
C5 Kurfürstendamm 64 11am–6pm Mon–Sat veronicapohle.com
This multi-label store specializes in fashionable evening and party dresses, for all occasions.

6. Suarezstraße
B4 suarezstrasse.com
To the west of Charlottenburg, this street has around 30 antique shops.

7. Bücherbogen
C4 Stadtbahnbogen 593 11am–7pm Mon–Sat buecherbogen.com
Berlin's leading seller of books on the arts and photography, Bücherbogen is situated under the S-Bahn arches at Savignyplatz.

8. Patrick Hellmann
C4 Bleibtreustr. 36 10am–7pm Mon–Fri, 10am–6pm Sat patrichhellmann.com
Gentlemen's fashions made from the best materials, including Hellmann's own collection, and clothes from well-known designers can be found here.

9. Rogacki
B4 Wilmersdorfer Str. 145/6 10am–6pm Tue–Thu, 9am–6pm Fri, 8am–2pm Sat rogacki.de
Established in 1932, Rogacki is a famous seafood delicatessen.

10. Goldhahn und Sampson
B4 Wilmersdorfer Str. 102–103 8am–8pm Mon–Sat, 8am–1:30pm Sat goldhahnundsampson.de
Wine and delicious produce are sold at this delicatessen.

Variety of coffees at Berliner Kaffeerösterei

Cafés and Coffee Shops

1. Berliner Kaffeerösterei
◘ C6 ⌂ Uhlandstraße 173 ◷ 9am–
8pm Mon–Sat, 10am–7pm Sun
ⓦ berliner-kaffeeroesterei.de
This place offers coffee beans from
around the world, and cakes and snacks.

2. Café Wintergarten im Literaturhaus
◘ C5 ⌂ Fasanenstr. 23 ◷ 9am–
midnight daily ⓦ cafe-im-
literaturhaus.de
Based in the conservatory of an old
city mansion, this beautiful café also
has garden seating in the summer.

3. Manufactum Brot und Butter
◘ C5 ⌂ Hardenbergstrasse 4-5
◷ 8am–8pm Mon–Sat
ⓦ manufactum.de
A bakery-café on the ground floor of
the Manufactum department store.

4. Café Maitre Münch
◘ B5 ⌂ Giesebrechtstr. 16 ◷ 11am–5pm
Tue–Sat ⓦ cafe-maitre-muench.de
Expect homemade desserts such as
cakes and macaroons, and a small but
hearty mains menu at this cosy spot.

5. Café Hardenberg
◘ C5 ⌂ Hardenbergstr. 10 ◷ 10am–
11pm Sun–Thu, 10am–midnight Fri–
Sat ⓦ cafe-hardenberg.com
A favourite of students and artists
since the 1850s, this café has a great
atmosphere and reasonable prices.

6. Espresso House
◘ C4 ⌂ Knesebechstraße 1–2
◷ 7am–7pm Mon–Fri, 8am–7pm
Sat & Sun ⓦ de.espressohouse.com
A Scandinavian gourmet coffee chain
serving speciality drinks and snacks.

7. Der Kuchenladen
◘ B4 ⌂ Kantstr. 138 ◷ 10am–
8pm daily ⓦ derkuchenladen.de
Enjoy delectable lemon tarts and
other delicious homemade delights
at this tiny café.

8. Café Kleine Orangerie
◘ B3 ⌂ Spandauer Damm 20
☎ (030) 322 20 21 ◷ 10am–6pm
Tue–Sun
A small, pleasant garden café at
the historic building of Charlottenburg
Palace serving light snacks and coffee.

9. A Never Ever Ending Love Story
◘ B4 ⌂ Kantstr. 25 ◷ 8am–5pm
daily ⓦ anevereverendinglove
story.com
This popular local spot, known for
its pancakes and delicious lattes, is
a favourite for brunch.

10. Schwarzes Café
◘ B4 ⌂ Kantstr. 148 ◷ 24 hours
ⓦ schwarzescafe-berlin.de
This alternative grungy café offers
excellent all-day breakfasts and
is often packed until dawn.

Restaurants

1. Francucci
☑ C5 **☐** Kurfürstendamm 90
◷ 4–11pm daily **Ⓦ** francucci.
com · €€

This popular Tuscan restaurant serves excellent pizza, home-made pasta and creative meat and fish dishes.

2. Lamazère Brasserie
☑ B4 **☐** Stuttgarter Platz 18 **◷** 6–11pm
Tue–Sun **Ⓦ** lamazere.de · €€€

With an interior shaped like a tunnel, this charming restaurant serves typical French cuisine. Book ahead.

3. Dicke Wirtin
☑ C4 **☐** Carmerstr. 9 **◷** 11am–midnight
daily **Ⓦ** diche-wirtin.de · €€

Enjoy classic German fare in a cosy wood-panelled interior, which will transport you to an old-world Berlin.

4. Die Nußbaumerin
☑ C4 **☐** Leibnizstr. 55 **◷** 5–11pm
Mon–Fri **Ⓦ** nussbaumerin.de · €€

Michelin-starred chef Johanna Nußbaum's menu features Tafelspitz (boiled beef broth) and Kaiserschmarrn (scrambled pancake).

5. Kuchi
☑ B4 **☐** Kantstr. 30 **◷** Noon–11pm
daily **Ⓦ** huchi.de · €€

This minimalist restaurant has a loyal clientele and the best sushi bar.

6. Lon Men's Noodle House
☑ B4 **☐** Kanstr. 33 **☎** (030) 31519678
◷ Noon–10pm Thu–Mon · €

This popular spot, known for its homemade noodles and dumplings, gets busy, but it's worth the wait.

7. Lubitsch
☑ C4 **☐** Bleibtreustr. 47
◷ Noon–midnight daily
Ⓦ restaurant-lubitsch.dem · €€

A small, elegant restaurant serving fresh, regional cuisine.

8. Mine Restaurant
☑ C5 **☐** Meinehestr. 10
◷ 5:30pm–11pm daily
Ⓦ minerestaurant.de · €€

Enjoy contemporary Italian dishes at this restaurant. The delicious food is complemented by a terrific wine list and amazing desserts.

9. Marjellchen
☑ B5 **☐** Mommsenstr. 9 **◷** 5–11pm
daily **Ⓦ** restaurant-marjellchen-berlin.de · €€

This delightful restaurant serves hearty dishes from East Prussia, Pomerania and Silesia.

10. Bruderherz
☑ B4 **☐** Leonhardtstr. 6 **◷** 6–11pm
Mon–Fri, 5–11pm Sat **Ⓦ** bruderherz-restaurant.de · €€

A relaxed atmosphere welcomes guests at this restaurant, which is run by two Polish brothers. It serves excellent pasta and other Italian dishes.

Outdoor seating at the elegant Lubitsch

KREUZBERG, SCHÖNEBERG AND NEUKÖLLN

Before the Wall fell, Kreuzberg was a hotbed of squatters, hippies and anarchists. Despite rapid gentrification it is still the city's most colourful area. Here, a diverse community of professionals, artists and students harmoniously coexists in renovated petit-bourgeois flats. The adjacent Neukölln is Berlin's trendiest area for art galleries, cool restaurants and dive bars, particularly along Weserstrae. Schöneberg is not as daring as Kreuzberg, but it still evokes a free-minded spirit. Here, Winterfeldtplatz is lined with inviting pubs, and Nollendorfplatz is the nexus of Berlin's lively LGBTQ+ scene.

1 Top 10 Sights
p133

1 Restaurants
p139

1 The Best of the Rest
p136

1 Pubs, Bars and Nightclubs
p138

1 Shops and Markets
p137

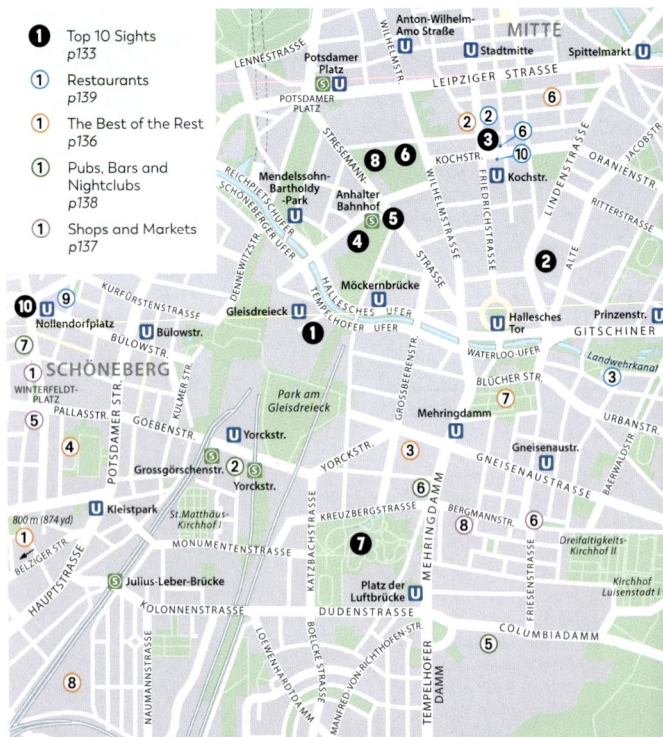

For places to stay in this area, see p176

Shipping and navigation exhibits, Deutsches Technikmuseum

1 Deutsches Technikmuseum

📍 F5 🏛 Trebbiner Str. 9 🕐 9am–5:30pm Tue–Fri, 10am–6pm Sat & Sun 🌐 technikmuseum.berlin/en ♿

The history of technology and crafts is the theme of this museum located in the grounds of a former railway goods yard. Visitors can learn about developments in aviation and admire 40 planes, including a Junkers Ju 52 and a "raisin bomber", the type of plane used in the Berlin airlift. Old ships and steam locomotives hark back to the Industrial Revolution. A must-visit is the Science Center Spectrum, where you can perform any of the 150 experiments on offer. There is no admission fee for those under 18.

2 Jüdisches Museum Berlin

The Jewish Museum's unique architecture and exhibitions *(p55)* aim to illustrate the repercussions of the Holocaust. Narrow, slanting galleries with zig-zag turns evoke a sense of dislocation, and are punctured by "voids" – empty spaces embodying the vacuum left behind by the destruction of Jewish life. Nearly 1,000 years of German-Jewish cultural history are documented here; a special exhibition evokes everyday Jewish life in Berlin from the end of the 19th century. Visitors can hear the sound of a shofar, and listen to ancient and modern Jewish music at the Music Room. After undergoing extensive renovation, a permanent exhibition opened in 2020.

3 Haus am Checkpoint Charlie

📍 G4 🏛 Friedrichstr. 43–45 🕐 10am–8pm daily 🌐 mauermuseum.de ♿

Founded shortly after the Berlin Wall was built, this museum details the history of the Wall and the means people used to escape to West Berlin, from a hot-air balloon to a car with a false floor. Of the former border only a replica control hut remains.

4 Berlin Story Bunker

F5 Schöneberger Str. 23A 10am–7pm daily berlinstory.de

Two exhibitions are installed in a former air raid bunker near the World War II ruins of Anhalter Bahnhof. The "Hitler: How Could It Happen?" exhibition tells the story of Hitler's rise to power, incorporating a model of the infamous Führerbunker.

5 Anhalter Bahnhof

F5 Ashanischer Platz 6–7

The giant structure was erected in 1880 by architect Franz Schwechten as a showcase station: official visitors to the Empire were meant to be impressed by the splendour and glory of the German capital. In 1943 it was damaged by bombs and in 1960 it was pulled down. The waste ground behind the façade was meant to become a park, but today the Tempodrom is based here, hosting concerts and live events.

6 Topographie des Terrors

F4 Niederhirchnerstr. 8 10am–8pm daily topographie.de/en

Between 1933 and 1945, three Nazi institutions of persecution and terror were located in this area: the Secret State Police Office; the SS leadership; and the Reich Security main office. After World War II, all the buildings were bulldozed. A striking documentation centre, designed by Berlin architect Ursula Wilms, was inaugurated in 2010 on this site, providing information about the headquarters of the National Socialist SS and police state during the Third Reich and showing the extent of the Nazi reign of terror throughout Europe.

7 Viktoriapark

F6 Kreuzbergstr.

This park was set up as a recreational space for workers in Kreuzberg in 1888–94 to plans by Hermann Mächtig. It has an artificial waterfall, and the Neo-Gothic Schinkel memorial, 66 m (216 ft) high, commemorates Prussian victory in the Wars of Liberation against Napoleon.

Remains of the Anhalter Bahnhof, once the gateway to south Germany

One of the mosaics on Martin-Gropius-Bau

8 Martin-Gropius-Bau

📍 F4 📍 Niederhirchnerstr. 7 🕐 Noon–7pm Mon & Wed–Fri, 11am–7pm Sat & Sun 🌐 berlinerfestspiele.de/gropius-bau 🔗

This beautifully ornamented former museum of arts and crafts often hosts modern art exhibitions.

9 Tempelhofer Feld

📍 G6 📍 Tempelhofer Damm 1 🌐 thf-berlin.de 🔗

Tempelhofer Feld was converted into a public park after the airport's closure in 2008. There are guided tours of the old terminal.

10 Nollendorfplatz

📍 E5

Nollendorfplatz and neighbouring Winterfeldtplatz are right in the centre of Schöneberg. "Nolli", as it's known, became central to Berlin's LGBTQ+ scene. A plaque at the Nollendorfplatz U-Bahn station honours the 5,000 homosexual victims killed in concentration camps by the Nazis. Today, LGBTQ+ life is concentrated more in the surrounding streets than the square itself. Nollendorfplatz was a centre of entertainment before World War II. The Metropol-Theater, now a club, was then helmed by famed theatre director Erwin Piscator. The writer Christopher Isherwood, whose *Berlin Stories* became the basis of *Cabaret*, the musical and film, lived next door.

A DAY IN KREUZBERG

Morning

Start at **Anhalter Bahnhof**, which you can reach by S-Bahn. Then, continue along Stresemannstraße towards the **Martin-Gropius-Bau**. Wander around the exhibitions here, then take a break in the museum café. Afterwards, visit the neighbouring **Topographie des Terrors** museum, which will bring you face to face with the dark Nazi past of this area. Continue along Niederkirchnerstraße, passing an original section of the Berlin Wall. Cross Wilhelmstraße and stop at **Haus am Checkpoint Charlie** (p133) at the former East–West border at Friedrichstrasse.

Afternoon

Have lunch at **Sale e Tabacchi** (p139) in Rudi-Dutschke-Straße. Before you continue east, make a detour south on Lindenstraße to the **Jüdisches Museum Berlin** (p50) and the **Berlinische Galerie** (p57). Then take the U6 from Hallesches Tor to Platz der Luftbrücke. **Viktoriapark** nearby is a good place for a rest, or stroll up Bergmannstraße for a coffee break. At the end of the street, turn north into Baerwaldstraße and continue to Carl-Herz-Ufer for a meal at the **Rutz Zollhaus** (p139) on the Landwehrkanal. Walk east along Planufer, turn left and cross the Kottbusser Brücke bridge to bar hop between Kottbusser Tor and Oranienstrasse in Kreuzberg's gritty heart.

The Best of the Rest

Cycling on the Oberbaumbrücke

1. Rathaus Schöneberg
D6 **John-F-Kennedy-Platz**
It was from this town hall in 1963 that US President John F Kennedy made his famous "I am a Berliner" speech, expressing his commitment to the freedom of West Berlin.

2. Asisi's Wall Panorama
G4 **Friedrichstr. 205** **10am–6pm daily** **die-mauer.de/en**
This is a life-size reproduction of the Berlin Wall as it appeared in the early 1980s, with sound and light installations.

3. Riehmers Hofgarten
F6 **Yorckstr. 83–86**
This estate, with over 20 buildings, was constructed as officers' quarters during the Gründerzeit era, following the establishment of the German Empire in 1871. Restored in the 1970s, it now features a pleasant hotel with an elegant restaurant.

4. Kammergericht
E6 **Elßholzstr. 30–33**
From 1947 to 1990, this magnificent supreme court, built in 1909–13, was used as the Allied Control Council.

5. Oberbaumbrücke
Warschauer/Shalitzer Str.
Pedestrians and cyclists can cross to the other side of the Spree River from Kreuzberg to Friedrichshain on this red-brick bridge, one of Berlin's loveliest, which was built in 1894–6. The bridge provides views of the TV Tower and the Molecule Man.

6. Mossehaus
L5 **Schützenstrasse 25**
One of Berlin's most influential publishing houses was based in this Jugendstil corner house in the former newspaper district.

7. Friedhöfe Hallesches Tor
G5 **Mehringdamm**
Many celebrities are buried in these four cemeteries, including the composer Felix Mendelssohn Bartholdy and the writer E T A Hoffmann, whose work inspired Offenbach to compose his opéra fantastique *The Tales of Hoffmann*.

8. Gasometer Schöneberg
E6 **Torgauer Str. 12–15**
Once a massive gas holder, this Schöneberg landmark was decommissioned in the 1990s and turned into a viewing platform.

9. Kottbusser Tor
H5
This iconic roundabout, located in the heart of Berlin's Turkish community in Kreuzberg, is surrounded by graffiti-covered brutalist tower blocks.

10. Mariannenplatz
H5
This park-like square with old trees is dominated by a large Gothic-style building. The former hospital and nursing school, Bethanien, is now a protected landmark and is used for various cultural and social initiatives.

Shops and Markets

1. Winterfeldtmarkt
⬛ E5 ⬛ Winterfeldtplatz ⬛ 8am–2pm Wed, 8am–4pm Sat
A favorite among Berlin locals, this artisanal market offers fresh fruit, vegetables, homeware, flowers and deli goods.

2. Türkischer Markt am Maybachufer
⬛ H5 ⬛ Maybachufer ⬛ 11am–6:30pm Tue & Fri
This vibrant, sometimes chaotic, market is the place to buy unleavened bread, fresh fruit and vegetables, and goat's cheese.

3. Hard Wax
⬛ H5 ⬛ Köpenicher Str. 70 Kraftwerk Berlin ⬛ 3–8pm Mon–Sat ⬛ hardwax.com
This famous record store is known for its curated collection of music. The selection mainly features electronic music, but also includes some reggae and disco.

4. Oranienplatz and Oranienstraße
⬛ H5 ⬛ Oranienstr./corner Oranienplatz
This bustling high street and famous square in Kreuzberg specializes in all things alternative.

5. Winterfeldt Schokoladen
⬛ E6 ⬛ Goltzstr. 23 ⬛ 10am–6pm Mon–Sat, noon–6pm Sun ⬛ winterfeldt-schokoladen.de
Choose from a variety of chocolates at this lovely store with an adjoining café.

6. Marheineke Markthalle
⬛ G6 ⬛ Marheinekeplatz ⬛ 8am–8pm Mon–Fri, 8am–6pm Sat ⬛ meine-markthalle.de
This is one of the few remaining market halls in Berlin. Marheineke has colourful fruit and vegetable stalls and a wide range of organic produce, as well as numerous snack bars.

7. Wesen
⬛ Tellstraße 7 ⬛ 11am–7pm Mon–Sat ⬛ format-favourites.de
Find ethically and locally produced jewels, bags or shoes here, manufactured by Fairtrade fashion brands.

8. Ararat
⬛ G6 ⬛ Bergmannstr. 99A ⬛ 10am–8pm Mon–Sat ⬛ ararat-berlin.de
One of Berlin's best-stocked and quirkiest stationery, curiosity and gift shops, the colourful Ararat has many lovely items for sale.

9. Depot2
⬛ H5 ⬛ Oranienstr. 9 ⬛ depot2.de
This small boutique sells the latest streetwear, trainers and hip-hop fashion by local labels.

10. Overkill
⬛ H4 ⬛ Köpenicher Straße 195A ⬛ 11am–8pm Mon–Sat ⬛ overkillshop.com
A haven for streetwear fans, this store has over 500 pairs of trainers, including many limited and rare editions from popular international brands.

Large selection of trainers on display at Overkill

Pubs, Bars and Nightclubs

Well-stocked bar at Ankerklause

1. Ankerklause
F H5 **A** Kottbusser Damm 104
O From 10am daily **W** ankerklause.de
An informal and popular late-night bar and café on the Landwehrkanal.

2. E. & M. Leydicke
F E6 **A** Mansteinstr. 4 **O** 7pm–1am daily **W** leydicke.com
This popular family-run bar hosts amazing parties.

3. Südblock
F H5 **A** Admiralstr. 1–2 **O** From 5pm Mon–Sat, 1pm Sun **W** suedblock.org
Right in the middle of Kottbusser Tor, this establishment is arguably one of Berlin's most beloved LGBTQ+ bars.

4. Van Loon
F G5 **A** Carl-Herz-Ufer 5–7
O 10am–11pm daily **W** vanloon.de
Savour a snack surrounded by nautical artifacts on this old barge moored in Urbanhafen.

5. SilverWings Club
F F6 **A** Columbiadamm 10
O 10pm–5am Sat **W** silverwings.de
Established in 1952, SilverWings is one of the oldest nightclubs in Berlin. It hosts various events and parties featuring rock 'n' roll and soul music.

6. Rauschgold
F F6 **A** Mehringdamm 62 **O** From 8pm daily **W** rauschgold.berlin
This popular bar, which caters to a predominantly queer crowd, is best visited late at night. It offers karaoke and themed nights and gets very crowded on weekends.

7. Green Door
F E5 **A** Winterfeldstr. 50
O From 7pm daily **W** greendoor.de
Do not miss out on the extensive drinks menu offered here. Happy hours are from 6 to 8pm.

8. SO36
F H5 **A** Oranienstr. 190 **W** so36.com
The SO36 is a very lively alternative music and dance club. Visitors can enjoy a range of concerts, shows and parties here.

9. Würgeengel
F H5 **A** Dresdener Str. 122
O From 7pm daily **W** wuergeengel.de
The drinks at the "Angel of Death" are not lethal, but the bar staff and clientele are straight out of a Buñuel film.

10. Klunkerkranich
A Karl-Marx-Str. 66 **O** Hours vary, chech website **W** klunkerkranich.org
This rooftop bar overlooks the city and offers stunning views at sunset. Take the lift to the top of Neukölln Arcaden, then walk the rest of the way through the car park. Note, the bar remains closed in January and February.

Enjoying the rooftop view from Klunkerkranich

Restaurants

1. Defne

⛨ H5 ⬧ Planufer. 92c ⬧ 4pm–midnight daily (winter: from 5pm) ⬧ restaurant-defne.business.site · €

A restaurant with an intimate setting, Defne serves modern Turkish food. It does not accept credit cards.

2. Entrecôte

⛨ G4 ⬧ Schützenstr. 5 ⬧ 11:30am–1am Mon–Fri, 5pm–1am Sat ⬧ entrecote.de · €€

Simple yet tasty meals are served at this French brasserie, located close to Checkpoint Charlie (p133).

3. Rutz Zollhaus

⛨ G5 ⬧ Carl-Herz-Ufer 30 ⬧ From 6pm Tue–Sat ⬧ rutz-zollhaus.de · €€

Formerly a border control point on the banks of the Landwehrkanal, the Rutz Zollhaus serves international and German fare. Be sure to try the house speciality, Oldenburger Ofenente (golden roast duck).

4. Zola

⛨ H5 ⬧ Paul-Linke-Ufer 39 ⬧ Noon–10pm daily · €

Excellent Neapolitan-style pizza draws crowds to this quaint place with lovely outdoor seating on the Landwehrkanal.

5. Lavanderia Vecchia

⛨ H6 ⬧ Flughafenstr. 46 ⬧ Lunch: 12:30–5pm Wed–Fri; Dinner: 5:30–10pm Wed–Sun ⬧ lavanderiavecchia.wordpress.com · €€

Set in an old laundry, this Italian restaurant excels in Roman staples.

Restaurant Tim Raue's sophisticated interior

6. Restaurant Tim Raue

⛨ G4 ⬧ Rudi-Dutschke-Str. 26 ⬧ Lunch: noon–3:30pm Sat; Dinner: 6pm–midnight Tue–Sat, 6:30pm–midnight Sat ⬧ tim-raue.com · €€€

This two-Michelin-starred restaurant offers a fusion of modern German flavors and Asian umami influences. Reservations are a must.

7. Max und Moritz

⛨ H5 ⬧ Oranienstr. 162 ⬧ 5–11pm Wed–Mon ⬧ maxundmoritzberlin.de · €€

A 120-year-old inn serving dishes such as Königsberger Klopse (braised meatballs with caper sauce) and local beers.

8. Horváth

⛨ H5 ⬧ Paul-Linche-Ufer 44a ⬧ 6:30–10:30pm Wed–Sun ⬧ restaurant-horvath.de · €€€

This Michelin starred restaurant serves elegantly presented Austrian dishes.

9. Frühstück 3000

⛨ E5 ⬧ Bülowstr. 101 ⬧ 9am–4pm daily ⬧ fruehstueck3000.com · €€

Great brunch spot serving omelets and eggs Benedict with caviar. Book ahead.

10. Sale e Tabacchi

⛨ G4 ⬧ Rudi-Dutschke-Str. 23 ⬧ Noon–1am Mon–Sat ⬧ sale-e-tabacchi.de · €€

Elegant Italian restaurant where you can dine in the courtyard in summer.

PRENZLAUER BERG

Even when the city was divided, this former workers' district in East Berlin was favoured by artists and an alternative crowd. While it continues to exert a similar pull today, Prenzlauer Berg is being steadily transformed by young professionals and families. Cafés and restaurants have taken over tenement blocks around Kollwitzplatz and Husemannstraße, giving the streets an almost Parisian flair, while Kastanienallee, also known as "Casting Alley", is the place for stylish Berliners to see and be seen.

- **1** Top 10 Sights p141
- **1** Restaurants p145
- **1** The Best of the Rest p144

For places to stay in this area, see p177

Neo-Gothic complex of Kulturbrauerei, designed by Franz Schwechten

1 Kulturbrauerei
🚇 H1 🚊 Schönhauser Allee 36–39 (entrance: Knaackstr. 97) 🌐 kultur brauerei.de/en

This complex of buildings originally housed the Schultheiss brewery, one of the breweries that made Prenzlauer Berg famous. The complex, parts of which are over 150 years old, was completely restored in 1997–9 and has become a lively and popular spot. Cafés, restaurants, a cinema, shops and even a theatre have sprung up in the red and yellow brick buildings and the numerous interior courtyards.

2 Kollwitzplatz
🚇 H2 🚊 Prenzlauer Berg

Once a quiet square, Kollwitzplatz is today the noisy heart of the district. All around the green square, locals congregate in the numerous cafés, pubs and restaurants. From the lavishly restored façades it is hard to tell that this was once one of the city's poorest areas. The artist Käthe Kollwitz (p64) once lived and worked at No 25 (now destroyed), from where she highlighted the poverty of the local workers in her sculptures, drawings and sketches.

3 Prater
🚇 H1 🚊 Kastanienallee 7–9 🕐 Restaurant: from 5pm Mon–Sat; noon Sun; Beer garden: from noon daily (only summer months)

The Prater is one of the few remaining entertainment complexes that were once common in big German cities. It was built in 1837 just outside the original city gates, and was first jokingly called "Prater" after its world-famous counterpart in Vienna. A concert hall was added in 1857 and by the turn of the century it had become so popular that the nickname stuck. Today, you can enjoy beer and food at the restaurant (p144) of the same name.

4 Schönhauser Allee
🚇 H1 🚊 Prenzlauer Berg

Schönhauser Allee, 3 km (2 miles) long and lined with shops and pubs, is the main artery of the district. Down the centre of the road runs the raised train tracks of the U2 U-Bahn line. A couple of buildings are still in their pre-1989 state and give a good impression of the old Prenzlauer Berg, especially between Senefelderplatz and Danziger Straße.

Passengers at the Schönhauser Allee U-Bahn station

PRENZLBERG OR PRENZLAUER BERG?

Many locals simply say Prenzlberg when talking about their quarter. But this name is used mainly by West Berliners and West Germans who moved here – the real name is Prenzlauer Berg, just as it is written. The supposed nickname is just a newfangled term for a neighbourhood that has become fashionable after the fall of the Berlin Wall.

5 Wasserturm

🅟 H2 🅐 Knaachstr.

The unofficial symbol of the district is this giant 30-m- (98-ft-) high water tower, built in 1877 as a water reservoir, but shut down in 1914. The engine house in the tower was used as an prison by the SA. The water tower stands on the Windmühlenberg (windmill hill). This round brick building has now been converted into trendy apartments.

6 Jewish Cemetery

🅟 H2 🅐 Schönhauser Allee 23–25 🅞 8am–4pm Mon–Thu, 7:30am–1pm Fri 🅦 jg-berlin.org

This small Jewish cemetery was set up in 1827, when the former Jewish cemetery in Große Hamburger Straße was closed. Two of the famous personalities who have found their final resting places here are the painter and printmaker Max Liebermann (1847–1935) and the composer Giacomo Meyerbeer (1791–1864).

7 Zionskirche

🅟 G2 🅐 Zionshirchplatz 🅞 2–6pm Mon–Sat, noon–6pm Sun 🅦 zionshirche-berlin.de

Zionskirche, dating from 1866–73, and the square of the same name form a tranquil oasis in the middle of the lively district. The Protestant church has always been a political centre too. During the Third Reich, resistance groups against the Nazi regime congregated here and, during the East German period, the alternative "environment library" (an information and documentation centre) was established. The church and other opposition groups who were active at Zionskirche played a decisive role in the political transformation of East Germany in 1989–90, which eventually led to the reunification of Germany.

8 Gethsemanekirche

🅟 H1 🅐 Stargarder Str. 77 🅞 2–6pm Mon–Thu; services: 10:30am–12:30pm Sun 🅦 ekpn.de

Outside this red-brick church, dating back to 1891–3, East German secret

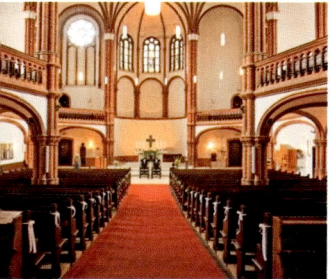

Interior of the stunning Gethsemanekirche

police beat up peaceful protesters. It was the starting point for the collapse of the East German regime.

9 Husemannstraße
☑ H1 🚇 Between Wörther and Danziger Str.

The East German regime undertook a perfect restoration of this idyllic street for Berlin's 750th anniversary celebrations. A stroll through the leafy roads lined with houses from the Gründerzeit (the years after the founding of the German Empire in 1871) is one of the loveliest ways to experience Prenzlauer Berg. Ancient-looking street lamps and signs, cobbled streets, antiquated shop signs and a few atmospheric pubs take visitors back to the late 19th century.

10 Synagoge Rykestraße
☑ H2 🚇 Ryhestr. 53
🌐 jg-berlin.org 📷

Built in 1904, this spectacular synagogue is one of the few Jewish places of worship to have survived Kristallnacht on 9 November 1938, the violent attacks on Jewish property by the Nazis. The temple's historic interior was built from red bricks in the shape of a Neo-Romanesque basilica. It is the best-preserved and the largest synagogue in Berlin. There are guided tours every Thursday.

Jewish Cemetery with its lush green cover

A DAY IN PRENZLAUER BERG

Morning
Set off from the U-Bahn station in **Senefelderplatz** (p144). From here, explore the old tenement blocks and backyards. Then continue west along Fehrbelliner Straße to Zionskirchplatz, and visit the eponymous **Zionskirche**. There are numerous cafés on the square, such as **Kapelle**, where you could stop for a coffee. Leave the square via Zionskirchstraße, then turn left onto colourful Kastanienallee. At the end of the street you could visit **Prater** (p144). Then turn right into Oderberger Straße, one of the area's best preserved streets. Continue east along Sredzkistraße until you reach **Husemannstraße**. Look around the old Berlin streets, you may find something interesting to buy.

Afternoon
Stop for lunch at a restaurant in **Kollwitzplatz** (p141): **Gugelhof** (p145) or **Zander**, the former for German and French cuisine, the latter for imaginative fish specialities. After lunch, walk along Knaackstraße to the **Synagoge Rykestraße**. From here it is a few paces back to the **Wasserturm**. Rest in the small green space around the tower before continuing along Belforter Straße and Kollwitzstraße to Schönhauser Allee. Finish your walk at the tranquil **Jewish Cemetery**.

The Best of the Rest

Distinctive dome of the Zeiss-Großplanetarium

1. Greifenhagener Straße
🔲 H1

Not the most beautiful, but one of the best-preserved red-brick residential streets of old Berlin.

2. Pfefferberg
🔲 H2 🔲 Schönhauser Allee 176
🌐 schankhalle-pfefferberg.de

This alternative cultural centre is set in a former brewery and hosts concerts, performance art events and festivals.

3. Senefelderplatz
🔲 H2

The wedge-shaped square is named after Alois Senefelder, a pioneer of modern printing techniques. At its centre is a "Café Achteck", a historic octagonal public urinal.

4. Zeiss-Großplanetarium
🔲 Prenzlauer Allee 80 🕐 Hours vary, check website 🌐 planetarium.berlin

Gaze at stars, planets and galaxies under the dome of this planetarium.

5. Mauerpark
🔲 G1 🔲 Am Falkplatz

The vast park near the former border, comprising Max Schmeling Hall and Jahn Sports Park, was built for the Berlin Olympic bid in 2000. Today, it hosts sports and music events, karaoke and a Sunday flea market.

6. Helmholtzplatz
🔲 H1

Along with the trendy cafés and bars, this area also has buildings reminiscent of a social housing programme.

7. Museum Pankow
🔲 H2 🔲 Prenzlauer Allee 227–228
🕐 10am–6pm Tue–Sun
🌐 berlin.de/museum-pankow

This museum charts the history of the district and its poor working-class inhabitants in the 19th century.

8. Konnopke's Imbiss
🔲 H1 🔲 At the southern exit of U-Bahn Eberswalder Straße
🕐 11am–6pm Tue–Fri, noon–7pm Sat 🌐 konnopke-imbiss.de

This legendary *Currywurstimbiss* was opened in 1930. The sausages served here are among the best in the city.

9. Oderberger Straße
🔲 G1–H1

This street is lined with cafés, boutiques and historic buildings. The old swimming baths were renovated in 2015.

10. Thälmannpark
🔲 H1 🔲 Prenzlauer Allee

One of few parks in the northeast of the city, dominated by Socialist prefabricated buildings. It has a monument to Ernst Thälmann, a Communist murdered by the Nazis.

Stall at the famous Sunday flea market in Mauerpark

Restaurants

1. Oderquelle

🗺 G1 🏠 Oderberger Str. 27 🕙 6–11pm
Mon–Sat, noon–11pm Sun
🌐 oderquelle.de · €€

Basic Berlin and German dishes are
served up in an alternative, relaxed
setting in this quaint little *Kiez*
(neighbourhood) place.

2. Kanaan

🏠 Schliemannstraße 15 🕙 Noon–
10pm Mon–Fri, 11am–10pm Sat & Sun
🌐 kanaan-berlin.de · €

Oz Ben David, an Israeli, and Jalil Dabit,
a Palestinian, run this small vegetarian
diner offering Middle Eastern food. They
claim to serve the best hummus in town.

3. Lucky Leek

🗺 H2 🏠 Kollwitzstra. 54 🕙 6–10pm
Wed–Sun 🌐 lucky-leek.com · €€

Experience vegan dining here. There
are no à la carte menus on Fridays and
Saturdays, but you can choose from
the three- or five-course meals.

4. 60 seconds to Napoli

🗺 H1 🏠 Oderberger Str. 61
🕙 11:30am–midnight daily
🌐 60secondstonapoli.de · €€

Surprises at the Prater include a beer
garden (Apr–Sep), a rustic restaurant
in the courtyard and free live concerts.
Credit cards are not accepted.

5. Sasaya

🗺 H1 🏠 Lychener Str. 50 🕙 Noon–3pm
& 6–11pm Thu–Mon 🌐 sasaya-berlin.
de · €€

Head to Sasaya for some of Berlin's
best sushi. Reservations needed.
Credit cards are not accepted.

**Streetside dining at Gugelhof,
a popular spot**

6. Gugelhof

🗺 H2 🏠 Knaackstr. 37 🕙 5–10pm
Mon–Wed & Thu, 5–11pm Fri,
noon–11pm Sat, noon–9pm Sun
🌐 gugelhofberlin.de · €€

The menu features an original
combination of German and
French cuisine.

7. Osmans Töchter

🗺 H1 🏠 Pappelallee 15 🕙 6–11:30pm
Mon–Sat 🌐 osmanstoechter.de · €€€

This modern, family-run restaurant
serves traditional Turkish cuisine.

8. Pasternak

🗺 H2 🏠 Knaackstr. 22 🕙 9am–
midnight daily 🌐 restaurant-
pasternak.de · €€

This Moscow-style venue has
borscht, Russian music and vodka.

9. Schankhalle Pfefferberg

🗺 H2 🏠 Schönhauser Allee
176 🕙 4–10:30pm Tue–Sat
🌐 schankhalle-pfefferberg.de · €€

Enjoy home-brewed beer and snacks
such as *Treberbrot* (bread made with
malt left over from brewing beer).

10. Anjoy

🏠 Ryhestraße 11 🕙 Noon–11pm
Mon–Sat, 11am–11pm Sun
🌐 anjoy-restaurant.de · €€

Enjoy traditional Vietnamese cuisine
and an interesting tea menu at Anjoy.

BERLIN'S SOUTHEAST

Berlin's east and south are considered to be remarkably different in character. Friedrichshain, Lichtenberg and Hohenschönhausen in the east are densely built-up, with their old tenement blocks evoking stark memories of World War II and perhaps even more of life during the bleak days of the East German DDR regime. Green Treptow and idyllic Köpenick in the far southeast, meanwhile, seem almost like independent villages and, together with the scenic Großer Müggelsee, have become one of the most popular day trip destinations for international visitors and Berliners alike.

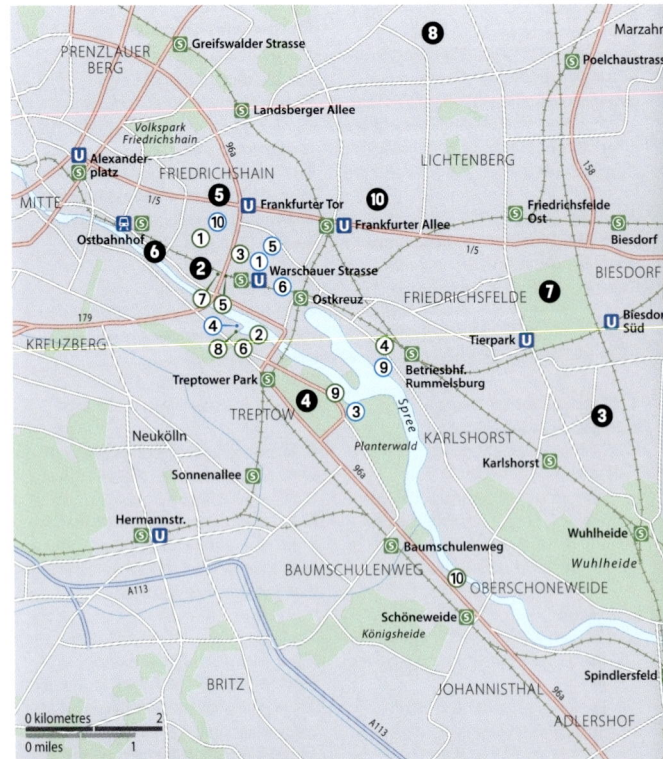

For places to stay in this area, see p177

Charming Köpenick on the banks of the Dahme

1 Köpenicker Altstadt and Köpenicker Schloss

🏛 Schloss: Schlossinsel ⏰ 11am–5pm Thu–Fri, 11am–6pm Sat & Sun 🌐 smb. museum 🔗

As early as the 9th century, people had settled on Schlossinsel. The village stayed independent until 1920. Its coat of arms still features two fish, and the Altstadt (Old Town) on the Dahme River has 18th–19th-century fishers' huts. On 16 October 1906, Wilhelm Voigt, dressed as a captain, led soldiers into the Rathaus (town hall) on Alt-Köpenick, arrested the mayor and "confiscated" the municipal coffers. The "Hauptmann von Köpenick" (Captain of Köpenick) is commemorated by a statue *(p151)* in front of the Rathaus. The 1904 structure is a good example of Gothic brick architecture from Brandenburg. The charming Baroque Köpenick palace, on Schlossinsel in the south of the district, was built in 1677–81 for the future King Frederick I by Dutch architect Rutger van Langervelt. It now houses collections from the Kunstgewerbemuseum *(p54)*.

2 Uber Arena

🏛 Mühlenstr. 12–30/O2-Platz 1 🌐 uber-arena.de

The city's largest entertainment arena, seating 17,000 people, hosts pop concerts and shows of all kinds, as well as being home to the Alba Berlin basketball team and the Eisbären Berlin ice-hockey club.

3 Museum Berlin-Karlshorst

🏛 Zwieseler Str. 4 ⏰ 10am–6pm Tue–Sun 🌐 museum-karlshorst.de

World War II ended here on 8 May 1945, when Germany signed its unconditional surrender. Documents, uniforms and photographs, displayed in the former officers' casino, relate the history of the war.

KAULSDORF

🚇 Kaulsdorf

MAHLSDORF

1/5

1/5

KAULSDORF SÜD

WALDESRUH

Mittelheide

🚇 Köpenick

Friedrichshagen 🚇

KÖPENICK

FRIEDRICHS-HAGEN

Spree

② ①

⑦

Kämmereiheide

⑧

⑨

Großer Müggelsee

Treptower Park, an attractive spot on sunny days

4 Treptower Park
📍 Alt-Treptow

Established in the 19th century for the city's working classes, Treptower Park is known for its Sowjetisches Ehrenmal (Soviet Memorial). In April 1945, 7,000 Red Army soldiers who died during the liberation of Berlin were buried here. Beyond the mass graves is a 12-m- (39-ft-) bronze statue of a Russian soldier holding a child and a sword with which he has destroyed the Nazi *Hakenkreuz* (swastika) symbol.

5 Friedrichshain
📍 H2

This area grew rapidly during the industrialization period. It became an Allied target during the war and was one of Berlin's most damaged districts. After the fall of the Wall, Friedrichshain attracted a young population, and it is now one of the city's most popular areas, home to trendy design and media companies, bars, clubs, and cafés, mostly set around Boxhagener Platz and Simon-Dach-Straße. Its Volkspark (*p67*) houses Ludwig Hoffman's Märchenbrunnen fountain, and the wooded Großer and Kleiner Bunkerberg hillocks.

6 East Side Gallery
📍 H4 📍 Mühlenstraße ⏰ 24 hours
🌐 eastsidegallery-berlin.de

A 1.3-km (0.8-mile) section of the Berlin Wall was left standing next to the Spree River. In 1990, 118 artists from around the world painted onto the concrete, making it a unique work of art. Particularly famous is a mural by Russian Dmitri Vrubel showing Erich Honecker and Leonid Brezhnev kissing. Most murals were restored by the original artists in 2009.

7 Tierpark Berlin
📍 Am Tierpark 125 ⏰ Hours vary, chech website 🌐 tierpark-berlin.de ↗

Located in the Friedrichsfelde Palace park, Europe's largest zoological garden hosts several rare species. The Siberian tigers in their rocky outdoor enclosures are worth a visit. The park is known for its successful elephant breeding programme. The 1695 palace sits in the middle of this estate.

8 Gedenkstätte Hohenschönhausen
📍 Genslerstr. 66 ⏰ Memorial: 10am–6pm daily 🌐 stiftung-hsh.de ↗↗

This former secret police prison for political prisoners was in use until 1990. Before 1951, it served as a reception centre for the Red Army. You can visit the watchtowers and cells – particularly horrifying are the windowless "submarine cells" for solitary confinement and torture. The prison is accessible only through guided tours. Check the website for up-to-date timings.

Morning

Begin your tour at Alexanderplatz. Sights on this tour are not always near each other, so using public transport is recommended. Take the U-Bahn line U5 to Magdalenenstraße station, from where it is a short walk to the **Stasimuseum Berlin**. Return to the station and continue on U5 to **Tierpark Berlin**, and explore both the zoological garden and the Schloss Friedrichsfelde, built in early Neo-Classical style. Then catch bus No. 296 from the Tierpark U-Bahn station to the Museum Berlin-Karlshorst.

Afternoon

From the museum, either walk (15 minutes) or take bus No. 296 southwest down Rheinsteinstraße to the S Karlshorst tram stop. No. 27 goes direct to Rathaus Köpenick. Stop for a German meal in the **Ratskeller** (p151), the town hall's cellar restaurant. Afterwards explore **Köpenick Old Town** (p147). The old fishing village is especially worth a visit. There are many cafés near **Köpenicker Schloss** (p147). Continue your journey by tram No. 60 to Friedrichshagen, the access point for the Großer Müggelsee. From here take one of the tourist boats for a trip around the lake before returning to Köpenick for the train back to the centre.

9 Großer Müggelsee

Treptow-Köpenich district

Nicknamed Berlin's "big bathtub", the Großer Müggelsee is the city's biggest lake. Müggelsee is not as popular as Großer Wannsee, mainly because it is further from the centre. It is known for the beer gardens on its south side, which can be reached on foot or by boat from Friedrichshagen. You can swim in the lake, and around it are great walking and cycling paths.

10 Stasimuseum Berlin

Ruschestr. 103, Haus 1
10am–6pm Mon–Fri, 11am–6pm Sat & Sun   stasimuseum.de

The former headquarters of the Stasi, East Germany's secret police, is now a memorial to the victims of the East German regime and of Erich Mielke, the minister in charge of the secret police. Visitors can see his offices, the canteen and spying equipment used by the Socialist regime.

Button spy camera exhibited at the Stasimuseum Berlin

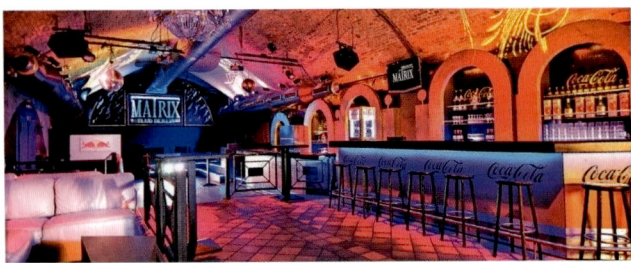

Matrix club in the Warschauer Straße railway station

Bars and Nightclubs

1. Berghain
🏠 Am Wriezener Bahnhof 🕐 Hours vary, chech website 🌐 berghain.berlin
With it's notoriously selective door policy, Berghain, Berlin's techno temple, is one of the world's best clubs.

2. Arena
🏠 Eichenstr. 4 🌐 arena.berlin
A riverside complex, Arena offers concert halls, a club ship (*Hoppetosse*) and a moored swimming pool (*Badeschiff*).

3. Cassiopeia
🏠 Revaler Str. 99 🕐 Hours vary, chech website 🌐 cassiopeia-berlin.de
This underground urban enclave is for ungentrified clubbing and live gigs.

4. Sisyphos
🏠 Hauptstraße 15 🕐 Hours vary, chech website 🌐 sisyphos-berlin.net
Inside a former factory, this popular club is famous for its weekend parties.

5. Matrix
🏠 Warschauer Platz 18 🕐 10pm–5am daily 🌐 matrix-berlin.de
A popular club, Matrix attracts a young crowd and Berlin's best DJs.

6. Festsaal Kreuzberg
🏠 Am Flutgraben 2 🕐 Hours vary, chech website 🌐 festsaal-hreuzberg.de
This venue hosts rock, alternative and indie bands. It has a lovely beer garden.

7. Monster Ronson's Ichiban Karaoke Bar
🏠 Warschauer Str. 34 🕐 From 7pm daily 🌐 karaokemonster.de
At this lively bar, karaoke fans either practise their art in soundproof booths that can fit up to 16 people, or sing on a stage. Try the Liquid Brunch party on Sundays.

8. Salon zur Wilden Renate
🏠 Alt Stralau 70 🕐 From 6pm Wed–Sun 🌐 renate.cc
Styled like a living room, this club plays house and techno music. It gets crowded shortly after opening.

9. Zenner
🏠 Alt Treptow 15 🕐 Beer garden: noon–6pm Mon–Fri, 11am–6pm Sat & Sun; Club: hours vary, chech website 🌐 zenner.berlin
One of the largest and oldest beer gardens in Berlin, Zenner is a leafy space situated in Treptower Park on the Spree River. There is also a hall where live music events take place on weekends.

10. Revier Südost
🏠 Schnellerstr. 137 🕐 Hours vary, chech website 🌐 reviersuedost.de
Set in the premises of the former Bärenquell brewery in the up-and-coming neighbourhood Schöneweide, Revier Südost hosts club nights, concerts and cultural events.

Restaurants

1. Il Ritrovo

⧉ Gabriel-Max-Str. 2 ⏲ Noon–11pm daily 🖥 ritrovo.de · €

Enjoy delicious, well-priced wood-fired pizza in a friendly and cosy atmosphere. There is also a wine bar here.

2. Ratskeller Köpenick

⧉ Alt-Köpenick 21 ⏲ Noon–10pm Tue–Sun 🖥 ratsheller-hoepenich.de · €€

Traditional fare is served in the vaulted cellars where Wilhelm Voigt famously conned (*p147*) local civil servants.

3. Klipper Schiffsrestaurant

⧉ Bulgarische Str. ⏲ 10am–midnight daily 🖥 hlipper-berlin.de · €

This two-masted 1890 boat has been turned into a restaurant; the menu features fish and game dishes.

4. Freischwimmer

⧉ Vor dem Schlesischen Tor 2 ⏲ From 6pm Mon–Fri, from 10am Sat & Sun 🖥 freischwimmer-berlin.com · €€

Head for brunch at this restaurant and bar floating on a wooden terrace.

5. Burgeramt

⧉ Krossener Str. 21–22 ⏲ 11am–1am Fri & Sat, 11am–11pm Sun–Thu 🖥 burgeramt.com · €

A wide variety of burgers are available at this burger joint, from beef patties to many vegetarian options.

6. Khao Taan

⧉ Gryphiusstr. 10 ⏲ 6–11pm Tue–Sat 🖥 khaotaan.de · €€

Impeccable Thai dishes served as a set menu. Diners need to book weeks in advance to secure a table here.

7. Krokodil

⧉ Gartenstr. 46–48 ⏲ 5–11pm Tue–Thu, 5pm–midnight Fri, 3pm–midnight Sat, 10:30am–10pm Sun 🖥 der-coepenicher.de · €€

Situated in Köpenick's Old Town, near the river baths in Gartenstraße, this is one of the nicest garden venues, especially in summer.

8. Bräustübl

⧉ Müggelseedamm 164 ⏲ Noon–11pm Mon–Sat, from 11am Sun 🖥 braeustuebl.wixsite.com · €€

This popular beer garden, belonging to the neighbouring Berliner Bürgerbräu brewery, serves excellent game dishes.

9. Hafenküche

⧉ Zur alten Flußbadeanstalt 5 ⏲ 6–11pm Wed–Fri, noon–11pm Sat & Sun 🖥 hafenhueche.de · €€

Tucked away along the Spree's waterfront on the city's east side, this port restaurant serves casual meals. The picnic baskets on offer are perfect to take on a weekend ride in a boat hired from the neighbouring shop.

10. Jäger & Lustig

⧉ Grünberger Str. 1 ⏲ 11:30am–midnight daily 🖥 jaegerundlustig.de · €€

A rustic restaurant and beer garden, Jäger & Lustig specializes in typical German cuisine; options include game and some vegetarian dishes.

Freischwimmer, a waterside restaurant on the Flutgraben Canal

GRUNEWALD AND DAHLEM

Berlin's green southwest, which includes the districts of Grunewald and Dahlem, is dotted with scenic lakes, rivers, residential villas, private estates and small castles. Grunewald and Dahlem have a charming suburban character that has always drawn affluent and famous Berliners. Visitors can enjoy extensive walks in the Grunewald forest, take a ferry ride across picturesque Wannsee to the romantic ruins at Pfaueninsel or relax at Europe's largest inland beach. Dahlem's Museum of Europäischer Kulturen has a terrific collection, while the Haus der Wannsee Konferenz and Alliiertenmuseum recall a darker period in Berlin's history.

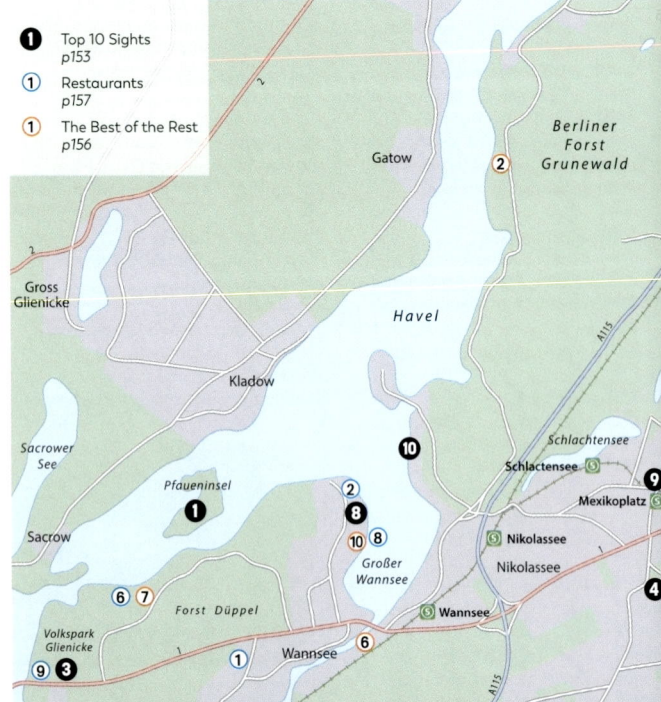

1 Top 10 Sights
p153

1 Restaurants
p157

1 The Best of the Rest
p156

For places to stay in this area, see p177

Friedrich Wilhelm II's palace on Pfaueninsel

1 Pfaueninsel
⌂ Pfaueninselchaussee
🌐 spsg.de

Visitors to Pfaueninsel are immediately enchanted by Friedrich Wilhem II's romantic palace and the eponymous peacocks that run around here. The Wannsee island, which can only be reached by ferry, is one of the most charming spots for a walk in Berlin.

2 Museum Europäischer Kulturen
⌂ Arnimallee 25 🕐 10am–5pm Wed–Fri, 11am–6pm Sat & Sun
🌐 smb.museum ♿

Out of the three museums that once had a home in Dahlem, only the Museum of European Cultures remains today (the Museum of Asian Art and the Museum of Ethnology moved to the Humboldt Forum *(p91)* in 2021). The museum's vast array of objects on display, including graphic art and jewellery, represent life in Germany and other European countries from the 18th century to the present day.

3 Schloss Glienicke
⌂ Königstr. 36 🕐 For tours: Apr–Oct: 10am–5:30pm Tue–Sun, Nov–Mar: 10am–5pm Sat & Sun
🌐 spsg.de ♿♿

One of Berlin's most beautiful Hohenzollern palaces, the Schloss Glienicke is a romantic castle built by Schinkel in 1824–60. It served as a summer residence for Prince Carl of Prussia. The landscaped garden was designed by Lenné and includes pavilions called "Große" and "Kleine Neugierde" (large and small curiosity), a restaurant and the Orangerie.

Schloss Glienicke, detail

Reconstructed medieval village at Museumsdorf Düppel

country house. Villa Maren at No 12 is a beautiful example of the Neo-Renaissance style. The villas on Furtwänglerstraße and Toni-Lessler-Straße are also worth visiting.

4 Museumsdorf Düppel

🏠 Clauertstr. 11 🕐 Late Mar–early Nov: 10am–6pm Sat & Sun 🌐 dueppel.de 🗺️

This lively open-air museum serves as a reminder that Berlin was once a series of villages dating back to the 13th century. Costumed actors enact the daily life of the Middle Ages, with bread-baking, pottery and basket-weaving demonstrations. The gardens are fascinating.

5 Alliiertenmuseum

🏠 Clayallee 135 🕐 10am–6pm Tue–Sun 🌐 alliiertenmuseum.de/en

This museum recalls the 50 or so years of partnership between West Berliners and the Western Allies. Based in a former US barracks, it uses uniforms, documents, weapons and military equipment to tell the story of Berlin's post-war history, though not only from the military point of view.

6 Grunewald Villas

Some of Berlin's most attractive 19th-century villas are found in the streets around the Grunewald S-Bahn station. Especially worth seeing are Nos 15 and 11 in Winklerstraße, the latter of which was built by Hermann Muthesius in the style of an English

7 Jagdschloss Grunewald

🏠 Hüttenweg 100, Grunewaldsee 🕐 For tours: Apr–Oct: 10am–5:30pm Tue–Sun; Nov–Mar: 10am–4pm Sat & Sun 🌐 spsg.de 🗺️🗺️

This small white 1542 palace is the oldest of its kind in the city area. It was once a hunting lodge for the Electors. Built in the Renaissance and Baroque styles, it holds paintings by Cranach the Elder and 16th–19th-century portraits of Hohenzollern rulers. Guided tours are the only way to visit – check the website for tour timings.

8 Haus der Wannsee-Konferenz

🏠 Am Großen Wannsee 56–58 🕐 10am–6pm daily 🌐 ghwk.de

It is hard to believe that something as abhorrent as the Holocaust could have been planned at this elegant villa. Built by Paul Baumgarten in 1914–15 in Neo-Baroque style for businessman Ernst Marlier, it hosted the Nazi elite, among them the infamous Adolf Eichmann, on 20 January 1942. They met to discuss the details

Sunseekers relaxing at Strandbad Wannsee

of the mass extermination of the Jews. An exhibition documents the conference and its consequences, as well as the history of the villa.

9 Mexikoplatz

Idyllic Mexikoplatz in the southern district of Zehlendorf is one of the most atmospheric and architecturally fascinating squares in Berlin. It is flanked by elegant semicircular Jugendstil apartment blocks, and in front of these stands Berlin's last remaining Art Deco-S-Bahn station. In summer, the buildings' balconies are decked with greenery and flowers. Some of Berlin's most magnificent mansion houses line Argentinische and Lindenthaler allees, the streets leading into the magnificent square.

10 Strandbad Wannsee

🏠 Wannseebadeweg 25
🕐 May–Oct: hours vary, check website
🌐 berlinerbaeder.de 🔗

Europe's largest inland beach, which is almost 2 km (1 mile) long and 80 m (262 ft) wide, is a picturesque spot on the edge of the city. It is covered with sand from the Baltic. The swim-ming baths were built in 1929–30 as a recreation area for workers. Visitors can enjoy sports activities such as beach volleyball and football here.

A DAY IN THE SOUTHWEST

Morning

Start your walk through Berlin's southwest by taking the S-Bahn (line S1) to **Mexikoplatz**. Admire the lovely villas and the green square before dropping in at **Café Krone** (*No 2 Argentinische Allee*) for a late breakfast. Then take bus No. 118 southwards to the open-air museum **Museumsdorf Düppel**. From there, take bus No. 115 north to the **Alliiertenmuseum**. Afterwards, a 20-minute walk through the park opposite leads right up to the beer garden **Luise** (*p157*) near Freie Universität, where you can have lunch.

Afternoon

Stop at the **Museum Europäischer Kulturen** (*p153*), a two-minute walk south of the café, or discover tropical flora in the giant greenhouses of the **Botanischer Garten** (*p66*), a 20-minute walk east. The seasonal displays are spectacular. Then find your way to the Botanischer Garten S-Bahn station to take the train to the Wannsee station, gateway to the sights of southwestern Berlin. Head to the beaches of **Strandbad Wannsee**. Alternatively, visit the **Haus der Wannsee-Konferenz** and then admire the park. Finally, hop on the bus for an early dinner at **Luther & Wegner Schloß Glienicke** (*p157*). Your best option for returning to the centre is the S-Bahn from Wannsee.

The Best of the Rest

1. Open Air Museum Domäne Dahlem
◻ Königin-Luise-Str. 49 ◻ Museum: 10am–5pm Wed–Sun; grounds: 7am–10pm daily ◻ domaene-dahlem.de ◻

Learn about modern organic farming at this historic working farm.

2. Grunewaldturm
◻ Havelchaussee ◻ 11am–7pm Mon–Thu, 11pm–8pm Fri–Sun

This Neo-Gothic brick tower was built in 1897 as a memorial to Kaiser Wilhelm I. There is also a viewing platform on top.

3. Onkel Toms Hütte
◻ Argentinische Allee

The "Uncle Tom's Hut" settlement, developed in 1926–32 according to designs by Bruno Taut and others, was intended to create a modern housing estate for workers.

4. Freie Universität
◻ Habelschwerdter Allee 45 ◻ Library: 9am–10pm Mon–Fri, 10am–8pm Sat & Sun ◻ fu-berlin.de

Berlin's largest university was founded in 1948 as a rival to the Humboldt University in East Berlin. It is worth looking at the 1950s Henry-Ford-Bau here, and the Philological Library, designed by Lord Norman Foster.

5. Teufelsberg
◻ 11am–sunset Mon–Fri, 11am–6pm Sat & Sun ◻ teufelsberg-berlin.de ◻

Situated on top of a hill, this Cold War-era listening tower is a landmark viewpoint. The surrounding forests are popular for biking and the Teufelsee lake for swimming and sunbathing.

6. Heinrich von Kleist's Grave
◻ Bismarchstr. 3, Am Kleinen Wannsee

German playwright Kleist and his companion Henriette Vogel committed suicide by shooting themselves in 1811; they are buried here together (near the S-Bahn overpass).

7. St-Peter-und-Paul-Kirche
◻ Nikolshoer Weg 17 ◻ 11am–4pm Mon–Thu, 9am–1pm Fri, 11am–2:45pm Sat & Sun ◻ kirche-nikolshoe.de

This stone church on the Havel was built in 1834–7 by Stüler and resembles Russian Orthodox churches.

8. Mahnmal Gleis 17
◻ Am Bahnhof Grunewald ◻ blochhaus-nikolshoe.de

Around 10,000 German Jews were deported from platform 17 at Grunewald S-Bahn station. A somber memorial marks the dates, destinations and the number of passengers on each departing train.

9. St-Annen-Kirche
◻ Königin-Luise-Str./Pacelliallee ◻ Noon–2pm Sat & Sun ◻ hg-dahlem.de

This 14th-century Gothic church has attractive murals depicting scenes from the life of St Anna, as well as late Gothic figures of saints and a Baroque pulpit.

10. Liebermann-Villa
◻ Colomierstr. 3 ◻ Apr–Sep: 10am–6pm Wed–Mon; Oct–Mar: 11am–5pm Wed–Mon ◻ liebermann-villa.de

The home of Berlin painter Max Liebermann, on the Wannsee shore, is now a museum of his art.

Beautiful garden at the Liebermann-Villa

Restaurants

PRICE CATEGORIES

For a three-course meal for one with half a bottle of wine (or equivalent meal), taxes and charges included.

€ under €30 €€ €30–60 €€€ over €60

1. Mutter Fourage

Chausseestrasse 15a 10am–6pm daily mutterfourage.de · €

Hidden in the yard of a market garden and an atelier, this charming café has a delicious selection of homemade cakes and snacks.

2. Haus Sanssouci

Am Großen Wannsee 60
From noon Wed–Sun
web.haussanssouci.com · €€

Offering great views of Wannsee, this idyllic cottage-style restaurant serves up mostly German food, but it has lobster nights and other specials too.

3. Floh

Am Bahnhof Grunewald 4
030 8929356 Noon–11pm daily · €

A rustic pub, Floh (Flea) is known for its homemade dishes. Its beer garden is right next to the Grundewald S-Bahn station.

4. La Gondola Due

Mexikoplatz 4 From 5pm Tue–Sat, 2–10pm Sun
lagondoladue.de · €€

This wonderful Italian restaurant is known for its great pastas, excellent wines and fantastic service.

5. Alter Krug Dahlem

Königin-Luise-Str. 52
Noon–11pm daily
alter-krug-berlin.de · €

Relax in the porch swings of this large beer garden. A barbecue provides the food at mealtimes.

Outdoor setting at the Alter Krug Dahlem

6. Blockhaus Nikolskoe

Nikolskoer Weg 15 Noon–6pm Wed–Sun (to 8pm Fri & Sat)
blockhaus-nikolskoe.de · €€

Traditional German fare is on offer at this historic cabin with a lakeside view.

7. Luise

Königin-Luise-Str. 40
11am–11:30pm Tue–Sun
luise-dahlem.de · €€

On the Freie Universität campus, Luise always has a good atmosphere. Try the great salads and sandwiches.

8. Café Max

Villa Liebermann, Colomierstr. 3
Apr–Sep: 10am–6pm Wed–Mon; Oct-Mar: 11am–5pm Wed–Mon
cafe-max-liebermann.de · €€

The café in the museum of the famous painter Max Liebermann has a lovely garden and lake views. Access to the café is with museum admission.

9. Luther & Wegner Schloß Glienicke

Königstr. 36 Noon–8pm Fri–Sun
schloss-glienicke.de · €€

Sophisticated surroundings and cuisine. Fish dishes and salads in summer, game and roasts in winter.

10. Chalet Suisse

Clayallee 99 From 5pm Wed–Fri, noon–10pm Sat & Sun chalet-suisse.de · €€

Enjoy local and Swiss cooking in a cosy atmosphere at Chalet Suisse.

POTSDAM AND SANSSOUCI

Potsdam is an important part of European cultural history – a splendid centre of the Enlightenment, which reached its climax in the 18th century in the architectural and artistic design of Frederick the Great's palace of Sanssouci. The palace complex, with its beautiful, extensive park, is both magnificent and playful. It has been designated a World Heritage Centre of Culture by UNESCO and enchants millions of visitors every year. The town of Potsdam, with more than 150,000 inhabitants, is the capital of the federal province of Brandenburg. This former garrison town has much to delight visitors, including small palaces and old churches, idyllic parks and historic immigrant settlements.

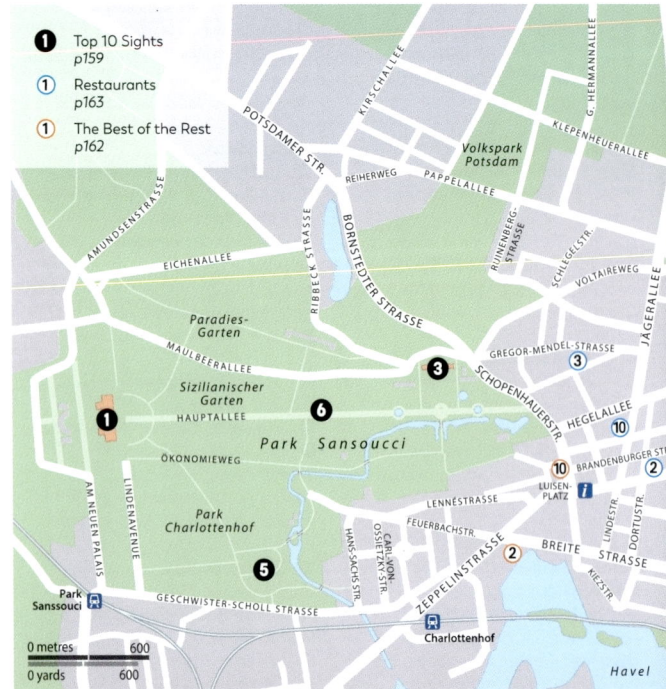

- **1** Top 10 Sights
  p159
- **1** Restaurants
  p163
- **1** The Best of the Rest
  p162

For places to stay in this area, see p177

Decadent Baroque Neues Palais in Park Sanssouci

1 Neues Palais

🏛 Am Neuen Palais ⏰ 10am–5:30pm Wed–Mon (Nov–Mar: to 4:30pm) 🌐 spsg.de 🚻♿

One of Germany's most beautiful palaces, the Baroque Neues Palais was built in 1763–9 for Frederick the Great by Johann Gottfried Büring, Jean Laurent Le Geay and Carl von Gontard. The vast structure has 200 rooms, including the Marmorsaal (marble hall), a lavish ballroom, and the Schlosstheater, where plays are once more performed today. Frederick's private chambers are equally splendid, especially his Rococo study, the upper gallery with valuable parquet flooring and the Oberes Vestibül, a room clad in marble.

2 Museum Barberini

🏛 Alter Markt, Humboldtstr. 5-6 ⏰ 10am–7pm Wed–Mon 🌐 museum-barberini.com ♿

This private art museum, once Palace Barberini, was built in 1771–72 by Frederick the Great. Destroyed during the war, it was reconstructed by Hasso Plattner, and opened to the public in 2017. The rooms house 250 paintings and sculptures from Plattner's collection and others on loan.

3 Schloss Sanssouci

🏛 Maulbeerallee ⏰ Apr–Oct: 10am–5:30pm Tue–Sun (Nov–Mar: to 4:30pm) 🌐 spsg.de 🚻♿

Frederick the Great wished to live "*sans souci*" (without worries) in a palace outside the city. In 1745, he commissioned architect Georg Wenzeslaus von Knobelsdorff to construct this Rococo palace using his own designs. The structure has a marble hall at the centre of the complex and pays homage to Rome's Pantheon. To its left and right are rooms designed by Johann August Nahl and von Knobelsdorff; these include the concert room and the king's library. Here, the monarch liked to play the flute or to philosophize with Voltaire. Works by Antoine Watteau adorn the palace walls.

Chinese House in the Roe Deer Garden of Schlosspark Sanssouci

4 Schloss Belvedere

📍 Im Neuen Garten ⏰ Hours vary, chech website 🌐 spsg.de

Completed in 1847, this summer palace exudes Italian Renaissance charm. Perched atop the Pfingstenberg Hill, the palace offers sweeping views over Potsdam, perfectly complemented by its stunning towers and elegant colonnades.

5 Schloss Charlottenhof

📍 Geschwister-Scholl-Str. 34a ⏰ May–Oct: 10am–5:30pm Tue–Sun 🌐 spsg.de

A Neo-Classical palace in Park Sanssouci, the Schloss Charlottenhof was built in 1829 by Schinkel for Friedrich Wilhelm IV. Particularly worth seeing here is the tent-like Humboldtsaal.

THE POTSDAM CONFERENCE

In July and August 1945, the heads of the governments of the United States (Harry Truman), the USSR (Joseph Stalin) and Great Britain (Winston Churchill) met in Schloss Cecilienhof in order to seal the future of Germany through a treaty. Vitally important points, such as the level of reparations to be paid by Germany, the demilitarization of the country, its new borders, the punishment of war criminals, and the resettlement of Germans from Poland were decided here.

6 Schlosspark Sanssouci

📍 Maulbeerallee ⏰ Hours vary, chech website 🌐 spsg.de

It is easy to spend a day in a park as large as this one. Among the many charming buildings hidden in the landscaped garden is the Rococo-style Chinesisches Haus (*Am Grünen Gitter*), built in 1754–6 by Johann Gottfried Büring. It originally served as a teahouse and dining room, and now houses an exhibition of East Asian porcelain. The Römische Bäder (*Lennéstr*), or Roman Baths, are lakeside pavilions modelled on an Italian Renaissance villa. They were built as bath- and guesthouses between 1829 and 1840 by Schinkel. The Orangerie (*An der Orangerie 3–5*), built in 1851–60 by Stüler, was also originally intended for the king's guests. Today it houses a small gallery of paintings.

7 Holländisches Viertel

📍 Friedrich-Ebert-Str., Kurfürstenstr., Hebbelstr., Gutenbergstr.

A pleasant way to explore Potsdam is a walk through the historic Old Town. Built between 1733 and 1742, the area originally served as a settlement for Dutch workers, after whom it is now named.

Interior of the Neo-Classical Nikolaikirche with its vast dome

8 Marmorpalais
🏛 Heiliger See (Neuer Garten) 🕐 May–Oct: 10am–5:30pm Tue–Sun; Nov–Mar: 10am–4pm Sat & Sun 🌐 spsg.de

This small, early Neo-Classical palace by the Heiliger See was built in 1791–7 by architect Carl Gotthard Langhans and others. It features an elegant concert hall as well as contemporary furniture and porcelain.

9 Marstall (Filmmuseum)
🏛 Breite Str. 1a 🕐 10am–6pm Tue–Sun 🌐 filmmuseum-pots dam.de

Set in the Baroque former stable buildings of the king's town residence, this small museum uses old cameras, props and projectors to document the history of German film.

10 Nikolaikirche
🏛 Am Alten Markt 🕐 9:30am–5pm Mon–Sat, 11am–5pm Sun 🌐 nikolaipotsdam.de

Potsdam's most attractive church, Nikolaikirche was designed by Schinkel in 1830 in Neo-Classical style. Its giant dome is particularly striking, and you can ascend it for a view over the Stadtschloss, which is now home to the parliament of Brandenburg.

A DAY IN POTSDAM

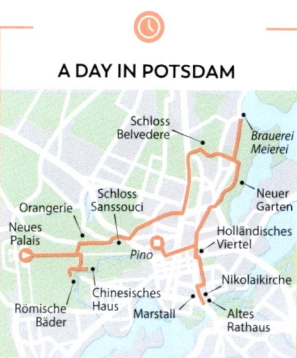

Morning
Begin your exploration in the Schlosspark Sanssouci as early as possible in order to get ahead of the daily influx of visitors. Start with **Neues Palais** and **Schloss Sanssouci** (p159) then visit the Chinesisches Haus, Römische Bäder and Orangerie. From Schlosspark walk along Voltaireweg to Neuer Garten in the northeast of Potsdam, where you can recover over a tasty lunch at **Brauerei Meierei** (Im Neuen Garten 10).

Afternoon
Start the afternoon at **Schloss Belvedere** and enjoy the sweeping vistas. Stop for a break at Heiliger See, then head to the centre of Potsdam, starting with the **Holländisches Viertel** (Dutch quarter) where you could pop into one of the numerous cafés. Stroll past the Propsteikirche St. Peter und Paul (p162), the Französische Kirche (p162), the **Nikolaikirche** and the **Altes Rathaus** (p162) to the **Marstall** film museum and **Museum Barberini**. If you have time, extend your tour by driving to nearby Babelsberg. You could either visit the **Filmpark** (p162), admire Schloss Babelsberg or walk up Telegrafenberg. Round off your day with a delicious meal at **Pino** (p163) in Potsdam.

The Best of the Rest

Brandenburger Tor, one of Potsdam's famous gates

1. Alexandrowka
🏛 Russische Kolonie/Puschhinallee
The Russian colony feels like a village in Tsarist Russia. Decorated log cabins with gardens were built here in 1826 for a Russian military choir. Don't miss the museum and the Alexander Newski church.

2. Dampfmaschinenhaus
🏛 Breite Str. 28 🕓 Hours vary, chech website 🌐 spsg.de
This building, resembling a mosque with minarets, is the water pumping station for Sanssouci. The 1842 pump can be seen inside.

3. Telegrafenberg
🏛 Albert-Einstein-Str. 🚻♿
The Einstein tower on top of Telegraph Hill was designed by Erich Mendelssohn in 1921-23. Einsteinturm tours organizes guided trips from October to March.

4. Schloss Babelsberg
🏛 Park Babelsberg 🕓 Hours vary, chech website 🌐 spsg.de
Built by Schinkel, this Neo-Gothic building sits in an idyllic park on the banks of the Havel River. The building is closed for renovation, but the park is open to visitors. Check the website for details of temporary exhibitions.

5. Potsdamer Stadtschloss
🏛 Neuer Marht
The Hohenzollern palace, once the residence of Frederick the Great, was badly bombed in World War II and had to be demolished in 1960. It is the cultural centre and the seat of the Potsdam legislative assembly.

6. Altes Rathaus
🏛 Am Alten Marht
The old town hall, built between 1753 and 1755, is decorated with sculptures and Potsdam's coat of arms – two gilded Atlas figures, each carrying a globe on its back. Today, it is home to the town's museum.

7. Filmpark Babelsberg
🏛 Großbeerenstr. 200, Potsdam 🕓 Hours vary, chech website 🗓 For events/event days, chech website 🌐 filmpark-babelsberg.de ♿
The Filmpark offers visitors a tour of the legendary UFA-Studios, complete with U-boat trips and stunt performances.

8. Französische Kirche
🏛 Am Bassinplatz 🕓 Late Mar–mid-Oct: 1:30–5pm Tue–Sun 🌐 reformiert-potsdam.de
In 1753, Johann Boumann completed this elliptical Huguenot church with its columned portico; Schinkel designed the beautiful interior in the 1830s.

9. Propsteikirche St. Peter und Paul
🏛 Am Bassinplatz 🕓 10am–6pm daily (winter: to 5pm) 🌐 potsdam.de/de/propsteikirche-st-peter-und-paul
Based on Haghia Sophia in Istanbul, the Catholic church of St Peter and St Paul was built in 1867–70 by Stüler.

10. Brandenburger Tor
🏛 Luisenplatz
The most attractive of Potsdam's five former town gates was built by Gontard and Unger between 1770-71 to celebrate Prussian victory in the Seven Years' War.

Restaurants

1. Kades am Pfingstberg
🏠 Große Weinmeisterstr. 43b
🕐 Noon–9pm Thu–Mon
🌐 restaurant-pfingstberg.de · €€
This spot features an outdoor terrace overlooked by lush trees, as well as an open fireplace inside. Wherever you sit, enjoy local dishes like venison goulash.

2. Zanotto
🏠 Dortustr. 53 🕐 From 6pm Wed–Sun 🌐 daszanottopotsdam.de · €€
This Italian restaurant uses fresh seasonal ingredients and home-made pasta.

3. Pino
🏠 Weinbergstr. 7 🕐 6pm–midnight Mon–Sat 🌐 pino-potsdam.de · €€
Close to Park Sanssouci, Pino serves a daily changing menu of exquisite Sicilian fare. The wine list reads like a Who's Who of Italian vintages.

4. Restaurant Juliette
🏠 Jägerstr. 39 🕐 5–10pm Wed–Fri, noon–2:30pm & 6–10pm Sat & Sun 🌐 restaurant-juliette.de · €€
Set in a former manor house this charming restaurant serves top-quality French classics.

5. Otto Hiemke
🏠 Karl-Gruhl-Str. 55 🕐 4–11pm daily (from noon Fri–Sun) · €
This welcoming pub has been family-run since 1896, and offers a traditional German menu.

Vintage Ford vehicle used by the Café Heider for advertising

6. Maison Charlotte
🏠 Mittelstr. 20 🕐 Noon–3pm & 4–10pm Mon–Sat 🌐 maison-charlotte.de · €€€
An old-world wine bar in a red-brick Dutch house with outdoor seating in a pleasant courtyard, Maison Charlotte serves French country fare and fine wines.

7. Höfts at Villa Kellermann
🏠 Mangerstr. 34 🕐 2–10pm Mon–Fri, 10am–11pm Fri–Sat, 10am–9pm Sun 🌐 villakellermann.de · €€€
This elegant Michelin-starred restaurant on Heiliger See features uniquely designed rooms. Locals come here to enjoy traditional German cuisine with a modern twist.

8. Waage
🏠 Am Neuen Markt 12 🕐 5–11pm Tue–Sat, noon–10pm Sun 🌐 restaurant-waage.de · €€
The regional meat and fish dishes at this attractive historic restaurant in central Potsdam are particularly worth trying.

9. Café Heider
🏠 Friedrich-Ebert-Str. 29 🕐 9am–9pm daily 🌐 cafeheider.de · €€
This lovely café in the middle of Potsdam's Old Town offers a fantastic breakfast, which you can enjoy outside on the terrace in summer.

10. La Madeleine
🏠 Lindenstr. 9 🕐 Noon–10pm daily 🌐 creperie-potsdam.de · €
A little bistro serving all sorts of crêpes, such as sweet with jam or savoury with ham – the ideal spot for a quick snack.

STREETSMART

Bagel seller cycling through the city

GETTING AROUND

Whether exploring Berlin by foot or public transport, and for a short city break or a longer stay, here is everything you need to know to navigate the city and its surrounding areas like a pro.

PUBLIC TRANSPORT COSTS
Tickets are valid on all forms of public transport in Berlin.

SINGLE

€3.50

(zones A–B)

DAY TICKET

€9.90

(zones A–B)

3-DAY TICKET

€36

(zones A–B)

SPEED LIMIT

MOTORWAY

130 km/h
(80 mph)

REGIONAL ROADS

70 km/h
(60 mph)

RURAL ROADS

100 km/h
(40 mph)

URBAN AREAS

50 km/h
(30 mph)

Arriving by Air

Berlin's two international airports, Tegel (TXL) and Schönefeld (SXF), were replaced in October 2020 by a new regional hub, the long-awaited **Berlin-Brandenburg (BER)**. Situated some 18 km (11 miles) southeast of the city on the former sight of Schönefeld airport, Berlin-Brandenburg is well connected and receives regular flights from Europe, North America and Asia. Schönefeld, which earlier operated as the fifth terminal, is now permanently closed.

The fastest way to travel to and from the airport is the S-Bahn lines S9 and S45, the regional trains RE8 and RE23, or the FEX Airport Express, direct to Berlin Hauptbahnhof every 30 minutes. Regular city buses link the airport to the U-Bahn network.
Berlin-Brandenburg (BER)
w berlin-airport.de

International Train Travel

International high-speed trains connect Berlin to other cities across Europe. Reservations are essential.

You can buy tickets and passes for mutiple international train journeys from **Eurail** or **Interrail**. Depending on the service, an additional reservation fee may apply. Always check that your pass is valid on the service you wish to travel with before boarding; travelling without reservations can incur a fine.

Eurostar runs a regular service from London, via the Channel Tunnel, to Brussels, where you can change for Berlin. **Deutsche Bahn**, Germany's national rail network, also runs a regular high-speed service to and from other European destinations.

Students and those under the age of 26 can benefit from discounted rail travel both to and in Germany. For more information on discounts, visit the Eurail or Interrail websites.
Deutsche Bahn
w bahn.com

Eurail
w eurail.com
Eurostar
w eurostar.com
Interrail
w interrail.eu

Long-Distance Bus Travel

FlixBus offers coach routes to Berlin from other European cities. Fares start from £19, with discounts for students, children and seniors. Other services include **Student Agency Bus** and **Ecolines**.

The **Zentraler Omnibus Bahnhof (ZOB)** is the city's largest long-distance bus station, with connections to towns all over Germany and the rest of Europe. Check online for timetables and tickets.

Ecolines
w ecolines.net
FlixBus
w flixbus.de
Student Agency Bus
w studentagencybus.com
Zentraler Omnibus Bahnhof (ZOB)
w zob-berlin.de

Public Transport

Berliner Verkehrsbetriebe (BVG) is Berlin's main public transport author-ity and service provider. Safety and hygiene measures, timetables, ticket information and transport maps can be found online.

BVG
w bvg.de

Tickets

Berlin is divided into three travel zones for the purposes of ticket pricing: A, B and C. Zone A covers the city centre, Zone B the outskirts of town and Zone C includes Berlin's suburban areas, Potsdam and its environs, as well as Berlin-Brandenburg airport. Tickets for any combination of zones are available and are valid on all forms of public transport, including trains, trams, S-Bahn, U-Bahn and ferries, for two hours, with unlimited changes.

Travel is only valid in one direction, so a second ticket is required for the return journey. Short-trip *(kurzstrecke)* tickets are cheaper, but can only be used for three stops on trains and six stops on buses and trams. Daily *(tageskarte)* and seven-day tickets *(7-Tage-Karte)*, costing €9.90 and €41.50 respectively for zones A–B, are better value if you are making multiple journeys. Seven-day tickets also allow you to travel with one extra adult or up to three children (under 14) for free after 8pm, on week-ends and on public holidays.

Discounted tickets are available with tourist cards that offer combined public transport and museum entry *(p173)*.

Ticket machines at train stations and on board trams accept cash only. Exact change is required on buses. Tickets can also be bought on the BVG ticket app. Tickets must be validated in the red or yellow time-stamping machine at platform entrances or on board buses. If caught without a valid ticket you face a fine.

Regional and Local Trains

Germany's railways are operated by Deutsche Bahn (DB). Regional Bahn and Regional Express (RB and RE) trains service the wider Berlin-Brandenburg region and beyond. Use this service for day trips to Potsdam and other towns near Berlin.

GETTING TO AND FROM BERLIN BRANDENBURG

Transport to city centre	Journey Time	Price
Airport Express (FEX)	30 mins	€3.80
RE8	35 mins	€3.80
RE23	35 mins	€3.80
S-Bahn (S9/S45)	50 mins	€3.80
Taxi	40 mins	€60

U-Bahn and S-Bahn

Don't let the name confuse you: Berlin's "underground" trains also run on elevated tracks above ground. There are nine U-Bahn lines, each connecting with the S-Bahn and other U-Bahn lines at points across Berlin. The service usually closes between 1am and 4am. On weekends all lines are open 24 hours except the U4 that closed in 2020. U-Bahn stations are marked by a rectangular blue sign with a large, white letter U.

The S-Bahn is faster than the U-Bahn, and its stations are further apart from one another. Berlin has 16 S-Bahn lines in total, running well beyond the confines of the city. Trains run every 10 or 20 minutes, or more frequently during peak travel times. S-Bahn stations are marked by a round, green sign, featuring a large, white letter S.

Buses

Several bus services operate in Berlin, and they all use the same ticket tariffs. City buses are marked by three-digit route codes and operate every 20 minutes between 5am and midnight. Major routes are serviced by Metro buses (marked by a letter M before the route number), operating 24 hours, and running every 10 to 20 minutes, while express buses (marked by a letter X) run every 5 to 20 minutes.

The night bus service operates every half an hour from midnight until 4am, when the U-Bahn service resumes. Regular tickets are valid on this service. Night bus tickets can also be bought from the driver (cash only).

All bus routes have a detailed timetable on display at each stop, and inner-city bus stops are equipped with digital screens indicating waiting times. Consult the BVG website (p167) for specific route information.

Trams

Despite only servicing the eastern parts of the city, trams (Straßenbahn) are a popular way to get around, particularly if you are travelling from Mitte to any part of Prenzlauer Berg. Important routes are serviced by 24 hour Metro trams, running every 10 minutes during the day and every 30 minutes from 12:30am. Other trams have different schedules and may have limited operating hours, so check the BVG website for timetables.

Public Ferries

An extensive system of canals and lakes links the city centre with neighbouring Potsdam, Spandau, Charlottenburg and Müggelsee, making boating not only a fun way to see the sights but also a viable way to get around.

Six ferry lines operate in Berlin as part of the city's integrated public transport system. Marked by a letter F, they provide cross-river connections in locations to the city's west and east.

Taxis

Official Berlin taxis are cream, have a "Taxi" sign on the roof and have a meter on the driver's dashboard. Taxi apps such as Uber and Bolt also operate.

Taxis can be hailed on the street, picked up at taxi ranks (taxistand) or booked in advance online or over the phone from firms such as **TaxiFunk Berlin** or **Würfelfunk**. If you are travelling 2 km (1 mile) or less, ask for a short trip (kurzstrecke) for €5 – this can only be requested in taxis that you have hailed on the street.

TaxiFunk Berlin
W taxifunk-berlin.de/en
Würfelfunk
W wuerfelfunk.de

Driving

Berlin is easily reached by car from most European cities via E-roads, which form the International European Road Network. Germany's regional roads (Landesstraßen) are marked with yellow road signs, while motorways (Autobahnen) are marked with blue road signs. Some stretches of motorway have variable speed limits depending on weather and road conditions; others have no enforced speed limit. German drivers therefore tend to zoom along at high speeds.

Drivers must carry their passport and insurance documentation if driving a foreign-registered vehicle. Driving licences issued by any of the EU member states are valid. If visiting from outside the EU, you may need to apply for an International Driving Permit. Check with your local automobile association before you travel.

You must be 21 or over and have held a valid driving licence for at least a year to rent a car in Germany. By law, drivers aged 21–22 must buy a Collision Damage Waiver (CDW). Drivers under 25 may incur a young-driver surcharge.

In the event of a breakdown or accident, or if you require assistance, contact **ADAC Auto Assistance**.

Berlin is surrounded by a circular motorway called the Berliner Ring, which has numerous signposted exits that lead straight to the city centre. While public transport is the easiest way to get around, Berlin is relatively straightforward to navigate by car; road layouts are clear and streets are well signposted. Parking is not hard to find and is relatively cheap. Always drive on the right. Unless otherwise signposted, vehicles coming from the right always have priority. Beware of cyclists and trams; trams take precedence, so take care when turning, and allow cyclists right of way. Seatbelts are compulsory, lights must be used in tunnels and the use of a mobile phone while driving is prohibited. The drink-drive *(p173)* limit is strictly enforced.

All drivers must have third-party insurance. Also compulsory is an environmental badge for vehicles driving within environmental green zones known as **Umweltzonen**. Most of downtown Berlin is an Umweltzone. Certification can be purchased online.

ADAC Auto Assistance
W adac.de
Umweltzonen
W umwelt-plakette.de

Cycling

Berlin is generally a very bike-friendly city, with many designated cycle lanes and traffic lights at intersections. If you get tired of pedalling, bikes can be taken on the U-Bahn, S-Bahn and trams (with an additional bicycle ticket), but they are prohibited on buses, except night buses, as long as there is space and at the driver's discretion.

Deutsche Bahn (DB) operates an excellent public bicycle system called **Nextbike**. Bikes can be picked up from train stations and major intersections, and dropped off at any of the Nextbike stations around the city. To rent a Nextbike, register by providing your credit card details. A one-off registration fee of €1 applies. The first 15 minutes cost €1. The maximum daily charge is set at €15 for 24 hours. You can also hire bikes at cycling shops for similar or cheaper rates; one of the most reliable is **Fahrradstation**. Be aware that drink-drive limits also apply to cyclists.

Cyclists should ride on the right. If in doubt, dismount: many cyclists cross junctions on foot; if you do so, switch to the pedestrian section of the crossing. Beware of tram tracks; try to cross them at an angle to avoid getting the wheels stuck. For your own safety, do not walk with your bike in a bike lane or cycle on pavements, on the left side of the road, in designated pedestrian zones or in the dark without lights. The locals usually don't bother, but wearing a helmet is highly recommended.

Fahrradstation
W fahrradstation.com
Nextbike
W nextbike.de/berlin/en

Walking

Berlin is one of the largest cities in Europe, but is still pleasantly walkable. Most of the major sights are located within a relatively small, mostly walkable area. Organized walking tours are also a popular option for those looking to explore the city on foot and learn its history along the way.

PRACTICAL INFORMATION

A little local know-how goes a long way in Berlin. On these pages you can find all the essential advice and information you will need to make the most of your trip to the city.

AT A GLANCE

CURRENCY
Euro (EUR)

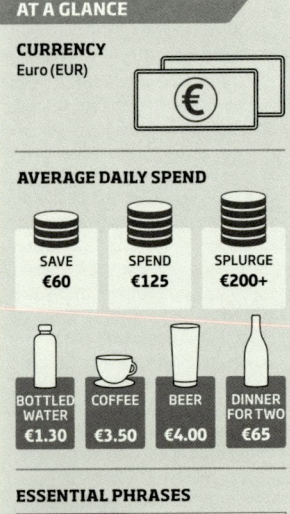

AVERAGE DAILY SPEND

SAVE	SPEND	SPLURGE
€60	€125	€200+

BOTTLED WATER	COFFEE	BEER	DINNER FOR TWO
€1.30	€3.50	€4.00	€65

ESSENTIAL PHRASES

Hello	Guten Tag
Goodbye	Auf Wiedersehen
Please	Bitte
Thank you	Danke
Do you speak English?	Sprechen Sie Englisch?
I don't understand	Ich verstehe nicht

ELECTRICITY SUPPLY
Power sockets are type F and L, fitting two-pronged plugs. Standard voltage is 230 volts.

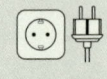

Passports and Visas
For entry requirements, including visas, consult your nearest German embassy or check the **German Federal Foreign Office** website. Citizens of the UK, US, Canada, Australia and New Zealand do not need a visa for stays of up to three months, but in future must apply in advance for the European Travel Information and Authorization System (**ETIAS**); roll-out has continually been postponed so check the website for details. EU nationals do not need a visa or an ETIAS.

ETIAS
W travel-europe.europa.eu/etias_en
German Federal Foreign Office
W auswaertiges-amt.de/en

Government Advice
Now more than ever, it is important to consult both your and the German government's advice before travelling. The UK Foreign, Commonwealth and Development Office (**FCDO**), the **US Department of State**, the **Australian Department of Foreign Affairs and Trade** and the German Federal Foreign Office offer the latest information on security, health and local regulations.

Australian Department of Foreign Affairs and Trade
W smarttraveller.gov.au
UK FCDO
W gov.uk/foreign-travel-advice
US Department of State
W travel.state.gov

Customs Information
You can find information on the laws relating to goods and currency taken in or out of Germany on the **Zoll** (Federal Customs Service) website.
W zoll.de/en

Insurance
We recommend taking out a comprehensive insurance policy covering theft, loss of belongings, medical

care, cancellations and delays, and read the small print carefully.

UK citizens are eligible for free emergency medical care in Germany, provided they have a valid European Health Insurance Card (EHIC) or UK Global Health Insurance Card (**GHIC**).

GHIC
🅦 ghic.org.uk

Vaccinations
No inoculations are needed for Germany.

Money
Major credit, debit and prepaid currency cards are widely accepted. Contactless payments are becoming the norm, too, though they are still not used on public transport, so it is always worth carrying some cash on you. Cash machines are located at various points throughout the city centre.

It's standard to tip around 10 per cent in restaurants if the service is good, or round up to the nearest euro for drinks in cafés and bars.

Travellers with Specific Requirements
Berlin is well-equipped for visitors with mobility requirements. Pavements are sloped at junctions and most public buildings, malls and cinemas are fitted with lifts, ramps and extra-wide doors. The **German Red Cross (DRK)** rents out wheelchairs.

S- and U-Bahn trains are wheelchair accessible, but not all stations have lifts. If you are in the U-Bahn, wait at the head of the platform, and the driver will put up a ramp. In the S-Bahn, speak to the station manager to have a ramp set up. BVG maps show all the accessible stations. Buses with a wheelchair symbol have a ramp. Download the free **accessBerlin** app (p172) for details of the most accessible routes around the city.

Berlin's charitable association for the blind and sight-impaired, the **Allgemeiner Blinden-und Sehbehindertenverein**, offers practical advice and useful information.

Allgemeiner Blinden-und Sehbehindertenverein
🅦 absv.de
German Red Cross (DRK)
🅦 drk-berlin.de/angebote/alltagshilfen/ hilfsmittelcentrum/reservierung.html

Language
German is the official language, but Berlin is a global city, and English is almost as prevalent as German. A lot of Berliners speak English, and you can easily get by in shops and restuarants without knowing a word of German, but it's always appreciated if you can handle a few niceties in the local language.

Opening Hours
From Monday to Saturday, small retailers generally open at 9am or 10am and shut by 7pm, while department stores close at 9pm. Large super-markets open 8am–10pm. Nearly all stores are closed on Sunday. Shops in large train stations and service stations and convenience stores (spätkauf) stay open until at least midnight, and are also open on Sundays.

Banks tend to have varied opening hours, so it's worth checking online if you need services beyond an ATM. Larger post offices work 8am–6pm Monday to Friday, and until at least noon on Saturday. Pharmacies open 9am–7pm Monday to Friday, and until 4pm on Saturday. Check online for those with a 24-hour service.

Public museums are generally open 10am–6pm; many close on Monday. On public holidays, schools, post offices and banks are closed for the day, and shops, museums and attractions either close early or are closed for the entire day.

Situations can change quickly and unexpectedly. Always check before visiting attractions and hospitality venues for up-to-date opening hours and booking requirements.

Personal Security

Berlin is a relatively safe city, but as in most cities, use common sense. Pickpocketing is common, particularly at tourist sites. Contact your embassy if your passport has been stolen, or in the event of a serious crime or accident.

Germans, and Berliners in particular, are generally accepting of all people, regardless of their race, gender or sexuality. While long celebrated as a liberal and tolerant country, Germany only legalized homosexuality in 1994. Despite the freedoms that the LGBTQ+ community enjoy in Berlin, acceptance is not always a given. If you do feel unsafe, the **Safe Space Alliance** pinpoints your nearest place of refuge.

The **Maneo** hotline run by **Mann-O-Meter** supports victims of homophobic behaviour. **Lesbenberatung** is a safe space that offers help, advice and counselling for lesbians, bisexual women, transgender, intersex, non-binary and queer people.

Lesbenberatung
🅦 lesbenberatung-berlin.de
Maneo
🅦 maneo.de
Mann-O-Meter
🅦 mann-o-meter.de
Safe Space Alliance
🅦 safespacealliance.com

Health

Berlin is known for its world-class health service. EU citizens can receive emergency medical treatment in Germany free of charge (*p171*), but you may have to pay upfront and claim on your insurance later. For visitors from outside the EU, payment of medical expenses is the patient's responsibility. It is therefore important to arrange good medical insurance (*p170*).

For minor ailments and prescriptions, go to a chemist or pharmacy (*Apotheken*). After 8pm, the address of the nearest all-night pharmacy is posted on the door of each outlet, or can be easily obtained on the **Apothekerkammer** website.

Apothekerkammer
🅦 akberlin.de

Smoking, Alcohol and Drugs

Germany has a smoking ban in all public places, including bars, cafés, restaurants and hotels, however, some designated smoking bars (Raucherkneipen) exist. Many pubs and bars, and even some cafés, are smoker-friendly. It's therefore

worth checking if where you're headed is smoke-free.

Recreational cannabis use was legalized in April 2024 for those 18 and older.

Possession of narcotics is strictly prohibited and could result in prosecution and a prison sentence.

Unless stated otherwise, it is permitted to drink alcohol on the streets and in public parks. A strict drink-drive limit of 0.05 per cent BAC (blood alcohol content) is enforced.

ID
Visitors are not required to carry ID, but in the event of a routine check you may be asked to show your passport. If you don't have it with you, the police may escort you to where your passport is kept so that you can show it to them.

Local Customs
Germany has very strict laws on hate speech and symbols linked to Hitler and Nazism. Disrespectful behaviour in public places can warrant a fine, or even prosecution. Be respectful when visiting Berlin's historical sights and monuments. Pay attention to signage indicating when photos aren't allowed and think carefully about how you compose your shots. Visitors have come under serious criticism for posting inappropriate photos taken in front of sites such as the Holocaust-Denkmal (p93) on social media.

Dress respectfully when visiting churches, synagogues and other religious buildings.

Mobile Phones and Wi-fi
Visitors travelling to Berlin with EU tariffs will be able to use their devices abroad without being affected by data roaming charges; instead they will be charged the same rates for data, SMS and voice calls as they would pay at home. Visitors with non-EU tariffs are advised to sign up for an international usage plan to keep costs down or purchase an e-sim.

Berlin has over 400 wireless internet hotspots, many of which are free. Cafés and restaurants are usually happy to permit the use of their Wi-Fi on the condition that you make a purchase.

Responsible Travel
In a city where zero-waste restaurants, flea markets and urban farms are the norm, it's no wonder Berlin is one of the world's most sustainable cities. Visitors can do their bit by cycling or walking around the city to reduce emissions, embracing locally and sustainably sourced cuisine, and using reusable water bottles and bags.

Post
German mail is efficient, reliable and fast. Buy stamps from a post office counter or vending machines.

Postboxes generally have two slots: *Postleitzahlen* (postal codes) 10000–16999 for addresses in Brandenburg and Berlin, and *Andere Postleitzahlen* (other postal codes) for destinations elsewhere in Germany and abroad.
Deutsche Post
🅦 deutschepost.de

Taxes and Refunds
VAT is 19 per cent in Germany. Non-EU residents are entitled to a tax refund subject to conditions. In order to do this, you must request a tax receipt and export papers (*Ausfuhrbescheinigung*) when you purchase your goods. When leaving the country, present these papers, along with the receipt and your ID, at customs to receive your refund.

Discount Cards
The **Berlin WelcomeCard** offers free entry to 30 major tourist attractions and discounted entry for over 180 more. It also includes unlimited access to the transport network while in Berlin.

Save up to 40 per cent on 15 of the city's leading tourist attractions and enjoy unlimited free travel on public transport with the **Berlin City Tour Card**.
Berlin City Tour Card
🅦 citytourcard.com
Berlin WelcomeCard
🅦 berlin-welcomecard.de

PLACES TO STAY

From luxurious hotels that recall the Golden Twenties to arty spots that celebrate an underground spirit, Berlin's accommodation is as exciting as the city itself. The best area depends on what you're after. Here for the nightlife? Book into buzzy hotels in Kreuzberg and Friedrichshain. Want to be near the bucket list sights? Opt for central Berlin areas like Alexanderplatz.

Historic hotels are everywhere, but take the chance to explore the city's quirky side too, staying at an indoor camping site or 19th-century former jail.

PRICE CATEGORIES

For a standard double room per night (with breakfast if included), taxes and extra charges.

€ under €120
€€ €120–€250
€€€ over €250

Central Berlin: Unter den Linden

Hotel Luc, Autograph Collection

🔲 L4 🏠 Charlottenstr. 50 🌐 marriott.com · €€€

With its bold splashes of deep Prussian blue on the walls, sofas and vases, Hotel Luc is a time capsule of Prussian elegance. A stay here will have you eager to learn more about Prussia's legacy, such as why the potato is the unofficial mascot for Prussian Germany; scan the QR code in the lobby, next to a basket of potatoes no less, to find out.

Château Royal Berlin

🔲 K3 🏠 Neustädtische Kirchstr. 3 🌐 chateauroyal berlin.com/de · €€€

No design detail has been overlooked at this sophisticated hotel, where individually styled rooms and suites feature contemporary art and custom-made oak furniture. It's all very refined and proper,

but stuffy it's not; the cocktail bar and rooftop are hangout spots for the city's artists.

Hotel de Rome

🔲 K4 🏠 Behrenstr. 37 🌐 roccofortehotels.com · €€€

Five stars come at a price at Hotel de Rome – fitting, given it's set in a 19th-century former bank. Elegant marble columns and an iron staircase are reminders of the building's past life, while upgrades have been given to the former jewellery vault (now housing a pool) and the bank directors' office (today, historic suites).

Central Berlin: Scheunenviertel

Monbijou Hotel

🔲 J5 🏠 Monbijoupl. 1 🌐 monbijouhotel.com · €

This affordable spot is at its most inviting in Berlin's chilling winter months, when a crackling fireplace keeps things cosy in the bar and lounge. Visiting in the summer? Make the most

of the rooftop, with 360-degree views of Berlin to blow your sandals off.

The Circus Hotel

🔲 G2 🏠 Rosenthaler Str. 1 🌐 circus-berlin.de · €

Yoga sessions, bike rentals, street art walking tours: this hotel will keep you busy from morning till night. When you're tired of all the action, take a break in the gorgeous garden courtyard or enjoy a beer at the Lost My Voice bar.

Gorki Apartments

🔲 G2 🏠 Weinbergsweg 25 🌐 gorkiapartments.com/ en · €€€

The luxurious Gorki Apartments come with all the trimmings: rain-forest showers, bathtubs, kitchenettes and Dyson hairdryers. With your very own doorbell and letterbox, as well as flea market finds dotting the interiors, it'll feel like a home away from home (albeit one located off Rosenthaler Platz, surrounded by some of Berlin's best restaurants).

St Christopher's Inn Berlin Mitte

Q J4 **A** Ziegelstr. 28
W st-christophers.co.uk/
berlin · €

If you're less bothered about the room itself and more about who you're sharing it with, this hostel is for you. Socializing is the beating heart of St Christopher's Inn, where guests chat on the rooftop terrace into the early hours, nurse drinks at the sports bar and bond on free walking tours offered through reception.

Hotel Telegraphenamt

Q J5 **A** Monbijoustr. 11
W telegraphenamt.com
· €€€

Set in a building that was once the biggest postal hub in Germany, this is a hotel you'll want to message home about. It's minutes from Museumsinsel, features impressive Neo-Baroque interiors and overlooks Monbijou Park. What makes it so special, though, is its stunning restaurant, ROOT, where global dishes are served under a conservatory roof.

Central Berlin: Around Alexanderplatz

Radisson Collection Hotel, Berlin

Q J6 **A** Karl-Liebknecht-Str. 3 **W** radissonhotels.com · €€

The Spree-side Radisson gets lots of ticks: central Mitte location, proximity to major sights, dreamy river and Berliner Dom views, sleek rooms and friendly staff. After a day of sightseeing, you can even indulge at the spa.

Tiergarten and the Federal District

Motel One Berlin-Potsdamer Platz

Q L3 **A** Leipziger Str. 132
W motel-one.com · €

Swap a night at the museum for a night at the mall with Motel One, located in the fabulous Mall of Berlin. It's not only budget-friendly (leaving you more money to shop with) but is also perfectly placed to tick off the city's key sights.

The Mandala Hotel

Q L2 **A** Potsdamer Str. 3
W themandala.de/de · €€

Looking for a peaceful getaway but still want to be in the thick of the action? The Mandala Hotel has got you covered. Though located on bustling Potsdamer Platz, it's a peaceful sanctuary inside, and has been known to host celebrities seeking the utmost privacy (the hot stone massages and the two Michelin-starred Facil only add to the attraction).

Arte Luise Kunsthotel

Q J3 **A** Luisenstr. 19
W luise-berlin.com/en · €

Known as a "gallery to stay overnight", this arty hotel is Berlin through and through. All 50 rooms have been individually designed by an artist, and there's even a gallery on-site that doubles as an event venue. Better yet, being close to Unter den Linden means you're never far from the city's iconic galleries and museums (not that you'll need them).

Lulu Guldsmeden Hotel

Q L2 **A** Potsdamer Str. 67
W guldsmedenhotels.com/lulu-guldsmeden · €

This hotel means business when it comes to sustainability. Bathroom products and bed linens are eco-friendly, the loft-style rooms incorporate natural materials such as bamboo, and organic food and drink options are Green Globe-certified. Even the *Guldsmeden* newspaper, which offers tips on the city, is eco-certified; read your copy in the peaceful garden courtyard.

SO/ Berlin Das Stue

Q E4 **A** Drakestr. 1
W so-berlin-das-stue.com · €€€

There's something to keep everyone happy here. For the kids, it's the setting, with floor-to-ceiling windows overlooking the Tiergarten and a private entrance to the Berlin Zoo. For the adults, it's the interiors, complete with a handsome bar and stunning white marble staircase.

InterContinental Berlin

⚐ D4 ⌂ Budapester Str. 2 🌐 ihg.com/intercontinent al/hotels/gb/en/berlin · €€€

The InterContinental has rolled out the red carpet over the decades, with everyone from George W Bush to Tom Hanks booking in. Follow suit and you're promised award-winning sustainable practices, a top-notch spa and a Michelin-starred restaurant with skyline views. If you don't spot a celeb, sipping a cocktail at the Marlene Bar (named after Berlin-born singer and actress Marlene Dietrich) is the next best thing.

Charlottenburg and Spandau

Max Brown Hotel Ku'damm

⚐ C6 ⌂ Uhlandstr. 49 🌐 maxbrownhotels.com/ hudamm-berlin · €

It's the little things that make a hotel feel like home: comfy beds to curl up in, dinky teapots to make the perfect cuppa, record players to listen to a collection of vinyl. Add to that bread baked on-site daily and stylish shops and bars on your doorstep and you'll want to move in.

Hotel Bristol Berlin

⚐ C5 ⌂ Kurfürstendamm 27 🌐 bristolberlin.com · €€

Hotel Bristol is a Berlin icon. The city's first new luxury hotel after World War II, it quickly became synonymous with the city's glitterati, hosting the likes of Alfred Hitchcock and Sophia Loren. It remains a glamorous spot today, in part thanks to its Ku'damm location and stunning indoor pool. The highlight? Having the famous Crêpes Suzette flambéed at your table at the Bristol Grill restaurant.

Wilmina Hotel

⚐ B4 ⌂ Kantstr. 79 🌐 wilmina.com · €€

Spending the night in jail doesn't ordinarily make for a happy holiday, unless you're staying at Wilmina. A women's prison from 1896 to 1985, the space has been creatively transformed, with original cell doors leading into elegant guest rooms. Enjoy contemporary German dishes served at the on-site restaurant.

Provocateur Hotel

⚐ B5 ⌂ Brandenburgische Str. 21 🌐 provocateur-hotel.com · €€

The spirit of the Golden Twenties is alive and well at the Provocateur. Velvet seating, a gold-accented bar and dark walls in the common areas set the scene for a seductive stay. The theme extends to the rooms, with chandeliers, plush red headboards and black-tiled bathrooms. Get to your suite via the gold lift, a fixture since 1911.

Sir Savigny Hotel

⚐ B4 ⌂ Kantstr. 144 🌐 sirhotels.com/en/ savigny · €

If you struggle to sleep in a hotel bed, book into Sir Savigny. Beds here are the stuff of dreams, with crispy 300 thread count cotton linens and pillows and mattresses you can sink into. It's the perfect place to retreat to after a day of exploring.

Kreuzberg, Schöneberg and Neukölln

Hüttenpalast

⌂ Hobrechtstr. 65/66 🌐 huettenpalast.de · €

Rain ruining your camping plans? You need Hüttenpalast, the world's first indoor caravan site. Here, restored vintage caravans are decked out with kitschy touches like furniture made of wine boxes, and communal areas are dotted with "trees" that light up at night. You can opt for one of the six traditional hotel rooms, each with its own bathroom, but where's the fun in that?

Orania Berlin

⚐ L5 ⌂ Oranienstr. 40 🌐 orania.berlin · €€€

Ideally located for Kreuzberg's vibrant nightlife scene, Orania will get your nights off to a great start. Live music concerts are held by jazz, soul and pop artists in the bar-lounge, the perfect place to mingle before hitting the nearby clubs and bars. When the early hours roll round, comfortable beds await.

The Yard Hotel

📍 L6 🏠 Alexandrinenstr. 125 🌐 hotel-theyard.berlin · €€

You wouldn't know that some of the city's top sights, from the Jewish Museum to Checkpoint Charlie, were only a few minutes' walk from here. This quiet Kreuzberg spot is a serene oasis with an emphasis on minimalism, natural light and greenery. If the earthy tones aren't calming enough, book into the wellness centre.

Prenzlauer Berg

Hotel Oderberger

📍 G1 🏠 Oderberger Str. 57 🌐 hotel-oderberger.berlin · €€

This hotel occupies a beautifully renovated 19th-century public bathhouse and as you'd expect its pool is a highlight. But there's so much more to shout about, such as vegan breakfast options, organic products in the bathrooms and in-room beauty treatments.

Linnen

📍 G1 🏠 Eberswalder Str. 35 🌐 linnenberlin.com · €€

Everything here is set up to feel like home. The reception area doubles as a cosy café, where the friendly owners welcome you warmly and offer tips for your stay. As for the lodgings, you can choose from six rooms,

plus apartments and studios, all stocked with organic toiletries.

Berlin's Southeast

Michelberger Hotel

🏠 Warschauer Str. 39–40 🌐 michelbergerhotel.com/en · €€

If you plan on partying at Berlin's best clubs, you'll be well positioned here in the heart of Friedrichshain. Set in a former factory, the space is as cool and stylish as its guests, who pass the time nursing a drink on the lobby's low sofas or reading a book from the communal shelves.

nhow

🏠 Stralauer Allee 3 🌐 nh-hotels.com/en/hotel · €

Want an electric guitar delivered to your room? Or a bluetooth speaker before a big night out? Europe's first music hotel has got you sorted. This Spree-side spot is wacky and wonderful, dotted with hot pink decor, funky furniture and lifts that have their own individual playlists.

Grunewald and Dahlem

Schlosshotel Berlin by Patrick Hellmann

🏠 Brahmsstr. 10 🌐 schlosshotelberlin.com · €€€

What do Josephine Baker, Paul McCartney and the Rolling Stones have in common? They

all stayed at this elegant Italian Renaissance hotel (although only one trashed valuable vases while here). Aside from its celebrity guestbook, Schlosshotel Berlin is loved for its easy access to Grunewald forest walking trails.

Potsdam and Sanssouci

Hotel Brandenburger Tor Potsdam

🏠 Brandenburger Str. 1 🌐 hotel-brandenburger-tor.de/en · €€

As impressive as the restored 18th-century hotel building is, the location sells this spot – stay here and you'll be within touching distance of the city's historic gate, Sanssouci Palace and the Dutch Quarter. Admire the surroundings with an aperitivo on the streetside terrace.

The niu Amity

📍 L3 🏠 Leipziger Str. 1/Bloch J 🌐 the.niu.de/hotels · €

If you're nostalgic for youthful days spent camping with friends, you'll love the niu Amity. Boy scout badges dot the walls, long breakfast tables invite guests to mingle and comfy chairs are set up around a cute indoor campfire. The hotel also rewards you for saving energy and water: opt out of having your room cleaned and you'll get a free drink at the bar. Cheers to that.

INDEX

PHRASE BOOK

In an Emergency

Where is the telephone?	Wo ist das Telefon?	voh ist duss tel-e-fone?
Help!	Hilfe!	hilf-uh
Please call a doctor	Bitte rufen Sie einen Arzt	bitt-uh roof'n zee ine-en artst
Please call the police	Bitte rufen Sie die Polizei	bitt-uh roof'n zee dee poli-tsy
Please call the fire brigade	Bitte rufen Sie die Feuerwehr	bitt-uh roof'n zee dee foyer-vayr
Stop!	Halt!	halt

Communication Essentials

Yes	Ja	yah
No	Nein	nine
Please	Bitte	bitt-uh
Thank you	Danke	dank-uh
Excuse me	Entschuldigung	Ent-shool-dee-goong
Hello	Guten Tag	goot-en tahk
Goodbye	Auf Wiedersehen	owf-veed-er-zay-ern
Good evening	Guten Abend	goot'n-ahb'nt
Good night	Gute Nacht	goot-un nukht
Until tomorrow	Bis morgen	biss morg'n
See you	Tschüss	chooss
What is that?	Was ist das?	voss ist duss
Why?	Warum?	var-room
Where?	Wo?	voh
When?	Wann?	vunn
today	heute	hoyt-uh
tomorrow	morgen	morg'n
month	Monat	mohn-aht
night	Nacht	nukht
afternoon	Nachmittag	nahkh-mit-tahk
morning	Morgen	morg'n
year	Jahr	yar
there	dort	dort
here	hier	hear
week	Woche	vokh-uh
yesterday	gestern	gest'n
evening	Abend	ahb'nt

Useful Phrases

How are you? (informal)	Wie geht's?	vee gayts
Fine, thanks	Danke, es geht mir gut	dank-uh, es gayt meer goot
Where is/are?	Wo ist/sind...?	voh ist/sind
How far is it to...?	Wie weit ist es...?	vee vite ist ess
Do you speak English?	Sprechen Sie Englisch?	shpresh'n zee eng-glish
I don't understand.	Ich verstehe nicht	ish fair-shtay-uh nisht
Could you speak more slowly?	Könnten Sie langsamer sprechen?	kurnt-en zee langsamer shpresh'n

Useful Words

large	gross	grohss
small	klein	kline
hot	heiss	hyce
cold	kalt	kalt
good	gut	goot
bad	böse/schlecht	burss-uh/shlesht
open	geöffnet	g'urff-nett
closed	geschlossen	g'shloss'n
left	links	links
right	rechts	reshts
straight ahead	geradeaus	g'rah-der-owss

Making a Telephone Call

I would like to make a phone call	Ich möchte telefonieren	ish mer-shtuh tel-e-fon-eer'n
I'll try again later	Ich versuche noch ein mal später	ish fair-zookh-uh nokh ine-mull shpay-ter
Can I leave a message?	Kann ich eine Nachricht hinterlassen?	kan ish ine-uh nakh-risht hint-er-lahss-en
answer phone	Anrufbeant-worter	an-roof-be-ahnt-vort-er
telephone card	Telefonkarte	tel-e-fohn-kart-uh
receiver	Hörer	hur-er
mobile	Handy	han-dee
engaged (busy)	besetzt	b'zetst
wrong number	Falsche Verbindung	falsh-uh fair-bin-doong

Sightseeing

library	Bibliothek	bib-leo-tek
entrance ticket	Eintrittskarte	ine-tritz-kart-uh
cemetery	Friedhof	freed-hofe
train station	Bahnhof	barn-hofe
gallery	Galerie	gall-er-ree
information	Auskunft	owss-koonft
church	Kirche	keersh-uh
garden	Garten	gart'n
palace/castle	Palast/Schloss	pallast/shloss
place (square)	Platz	plats
bus stop	Haltestelle	hal-te-shtel-uh
national holiday	Nationalfeier-tag	nats-yon-ahl-fire-tahk
theatre	Theater	tay-aht-er
free admission	Eintritt frei	ine-tritt fry

Shopping

Do you have/ Is there...?	Gibt es...?	geept ess
How much does it cost?	Was kostet das?	vass kost't duss?
When do you open/ close	Wann öffnen Sie/ schliessen Sie?	vann off'n zee shlees'n zee
this	das	dass
expensive	teuer	toy-er
cheap	preiswert	price-vurt
size	Grösse	gruhs-uh
number	Nummer	noom-er
colour	Farbe	farb-uh
brown	braun	brown
black	schwarz	shvarts
red	rot	roht
blue	blau	blau
green	grün	groon
yellow	gelb	gelp

Types of Shop

antique shop	Antiquariat	antik-var-yat
chemist (pharmacy)	Apotheke	appo-tay-kuh
bank	Bank	bank
market	Markt	markt
travel agency	Reisebüro	rye-zer-boo-roe
department store	Warenhaus	vahr'n-hows
chemist's drugstore	Drogerie	droog-er-ree
hairdresser	Friseur	freezz-er
newspaper kiosk	Zeitungskiosk	tsytoongs-kee-osk
bookshop	Buchhandlung	bookh-hant-loong
bakery	Bäckerei	beck-er-eye
post office	Post	posst
shop/store	Geschäft/Laden	gush-eft/lard'n
film processing shop	Photogeschäft	fo-to-gush-eft
self-service shop	Selbstbedie-nungsladen	selpst-bed-ee-nungs-lard'n
shoe shop	Schuhladen	shoo-lard'n
clothes shop store	Kleiderladen Boutique	klyder-lard'n boo-teek-uh
food shop	Lebensmittel-geschäft	lay-bens-mittel-gush-eft
glass, porcelain	Glas, Porzellan	glars, Port-sellahn

Staying in a Hotel

Do you have any vacancies?	Haben Sie noch Zimmer frei?	harb'n zee nokh tsimm-er-fry
with twin beds?	mit zwei Betten?	mitt tsvy bett'n
with a double bed?	mit einem Doppelbett?	mitt ine'm dopp'lbet
with a bath?	mit Bad?	mitt bart
with a shower?	mit Dusche?	mitt doosh-uh
I have a reservation	Ich habe eine Reservierung	ish harb-uh ine-uh rez-er-veer-oong
key	Schlüssel	shloos'l
porter	Pförtner	pfert-ner

Eating Out

Do you have a table for …?	Haben Sie einen Tisch für…?	harb'n zee ine-uhn Tisch für…?
I would like to reserve a table	Ich möchte eine Reservierung machen	ish mer-shtuh ine -uh rezer-veer-oong makh'n
I'm a vegetarian	Ich bin Vegetarier	ish bin vegg-er-tah-ree-er
Waiter!	Herr Ober!	hair oh-bare!
The bill (check), please	Die Rechnung, bitte	dee resh-noong bitt-uh
breakfast	Frühstück	froo-shtock
lunch	Mittagessen	mit-targ-ess'n
dinner	Abendessen	arb'nt-ess'n
bottle	Flasche	flash-uh
dish of the day	Tagesgericht	tahg-es-gur-isht
main dish	Hauptgericht	howpt-gur-isht
dessert	Nachtisch	nahkh-tish
cup	Tasse	tass-uh
wine list	Weinkarte	vine-kart-uh
tankard	Krug	khroog
glass	Glas	glars
spoon	Löffel	lerff'l
teaspoon	Teelöffel	tay-lerff'l
tip	Trinkgeld	trink-gelt

knife	Messer	mess-er
starter (appetizer)	Vorspeise	for-shpize-uh
the bill	Rechnung	resh-noong
plate	Teller	tell-er
fork	Gabel	gahb'l

Menu Decoder

Aal	ahl	eel
Apfel	apf'l	apple
Apfelschorle	apf'l-shoorl-uh	apple juice with sparkling mineral water
Apfelsine	apf'l-seen-uh	orange
Aprikose	apri-kawz-uh	apricot
Artischocke	arti-shokh-uh	artichoke
Aubergine	oh-ber-jeen-uh	aubergine (eggplant)
Banane	bar-narn-uh	banana
Beefsteack	beef-stayk	steak
Bier	beer	beer
Bockwurst	bokh-voorst	a type of sausage
Bohnensuppe	bow-nen-zoop-uh	bean soup
Branntwein	brant-vine	spirits
Bratkartoffeln	brat-kar-toff'ln	fried potatoes
Bratwurst	brat-voorst	fried sausage
Brötchen	bret-tchen	bread roll
Brot	brot	bread
Brühe	bruh-uh	broth
Butter	boot-ter	butter
Champignon	shum-pin-yong	mushroom
Currywurst	kha-ree-voorst	sausage with curry sauce
Dill	dill	dill
Ei	eye	egg
Eis	ice	ice/ ice cream
Ente	ent-uh	duck
Erdbeeren	ayrt-beer'n	strawberries
Fisch	fish	fish
Forelle	for-ell-uh	trout
Frikadelle	Frika-dayl-uh	rissole/ hamburger
Gans	ganns	goose
Garnele	gar-nayl-uh	prawn/shrimp
gebraten	g'braat'n	fried
gegrillt	g'grilt	grilled
gekocht	g'kokht	boiled
geräuchert	g'rowk-ert	smoked
Geflügel	g'floog'l	poultry
Gemüse	g'mooz-uh	vegetables
Grütze	grurt-ser	groats, gruel
Gulasch	goo-lash	goulash
Gurke	goork-uh	gherkin
Hammelbraten	hamm'l-braat'n	roast mutton
Hähnchen	haynsh'n	chicken
Hering	hair-ing	herring
Himbeeren	him-beer'n	raspberries
Honig	hoe-nikh	honey
Kaffee	kaf-fay	coffee
Kalbfleisch	kalp-flysh	veal
Kaninchen	ka-neensh'n	rabbit
Karpfen	karpf'n	carp
Kartoffelpüree	kar-toff'l-poor-ay	mashed potatoes
Käse	kayz-uh	cheese
Kaviar	kar-vee-ar	caviar
Knoblauch	k'nob-lowkh	garlic
Knödel	k'nerd'l	dumpling
Kohl	koal	cabbage
Kopfsalat	kopf-zal-aat	lettuce
Krebs	krayps	crab
Kuchen	kookh'n	cake

Lachs	*lahkhs*	salmon
Leber	*lay-ber*	liver
mariniert	*mari-neert*	marinated
Marmelade	*marmer-lard-uh*	marmalade, jam
Meerrettich	*may-re-tish*	horseradish
Milch	*milsh*	milk
Mineral-wasser	*minn-er-arl-vass-er*	mineral water
Möhre	*mer-uh*	carrot
Nuss	*nooss*	nut
Öl	*erl*	oil
Olive	*o-leev-uh*	olive
Petersilie	*payt-er-zee-li-uh*	parsley
Pfeffer	*pfeff-er*	pepper
Pfirsich	*pfir-zish*	peach
Pflaumen	*pflow-men*	plum
Pommes frites	*pomm-fritt*	chips/ French fries
Quark	*kvark*	soft cheese
Radieschen	*ra-deesh'n*	radish
Rinderbraten	*rind-er-brat'n*	joint of beef
Rinderroulade	*rind-er-roo-lard-uh*	beef olive
Rindfleisch	*rint-flysh*	beef
Rippchen	*rip-sh'n*	cured pork rib
Rotkohl	*roht-koal*	red cabbage
Rüben	*rhoob'n*	turnip
Rührei	*rhoo-er-eye*	scrambled eggs
Saft	*zaft*	juice
Salat	*zal-aat*	salad
Salz	*zalts*	salt
Salzkartoffeln	*zalts-kar-toff'l*	boiled potatoes
Sauerkirschen	*zow-er-keersh'n*	cherries
Sauerkraut	*zow-er-krowt*	sauerkraut
Sekt	*zekt*	sparkling wine
Senf	*zenf*	mustard
scharf	*sharf*	spicy
Kebab	*kay-bab*	kebab
Schlagsahne	*shlahgg-zarn-uh*	whipped cream
Schnittlauch	*shnit-lowkhh*	chives
Schnitzel	*shnitz'l*	veal or pork cutlet
Schweinefleisch	*shvine-uh-flysh*	pork
Spargel	*shparg'l*	asparagus
Spiegelei	*shpeeg'l-eye*	fried egg
Spinat	*shpin-art*	spinach
Tee	*tay*	tea
Tomate	*tom-art-uh*	tomato
Wassermelone	*vass-er-me-lohn-uh*	watermelon
Wein	*vine*	wine
Weintrauben	*vine-trowb'n*	grapes
Wiener Würstchen	*veen-er voorst-sh'n*	frankfurter
Zander	*tsan-der*	pike-perch
Zitrone	*tsi-trohn-uh*	lemon
Zucker	*tsook-er*	sugar
Zwieback	*tsvee-back*	rusk
Zwiebel	*tsveeb'l*	onion

Numbers

0	null	*nool*
1	eins	*eye'ns*
2	zwei	*tsvy*
3	drei	*dry*
4	vier	*feer*
5	fünf	*foonf*
6	sechs	*zex*
7	sieben	*zeeb'n*
8	acht	*ahkht*
9	neun	*noyn*
10	zehn	*tsayn*
11	elf	*elf*
12	zwölf	*tswerlf*
13	dreizehn	*dry-tsayn*
14	vierzehn	*feer-tsayn*
15	fünfzehn	*foonf-tsayn*
16	sechzehn	*zex-tsayn*
17	siebzehn	*zeep-tsayn*
18	achtzehn	*ahkht-tsayn*
19	neunzehn	*noyn-tsayn*
20	zwanzig	*tsvann-tsig*
21	einundzwanzig	*ine-oont-tsvann-tsig*
30	dreissig	*dry-sig*
40	vierzig	*feer-tsig*
50	fünfzig	*foonf-tsig*
60	sechzig	*zex-tsig*
70	siebzig	*zeep-tsig*
80	achtzig	*ahkht-tsig*
90	neunzig	*noyn-tsig*
100	hundert	*hoond't*
1000	tausend	*towz'nt*
1,000,000	eine Million	*ine-uh mill-yon*

Time

one minute	eine Minute	*ine-uh min-oot-uh*
one hour	eine Stunde	*ine-uh shtoond-uh*
half an hour	eine halbe Stunde	*ine-uh hallb-uh shtoond-uh*
Monday	Montag	*mohn-targ*
Tuesday	Dienstag	*deens-targ*
Wednesday	Mittwoch	*mitt-vokh*
Thursday	Donnerstag	*donn-ers-targ*
Friday	Freitag	*fry-targ*
Saturday	Samstag/ Sonnabend	*zams-targ zonn-ah-bent*
Sunday	Sonntag	*zon-targ*
January	Januar	*yan-ooar*
February	Februar	*fay-brooar*
March	März	*mairts*
April	April	*april*
May	Mai	*my*
June	Juni	*yoo-ni*
July	Juli	*yoo-lee*
August	August	*ow-goost*
September	September	*zep-tem-ber*
October	Oktober	*ok-toh-ber*
November	November	*no-vem-ber*
December	Dezember	*day-tsem-ber*
spring	Frühling	*froo-ling*
summer	Sommer	*zomm-er*
autumn (fall)	Herbst	*hairpst*
winter	Winter	*vint-er*

ACKNOWLEDGMENTS

This edition updated by

Contributor Alexander Rennie

Senior Editors Dipika Dasgupta, Alison McGill

Senior Designer Vinita Venugopal

Project Editor Tijana Todorinović

Project Art Editor Bharti Karakoti

Assistant Editor Gauri Shukla

Assistant Picture Research Administrator
Manpreet Kaur

Senior Picture Researcher Nishwan Rasool

Deputy Picture Research Manager
Virien Chopra

Publishing Assistant Simona Velikova

Jacket Designer Laura O'Brien

Senior Cartographer Subhashree Bharati

Cartography Manager Suresh Kumar

Pre-Production Coordinator Tanveer Zaidi

Pre-Production Designer Rohit Rojal

Senior Production Controller Samantha Cross

Deputy Managing Editor Dharini Ganesh

Managing Editor Beverly Smart

Managing Art Editor Gemma Doyle

Senior Managing Art Editor Priyanka Thakur

Editorial Director Hollie Teague

Art Director Maxine Pedliham

Publishing Director Georgina Dee

DK would like to thank the following for
their contribution to the previous editions:
Petra Falkenberg, Gabby Innes, Helen Peters,
Anna Streiffert, Debra Wolter

The publisher would like to thank the
following for their kind permission to
reproduce their photographs:

Key: a-above; b-below/bottom; c-centre; f-far;
l-left; r-right; t-top

123RF.com: fritzundkatze 153br, jarino47 51t,
stavrida 84.

Alamy Stock Photo: © Adam Eastland 156,
Agencja Fotograficzna Caro / Christoph Eckelt
107, Agencja Fotograficzna Caro / Muhs 121,
Agencja Fotograficzna Caro / Ponizak 139,
Agencja Fotograficzna Caro / Schwarz 26cla,
Agencja Fotograficzna Caro / Sorge 31tr,
Art Kowalsky 97, Bildagentur-online / Joko 32t,
Bildagentur-online 33cr, Bildagentur-online /
Joko 39tr, Bildagentur-online / Joko 94,
Bildagentur-online / McPhoto 44b, Bildagentur
online / Schoening 99, Bildagentur-online /
Schoening 124, Bildagentur-online / Schoening
142, Eden Breitz 105t, Eden Breitz 105b, Eden
Breitz 106t, Jo Chambers 39cra, charistoone-
images 60b, CMA / BOT 28b, Ian G Dagnall
85, Peter Delius 34-35t, dpa picture alliance
154–155b, edpics 70b, edpics 71b, Oscar Elias
34b, EPX 23br, FALKENSTEINFOTO 9tl, Folio
Images 38, Eddy Galeotti 12br, Angela Serena
Gilmour 40, Angela Serena Gilmour 47b,
Giovanni Guarino Photo 63b, Andrew Hasson
13cl, Maisant Ludovic / Hemis.fr 13tl, Juergen
Henkelmann 37b, Juergen Henkelmann 39cla,
Historic Images 9cr, Kate Hockenhull 129, Peter
Horree 106b, IanDagnall Computing 10cl, Image
Professionals GmbH / travelstock44 25br,
Image Professionals GmbH / LOOK-foto 62,
Imagebroker / Arco / Schoening 13clb (9),
Imagebroker / Arco / Schoening Berlin 17,
imageBROKER / Henning Hattendorf 95tl,
imageBROKER / Karl-Heinz Spremberg
104, imageBROKER / Schoening 119tl,
imageBROKER / Schoening 157, image-
BROKER / Schoening Berlin 79b, imageBROKER.
com GmbH & Co. KG / Norbert Michalke 11,
imageBROKER.com GmbH & Co. KG / Peter
Schickert 143tl, imageBROKER / Ingo Schul
33b, Imago 125b, INTERFOTO / Personalities
45, Joko 103b, Jon Arnold Images Ltd / Michele
Falzone 53, Albert Knapp 56t, Ton Koene 32b,
Lebrecht Music & Arts 10br, Iain Masterton 35b,
Iain Masterton 46b, Iain Masterton 47t, Iain
Masterton 56b, Iain Masterton 136, Iain
Masterton 149b, mauritius images GmbH /
Günter GräfenhainDate 160, mauritius images
GmbH / Rene Mattes 27t, Niday Picture Library
8, Cum Okolo 13cla, Werner Otto 41b, Panther
Media GmbH / Joerg Hackemann / meinzahn
63t, peter.forsberg 69t, Pictorial Press 64t,
Pictorial Press 65, Pictorial Press Ltd 10tl, PjrArt
127b, robertharding / Frank Fell 13bl,
robertharding / Frank Fell 66, S.Popovic RM
98, Joern Sackermann 25t, Schoening 114,
Schoening 128, Dave Stamboulis 101, Marek
Stepan 102, Sueddeutsche Zeitung Photo /
Blanc Kunstverlag 64b, travelstock44.de /
Juergen Held 68, travelstock44.de / Juergen
Held 83b, travelstock44.de / Juergen Held
113t, travelstock44.de / Juergen Held 151,
Urbanmyth 12cr, UtCon Collection 9tr.

Ankerklause: Wolfgang Borrs 138t.

AWL Images: Jon Arnold 165, Sabine
Lubenow 6–7.

erlinale: Andreas Teich 86.

erliner Kaffeerösterei: 130.

Corners: Massimo Ripani 1

epositphotos Inc: Patryk_Kosmider 91,
naxsol7 81b.

eutsche Oper: Marcus Lieberenz 72.

reamstime.com: 54, AGfoto 81t, Belusuab
4t, Cbechinie 115, Ccat82 117t, Claudiodivizia
9cr, Danielal 13clb, Danielal 144b, Davidstiller
1cb, Dennis Dolkens 21br, Draghicich 153t,
Elenaburn 110t, Elxeneize 10bl, Elxeneize 89,
Erix2005 162, Santiago Rodríguez Fontoba 59b,
Giuseppemasci 58, Diego Grandi 16tl, Diego
Grandi 42br, Diego Grandi 43b, Gunold 113b,
Hanohiki 57b, Hel080808 93b, Javarman 111b,
osefkubes 141b, Junede 126-127t, Konrad
Kerker 123t, Sergey Kohl 87, Anna Krivitskaia
7tl, Madrabothair 23bl, Vasilii Maslak 14cb
Philharmonie), Mateuszolszowy 49b, Aliaksandr
Mazurkevich 70t, Mistervlad 161b, Jaroslav
Moravcik 14bc, Luciano Mortula 55t, Luciano
Mortula 133t, Luciano Mortula 147t, Peter Moulton
7b, NGSpacetime 110b, Sergiy Palamarchuk
2cra, Anna Para 37cl, Sean Pavone 159t,
undapanda 67, Roberto Rizzi 80, Rudi1976 60t,
ergiomonti 23cb, Tomas1111 92, Val_th 141t,
anderWolfImages 16ca, Hilda Weges 109t,
ylvia Wendorf 144t, Kim Willems 26b,
irestock 20cla, Noppasin Wongchum 12crb,
orgy67 44t, Alex Zarubin 118.

etty Images: Corbis Documentary /
aremagnum 30t, Sean Gallup / Staff 28t,
ulton Archive / Estate of Emil Bieber / Klaus
ermann 9br, Hulton Fine Art Collection / Fine
t Images / Heritage Images 48b, Hulton Fine
t Collection / Heritage Images 29, Schöning /
stein bild 154t, Westend61 148–149t.

etty Images / iStock: Andrey Danilovich
t, E+ / mbbirdy 19, E+ / Nikada 5, Heiko119
crb, holgs 20br, ka_ru 120b, Nikada 21clb,
oppasin 14cb, Leonardo Patrizi 22, Robert
ygoda 21ca.

ugelhof: 145.

estaurant & Café Heider: 163.

OW: 76.

wish Museum Berlin: Spertus Institute
hicago / Roman März 51br, Yves Sucksdorff
–51b.

unkerkranich: Julian Nelken 138b.

atrix: 150.

in Haus am See: 77t.

erkill GmbH: 137.

estaurant Lubitsch Berlin: 131.

bert Harding Picture Library:
o Schulz 41t.

Schwules Museum: Tobias Wille 75.

Shutterstock.com: Alizada Studios 36,
KievVictor 96, LuisPinaPhotography 112, Mo
Photography Berlin 30b, 120t, Grzegorz_Pakula
42–43t, Ugis Riba 24–25b, Manfred Roeben 134,
Scharfsinn 16cla, Noppasin Wongchum 15.

Victoria Bar: 79t.

Sheet Map Cover Image:
Getty Images: The Image Bank /
Sylvain Sonnet

Cover Images:
Front and Spine: **Getty Images:**
The Image Bank / Sylvain Sonnet.
Back: **Alamy Stock Photo:** robertharding /
Frank Fell tl; **Getty Images / iStock:** E+ /
mbbirdy cl; **Shutterstock.com:** Scharfsinn tr.

First edition 2002

Published in Great Britain by Dorling Kindersley Limited,
DK, 20 Vauxhall Bridge Road, London SW1V 2SA, UK

The authorised representative in the EEA is
Dorling Kindersley Verlag GmbH. Arnulfstr.
124, 80636 Munich, Germany

Published in the United States by
DK Publishing, 1745 Broadway, 20th Floor,
New York, NY 10019, USA

A CIP catalogue record is available
from the British Library.

A catalogue record for this book is available
from the Library of Congress.

ISSN: 1479-344X

ISBN: 978-0-2417-4438-3

Printed and bound in China

www.dk.com